Maxine Hong Kingston

Twayne's United States Authors Series

Frank Day, Editor

Clemson University

TUSAS 711

MAXINE HONG KINGSTON
Jane Scherr

Maxine Hong Kingston

Diane Simmons

City University of New York–Borough of
Manhattan Community College

Twayne Publishers
New York

Twayne's United States Authors Series no. 711

Maxine Hong Kingston
Diane Simmons

Copyright © 1999 by Twayne Publishers

Twayne Publishers
1633 Broadway
New York, NY 10019

Library of Congress Cataloging-in-Publication Data

Simmons, Diane, 1948–
    Maxine Hong Kingston / Diane Simmons.
        p.   cm. — (Twayne's world authors series ; TUSAS 646)
    Includes bibliographical references (p.   ) and index.
    ISBN 0-8057-4621-8 (alk. paper)
        1. Kingston, Maxine Hong—Criticism and interpretation. 2. Women and literature—United States—History—20th century. 3. Chinese Americans in literature. I. Title. II. Series.
    PS3561.I52Z88   1999
813'.54—dc21   99-14329
                                                                          CIP

This paper meets the requirements of ANSI/NISO Z3948-1992 (Permanence of Paper).

10 9 8 7 6 5 4 3 2 1

Printed in the United States of America

For Burt and Jane

Contents

Acknowledgments

My thanks to Maxine Hong Kingston and Earll Kingston for a gracious welcome, good talk, and a glass of raspberry tea on a hot California morning; to Norbert Elliot, who thought writing was important enough to find time for; to my editor Frank Day for his patience—most of the time—with the punctuationally challenged; to Jeffrey Kinkley for his generous help with questions of romanization; to my husband, Burt Kimmelman, who keeps holding up the other half of the sky.

Permission to quote at length from the following material protected by copyright has been granted by Maxine Hong Kingston: *China Men* (New York: Ballantine Books, 1981); "Cultural Mis-Readings by American Reviewers," in *Asian and Western Writers in Dialogue: New Cultural Identities*, ed. Guy Amirthanayagam (London: Macmillan, 1982); *Hawai'i One Summer: 1978* (San Francisco: Meadow Press, 1987); "The Novel's Next Step," *Mother Jones*, December 1989; *Through the Black Curtain* (Berkeley, Calif.: Friends of the Bancroft Library, 1987); *Tripmaster Monkey: His Fake Book* (New York: Vintage, 1990); *The Woman Warrior* (New York: Vintage, 1989).

Permission to quote from the following is also gratefully acknowledged: King-Kok Cheung, "The Woman Warrior vs. the Chinaman Pacific: Must a Chinese American Critic Choose between Feminism and Heroism," in *Conflicts in Feminism*, ed. Marianne Hirsch and Evelyn Fox Keller (New York: Routledge, 1990), 234–51; Marilyn Chin, "A *MELUS* Interview: Maxine Hong Kingston," *MELUS* 16 (Winter 1989–1990): 57–74; "The Ballad of Mulan," in *Sunflower Splendor: Three-Thousand Years of Chinese Poetry*, ed. Wu-chi Liu and Irving Lo (Bloomington: Indiana University Press, 1975), 77; Donna Perry, "Maxine Hong Kingston," in *Backtalk: Women Writers Speak Out: Interviews by Donna Perry*, ed. Donna Perry (New Brunswick, N.J.: Rutgers University Press, 1993), 172–93; Paula Rabinotwitz, "Eccentric Memories: A Conversation with Maxine Hong Kingston," first published *Michigan Quarterly Review* Vol. 26, No. 1, Winter 1987.

Chronology

1940   Maxine Hong born to Chinese immigrants Tom and Ying Lan (Brave Orchid) Hong in Stockton, California, the eldest of six children born to the couple in the United States. Two children born earlier died in China.

1955   Wins five-dollar prize from *Girl Scout Magazine* for essay, "I Am an American."

1958   Wins full scholarships to attend the University of California at Berkeley. Begins as an engineering major, but changes to English.

1962   Marries actor Earll Kingston. Teaches high school English and math.

1963   Gives birth to son, Joseph.

1967   With her husband and son leaves Berkeley to "drop out" in Hawaii. Teaches high school and writes.

1976   Publishes *The Woman Warrior: Memoir of a Girlhood among Ghosts,* which wins the year's National Book Critics Circle Award for nonfiction.

1977   Wins *Mademoiselle* Magazine Award. Wins National Education Association Award.

1978   Writes diaristic accounts that will be published in 1987 as *Hawai'i One Summer.* Wins Anisfield-Wolf Race Relations Award.

1979   *The Woman Warrior* is named by *Time* magazine as one of the top 10 nonfiction books of the decade.

1980   Publishes *China Men.* Named a Living Treasure of Hawaii by a Honolulu Buddhist sect. Endowment for the Arts writing fellow. *China Men* named to American Library Association Notable Books List.

1981   Wins American Book Award for nonfiction for *China Men.*

1984   Visits China for the first time along with other writers as a guest of the Chinese Writers Association.

1987   Publishes *Hawai'i One Summer* and *Through the Black Curtains.*

1989   Publishes her first novel, *Tripmaster Monkey: His Fake Book.* PEN USA West award for fiction.

1991   *The Book of Peace,* a novel set during the Vietnam War, is destroyed in a wildfire that burns Kingston's Oakland, California, home to the ground. Kingston begins work on another book, which she tentatively titles *Another Book of Peace* or *The Fifth Book of Peace.*

1993   Receives Lila Wallace Reader's Digest Award, which allows Kingston to begin writing workshop for Vietnam veterans.

1995   Dramatized version of *The Woman Warrior* named best play of the year by *USA Today.*

1997   Receives National Humanities Medal.

1998   Receives Fred Cody Lifetime Achievement Award. Wins John Dos Passos Prize for Literature for *Tripmaster Monkey.*

1999   *Hawai'i One Summer* re-issued in paperback.

Chapter One

"How Do You Come Back from War?"

A Biographical Essay

Living in Hawaii in 1978 Maxine Hong Kingston was shocked to hear that a small island off the shore of Oahu was called "Chinaman's Hat." She recoiled, remembering the times the word *chinaman* had been used as a slur back home in Stockton, California: "At first I watched expressions and tones of voice for a snide reference to me. But the locals were not yelling at me or spitting at me or trying to run me down with a bike saying, 'Chinaman.' "[1]

By the summer of 1978 *The Woman Warrior* had appeared to immense acclaim, and at 38 Kingston—1960s radical, mother, high school teacher, Vietnam War protester—was an overnight literary sensation. Despite her mother's injunction, "Don't tell," Kingston told and was, in this first summer of fame, reaping the fruits of her boldness. Media critics hailed her as a genius—if sometimes an "inscrutable" one—and feminist literary critics claimed her as a pioneering voice in women's autobiography, revealing at last women "as they 'are' and not as they have been defined by a sexist society."[2] She was also immediately excoriated by a group of male Chinese writers, led by playwright Frank Chin, as a purveyor of "white racist art," a latter-day "Pocahontas," selling out Chinese Americans to pander to white readers.[3]

It is during this first summer of fame that Kingston—not especially confident in the water—decides to don snorkeling gear and swim out to Chinaman's Hat. She describes the trip: "Snorkeling is like flying; the moment your face enters clear water, you become a flying creature. . . . We swam through spangles of silver white fish. I hovered in perfect suspension over forests, flew over spring forests and winter forests. No sound but my own breathing. Sometimes we entered blind spots, darkness, where the sand churned up gray fog, the sun behind clouds. Then I had to lift my head out of the water to see and not be afraid." But then

2   MAXINE HONG KINGSTON

she would go below again, for the "dark hallways" could open out into "golden rooms" where "specks of sand shone like gold and fell like motes, like the light in California" (HS, 24). The wonder and beauty outweighed the fear, and Kingston made other trips out to Chinaman's Hat, even when she learned that the waters, a spawning place for sharks, concealed real dangers: "We continued to swim home with the fish we'd caught tied to our belts, and they did not attract sharks though pilot fish swam ahead of us" (HS, 25).

The story is an illuminative one, for in her writing—as in her swimming—Kingston continually works to transform paralyzing fear into boldness, beauty, and, sometimes, free, magical flight. This transformative energy—this mission to save herself and the world—is fundamental to who Kingston is as a person and as a writer. "I think maybe I'm not crazy," she says, "because I wrote the unspeakable out."[4]

Kingston seeks not only to face fear with a cheerful boldness—"We are heroes," she says, "in a big human adventure"[5]—but also to find a way to survive fear and violence without being brutalized. Throughout her work Kingston strives to humanize those whose humanity is in danger of being erased by fear or violence, by physical or psychological warfare.

In The Woman Warrior Kingston claims identity and power for Chinese women, who are in danger of being demeaned and even destroyed by "the oldest, most highly developed, male-dominated kinship system in history."[6] She breathes life into the figure of the outcast aunt, No Name Woman, who is erased from family memory for failing—whatever the cause, whoever the culprit—to play her assigned role in society. No longer merely a cautionary example of female subjugation, No Name in Kingston's hands has been granted subjectivity, passion, and even desire. With the figure of the woman warrior—the central motif of her first book and perhaps her life—Kingston seeks to show not only a woman who could fight to defend herself and her family but also one who "could come back and was not brutalized," who "could still be a woman, a family person, a communal person, not dehumanized."[7]

Kingston also seeks to humanize those who have born the brunt of American racism, particularly Chinese men who began coming to the United States in great numbers in the nineteenth century. In China Men Kingston imagines an inner, secret self for her own silent, angry father, linking him to the exiled poets of Chinese tradition. And she lifts her immigrant grandfathers above the black waters of stereotype, imagining for them lives of passion, rebellion, and longing. In Tripmaster Monkey she sympathizes with the angry young Chinese American beatnik playwright Wittman Ah Sing, first depicting his struggles in a racist and materialist society, then teaching him to transform his anger into community-building art.

Following *Tripmaster Monkey*, Kingston turned her attention to questions of war and peace, as, she says, she is "integrating a larger and larger chunk of the world" into her writing.[8] For Kingston, the Vietnam War, an Asian land war reminiscent of the warfare in China that dominated her young consciousness, provides an excellent opportunity for studying the central question of how one survives brutality intact. As she put the question in an interview: "How do you do that? Come back from war?" (Moyers). Her present concern with war, Kingston says, is only an enlargement of themes that have always been present in her life and work:

> The whole question of war and peace begins in *The Woman Warrior* [as Kingston's young protagonist deals with fears associated with World War II]. That little child is really worried. There's bombs going off. What war is this? How come is this [war] called World War Two? Was there a One? Will there be a Three? What's going on here? And I write about the trauma of seeing my first movie, which was a war movie. I'm wasting all my wishes on war. And so I see that I have had the same concerns from the very start and I'm bringing them more and more into mature thinking. (Simmons)

Kingston draws on a variety of models in her task of confronting and transforming fear. Like the mythical heroine of *The Woman Warrior*, Fa Mu Lan, the author takes it as her duty to step out of her role as "Little Sister" and save her people and the world through the power of story. Like Little Hill, the filial daughter in the early-nineteenth-century Chinese novel *Flowers in the Mirror* by Li Ruzhen, she sets out to rescue and rehabilitate a disappointed and despairing lost father. And like the madcap trickster Monkey from the traditional Chinese novel *Journey to the West*—who works dozens of changes to overcome adversaries on the road to enlightenment—Kingston imbues her work, particularly *Tripmaster Monkey: His Fake Book,* with an audacious playfulness that softens the difficulties to be overcome.

But Kingston's models are not all Eastern. Like her literary hero Walt Whitman who, she believes, had "a vision of a new kind of human being formed in this country," she seeks to end division by imagining new ways for people to join together. In writing *Tripmaster Monkey,* she says, "I just lifted lines from *Leaves of Grass*. You would think they were modern sixties slang".[9] Following another hero, William Carlos Williams, who Kingston sees demythologizing America in his book *In the American Grain*,[10] she believes that "we can change the past by figuring out new meaning to events that took place" (Moyers). And like Virginia Woolf in *Orlando,* a book she rereads to revive herself at low points, Kingston strives to break "through constraints of time, of gender, of culture. . . . I love the way she can make one character live for four hundred years, and that Orlando can be a man, Orlando can be a woman" (Fishkin, 784).

In addition to literary models, Kingston also seeks to emulate the pacifists and protesters of the antiwar 1960s, as she works to counter violence through an expanded perception, believing that "chang[ing] human consciousness" is a step toward "changing the material world" (Fishkin, 783). Like Allen Ginsberg, who sought to stop the Vietnam War by declaring it over, and to levitate the Pentagon through chants, Kingston seeks the right words that will end violence forever. Here, too, her Western antiwar models have an Eastern counterpart, for in the East there is a tradition of the right words changing the world: "The Chinese have this tradition," Kingston says, "that once upon a time there were these three books of peace that had all kinds of directions on how to have nonviolent communication. The myth is that these books were burned, and so we don't know what was in them—we don't know their effects. So I think of it as, that's what I have to do. I have to rewrite them, to try and figure out what was in them, to bring them back."[11]

In her three major books—*The Woman Warrior, China Men,* and *Tripmaster Monkey*—Kingston works a variety of transformations to save her characters from the dehumanization of fear and violence. In *The Woman Warrior* she transforms the silence, subservience, and even shame that are forced upon women in a male-dominant society into bold and forceful action: No Name Woman may have actually been a rebel. Any quiet girl may become a woman warrior leading her people, defending her family, punishing leering sexists with death. Brave Orchid can face down—even humiliate and belittle—the ghosts that would suffocate the life out of her. The girl, Maxine, can finally speak, shouting out her pent-up list of grievances like a heroine in Chinese opera. Finally, like the captured princess Ts'ai Yen, both Maxine and Brave Orchid can make their voices heard and understood, so that even barbarians must recognize their humanity.[12]

But it is not only women who are transformed. In *China Men* Kingston reworks the image of her father, Tom Hong, from the angry silent man whose only speech was a curse into a despairing poet in exile like the fourth-century B.C. figure, Ch'ü Yuan, the author of the poem *Li Sao,* who was too pure for the "muddy world" of war and politics.[13] The father's black silences are transformed into the still-dark, but now partially knowable, secret places where a sensitive man protects himself from a brutal world. Also in *China Men* Kingston obliterates the racist stereotype of the immigrant Chinese man as a silent, all-enduring coolie with no inner life. The immigrant grandfathers that Kingston creates do not see themselves as soulless slaves but as repositories of love and of family and cultural memory. They defy the order to work in silence, shouting out their pain and their love, their passion intimidating their white oppressors. Although the Chinese men are seen as little more than beasts of burden by the Americans with whom they build the transcontinental railroad, they confidently view themselves as the true muscle and soul of the new America; they are the ones who drive in the iron spike that actually completes the transcontinental railroad, once the ceremonial gold spike has been removed.

In *Tripmaster Monkey* Kingston transforms the depressed, suicidal Wittman Ah Sing from an angry young man lost in early 1960s America to the architect of his own loving, supportive, and inclusive community that he constructs through the transformative magic of theater. In the process Wittman transforms himself from an outsider in American life, to a savior of the American soul, which he believes has been co-opted by a corporate and militaristic mentality. As black Americans have "integrated" the American imagination with their music, providing American culture with the rich emotionality of jazz and blues, so Kingston sees the Chinese stories of heroism, loyalty, and community lifting and uniting lonely isolated Americans. Stories from Chinese novels are particularly appropriate for this purpose, as fiction was traditionally seen as a lowbrow form of literature. "This," Jeffrey Kinkley notes, "is China from the underside, indeed, from the rebellious side."[14]

Drawing the Black Curtain

Maxine—her family called her "Ting Ting"—Hong was born into a world that was full of drama and beauty, and also of fear and struggle. Her parents were immigrants from China; her father arrived in the United States in 1924, her mother in 1939, a year before the arrival of Maxine, the first of six American-born children. (Two previous children had died in China.) Tom Hong, who renamed himself after Thomas Edison, had been a scholar and teacher in the village of Sun Woi near Canton. In New York he worked for 15 years in a laundry before sending for his wife, Ying Lan (Brave Orchid). In the interim Brave Orchid, like the figure in *The Woman Warrior,* studied and practiced medicine, a groundbreaking accomplishment for a woman at that time. The Hongs lived first in New York City. Then, after being cheated out of their stake in the New York laundry, Tom Hong and his wife moved to Stockton, California, where he managed a gambling house for a time, naming his daughter after a particularly lucky blonde gambler.[15] The family later owned and operated the New Port Laundry in Stockton, where the Hong children put in long, grueling hours: "It was *awfully* hard work," Kingston remembers. "I used to make up kids games to keep myself going. If I did ten T-shirts I'd allow myself to take a break, okay? The laundry also influenced how I thought about money. Twenty five cents was one white starched shirt."[16]

But the laundry was not only a site of drudgery. It was also a meeting place for Stockton's Chinese community, where Kingston heard the "talk-stories" she would later draw on in her writing. She defines talk-story as

> a tradition that goes back to prewriting time in China, where people verbally pass on history and mythology and genealogy and how-to stories and bedtime stories and legends. They pass them down through the generations, and it keeps the community together. The tradition was so strong in China that people brought it to America, where the stories changed and became American stories. [At the laundry] I would hear talk-story from everyone who came in. So I inherited this amazing amount of information, culture, history, mythology, and poetry.[17]

Kingston grasped the power of storytelling not only to transform the drudgery of the moment but also to create myths with the power to transform both the past and the future. The Cantonese, who until the 1960s made up most of America's Chinese population, are, Kingston says, "wildly imaginative. . . . [They had the] imagination to make up the Gold Mountain [the term used for the United States] and then go find it."[18]

Kingston listened to the talk in the laundry and also to her parents, who were always singing what their daughter took to be "village ditties. They sing that on the farm. . . . I never knew, until I got to college and was taking Asian Lit Class, that that was important poetry. I just thought it was my parents' tales. . . . And then I thought later, oh, Tu Fu, and Li Po[19]—this is important stuff."[20] "Now I realize how rare that is. Priceless gifts they strewed into your path" (Bonetti).

Two ancient stories in particular made an impression on Kingston: "The Adventures of General Yue Fei," and "The Ballad of Mulan." In the first a mother writes a charge of loyalty on her son's back, cutting the characters into his flesh. In the second a young woman disguises herself as a man and goes to war to defend her family. "I learned to talk by repeating those things," Kingston says (Marilyn Chin, 70). Both stories were eventually conflated into Kingston's account of the woman warrior.

Kingston does not find it at all inappropriate to use these heroic works in writing about her own family. "My family," Kingston says, "is more imaginative and brave than most people. They've had more adventures, more triumphs and defeats. They've traveled halfway round the world. They're people with big lives. and I guess I think this about all Chinese people. They have an amazing amalgam of practicality and imagination. Maybe that's the Chinese spirit—to embody those two wildly different world views."[21]

If Kingston's childhood was energized by her parents' "strong life force, passionate, dramatic, drama before your eyes" (Bonetti), it could also be a place of fear and displacement, where the child Ting Ting experienced both the need to hide from the dangers of the world and the sense that much of the world was hidden from her.

As a child, Kingston could not be sure what her fate as a female would be. Although the talk of her parents and the others in the laundry imparted a rich, dramatic sense of life, it also transmitted the cultural conception—noted by many Chinese and Chinese American women authors—that girls were inferior, a useless drain on family resources. The young Maxine, like the protagonist of *The Woman Warrior,* grew up hearing from men and women alike remarks such as "Feeding girls is like feeding cowbirds" and "Better to raise geese than girls."[22] Ting Ting also heard that poor families sometimes sell their daughters as slaves and vowed to do anything to prevent that from happening. One way Kingston tried to protect herself was through writing. She began to write at around the age of eight, she says, because "I felt there was no room for me in my house. I felt displaced by the five brothers and sisters who came after me. I always felt I had no place of my own and had to hide. I had to make a big invisible world and that was the writing. I would scrunch up in a little place and be very secretive and make up a world that didn't take up much room" (Talbot, 12).

Kingston also sought to escape through reading, but here the harsh realities of the outer world could intrude. Even immersed in nineteenth-century fiction she would be reminded of the racism continuing to pervade the Stockton streets beyond her door, as well as American society in general. Engrossed in Louisa May Alcott's *Little Men* one day, Kingston was "reading along, identifying with the March sisters, when I came across this funny-looking little Chinaman. It popped out of the book. I'd been pushed into my place. I was him, I wasn't those March girls" (Hoy, 142).

It may be from this tension—the need to hide, the sense that the world is hidden—that one of the central images of Kingston's work comes, that of "black curtains that hang over something wonderful, some amazing show about to open." It was an image that came to her, Kingston says, before she could "read or write or even speak much. . . . All my life, I've looked for those black curtains; I want to part them, and to see what is on the other side."[23]

In *The Woman Warrior* Kingston describes her early school years when she would cover all of her paintings with black. Here the image of black curtains, linked to the silence of the girl who does not speak the school language of English, is both self-imposed and imposed from without. She must protect her creations from the alien English speakers who will not be able to truly know her and her work; at the same time she is closed out of the larger world that school, English, and education represent in *The Woman Warrior.* She recalls:

> My silence was thickest—total—during the three years that I covered my school paintings with black paint. I painted layers of black over houses and flowers and suns, and when I drew on the blackboard, I put a layer of chalk on top. I was making a stage curtain, and it was the moment before the curtain parted or rose. The teachers called my parents to school, and I saw they had been saving my pictures, curling and cracking, all alike and black. The teachers pointed to the pictures and looked serious, talked seriously too, but my parents did not understand English. ("The parents and teachers of criminals were executed," said my father.) My parents took the pictures home. I spread them out (so black and full of possibilities) and pretended the curtains were swinging open, flying up, one after another, sunlight underneath, mighty operas. (*WW,* 165)

The image of black curtains, Kingston says, probably had its literal source in the blackout curtains of World War II, a war that not only threatened the United States but had for several years before the American entry devastated the Hong family's Chinese homeland. The curtains represented protection from the potential violence of the outside world, as well as the sense of being cut off from the rest of the world. But for all the danger associated with the curtains, the young Kingston was already at work transforming fear into creative energy and magical beauty. The blackout curtains signaled danger but at the same time suggested the excitement of great events: "My mother and father laughed and talked while climbing up and down the ladder and unfurling lengths and folds of drapery. They hadn't owned curtains before. Sun rays shot out the top and side edges. We were safe from the street, the city, strangers, World War II" (*BC*, 5).

Not only did the 32 curtains black out World War II, but they also protected the family from the street in Stockton's tough south side, which may have felt like a war zone to a young child. "It was no suburban, middle-class background," Kingston says; Rupert Garcia, the painter who grew up in the same neighborhood and graduated from Edison High School a year later than Kingston, describes the neighborhood as "horrific."[24] Inducted along with Kingston into Edison High School's first Hall of Fame in 1987, Garcia included in his acceptance speech a reading of the names of those class members who "had been killed or jailed," who had not survived the dangers of the neighborhood.[25] It is here that Kingston learned to recoil from the word "Chinaman" and to fear being spat at or run down by a bike. In *The Woman Warrior* her protagonist recounts being shooed away from corpses of "dead slum people" found on the streets, tells of having to fight, especially in junior high school, and remembers that she "always cried" (*WW*, 51). In *Hawai'i One Summer* Kingston recalls having to deal with a "race thing," remembering how in high school, "suddenly the colored girls would walk up, and my colored girlfriends would talk and move differently. Well, they're athletes, I thought; they go to the same parties. The only place I ever considered sitting for lunch was at the Chinese table. There were more of us than places at that table. Hurry and get to the cafeteria early or go late when somebody may have finished or left a seat. Or skip lunch" (*HS*, 10).

But war, racism, and the struggle with an alien language and a tough neighborhood did not exempt Kingston from the more commonplace agonies of adolescence. Writing 20 years later, Kingston, by this time a famous author, still does not know whether she can face her high school reunion. She asks her year-younger sister what kind of image she had in high school, and the sister replies, " 'Well, when I think of the way you

looked in the halls, I picture your slip hanging' " (HS, 10). Contemplat-
ing the reunion, Kingston asks herself if everything will be different as a
result of her writing success. The reply: "I was writing in high school.
Writing did not protect me then, and it won't protect me now" (HS,
10). When it seems that her husband will not be able to accompany her,
she writes, "Alone at the dance. Again" (HS, 10).

If social life continued to be difficult in the upper grades, academic
life was much improved. From a first grader who scored zero on intelligence exams after she colored the entire test page black, Kingston—
once she learned English around the age of eight—excelled in her classes
and was eventually awarded 11 scholarships to attend the University of
California at Berkeley. With the ability to speak and write in English
came a feeling of power, and she began to write in a variety of genres.
Once she had mastered English she felt liberated. English was so simple:

> [It seemed] bright, full of freedom. I felt freedom because the English
> language is so easy, and I thought, My gosh, everything I hear I can
> notate it! I can notate Chinese. I can write Chinese in English. I can write
> English in English and I never had that power when I spoke only Chi-
> nese. You speak Chinese and then the written language is completely dif-
> ferent. There's no system. It's one word at a time. But all of a sudden,
> with the 26 letters in the English alphabet you can write anything.[26]

Her teachers encouraged her writing, and at 15 she won a five-dollar
prize from *Girl Scout Magazine*. The essay was entitled "I Am an American" (Morey and Dunn, 74).

Through reading Kingston also began to find her eventual direction
as a writer. Of central importance was Jade Snow Wong's *Fifth Chinese
Daughter* (1945), the autobiographical account of a Chinese American
girl growing up in the 1930s. Wong's book has recently been seen by
some critics as a somewhat toadying attempt to explain Chinese Americans to a white reading audience, who in the midst of World War II
needed to be able to distinguish between friendly Chinese and enemy
Japanese. But whatever the present take on Wong's work, Kingston
does not forget the impact of *Fifth Chinese Daughter* on a young girl looking for her place in the world and in literature. Wong's book, she says,
"saved my life." While Alcott's *Little Women* had made her feel "pushed
out of literature" (Saffa), *Fifth Chinese Daughter* allowed Kingston "for
the first time [to] see a person somewhat like myself in literature. I had
been trying to write about people who were blonde, or a beautiful red-
head on her horse, because those were the people who were in the books.

So I was lucky that at a young age I could see a Chinese American" (Hoy, 142). Reading Wong, Kingston saw something else with which she could identify, the Chinese habit of favoring boys over girls. Kingston noticed that, in Wong's book, the boys got all the meat of a chicken; the girls got the feet. Maxine, at least, got the wing (Saffa).

The 1960s at Berkeley: Questions of Speech and Power

At the University of California at Berkeley, Kingston first studied engineering, her parents' idea of a good career choice: "{T}hey wanted all their children to be mathematicians, engineers." But engineering made her "miserable," even though she felt it was her duty to help the United States catch up with the Soviets in space exploration.[27] She also considered journalism and was given the night shift on the college newspaper, but she couldn't stay awake and couldn't get use to writing about facts (Loke, 55). Although she always loved English literature, she felt that "there was no good reason for doing it. When I went from engineering to English, I felt I had abdicated all my responsibilities. I was just living life for the fun of it. I guess it was the way I was raised, but everything had to be hard. But English was easy for me, so I shouldn't do anything that was easy. . . . There was something wrong with me if I did something that was easy and fun" (Marilyn Chin, 69).

But there was more to Berkeley in the early 1960s than study, and Kingston, for whom silence had been a kind of torture and who had not yet fully broken her own silence, became an enthusiastic member of the Free Speech movement and an admirer of the stream-of-consciousness monologues of the comedian Lenny Bruce. These were also heady days for the Civil Rights movement, a struggle that reverberated with Asian American students, some of whom sought to imitate the confrontational style of the Black Panthers. And along with thousands of other students, she joined in protests against the Vietnam War. For her, however, there was a special agony to the war as Americans went to kill Asians— "gooks"—and as the media churned out images of strange small people in silly pajama-like garb, who, it was widely expressed, did not value human life in the same way that Americans did.

At Berkeley in the early 1960s, then, the whole world seemed to be concerned with the issues that had bedeviled Kingston throughout her life: the ability of those in power to demand a complicit silence from those they dominated, the dehumanization and brutalization of Asians, and the contradiction of racism persisting in the land of the free. At Berkeley everyone seemed to be trying to change the perceptions that allowed these things to happen, and Kingston seems to have identified completely with this effort: "We were trying to figure out how to stop the war," she says looking back. "What if I change perception, can I change reality?"[28]

Kingston reveled in the sense of freedom of the early 1960s, the politics, and the language being invented to describe new sensations and new actions. "One of the wonderful things about the 1960s was language," she says. "There was a new language and there were wonderful new ways of describing psychedelic states, spiritual states, trying to find new words for political actions like those of Gandhi and Martin Luther King. What do you call that when you sit at the lunch counter and you don't move and you do it with peace and love?" (Seshachari, 17). Although the counterculture movement of the 1960s has been much maligned, Kingston continues to see the period as a wonderful moment, a time of "peace on earth" and "friendship" during which she and her friends "thought we were going to change the world. People spoke without cynicism. I keep seeing various people I try to tell about that time and I think they diminish it, or they dismiss it" (Loke, 55). And she sees that the spirit of monkey—the legendary Chinese trickster figure whose "task it is to bring chaos to establishment"—was abroad in the 1960s: "Abby Hoffman, Allen Ginsberg. . . . They were monkey spirits, trying to change the world with costumes and street theater" (Marilyn Chin, 61).

Kingston also took part in the drug culture of the 1960s, particularly the experimentation with psychedelics: "We were all on drugs in the '60s; [the drugs] messed with our minds and time and space, our perception of events were changed and expanded" (Vitale). The title of her third book, *Tripmaster Monkey,* is based in part on a role created by the 1960s drug culture: "People would be on acid, and there's a tripmaster who suggests trips for them and who guides them and keeps them from flipping out. I feel that I myself was very good at doing that. Often I would be the one who would not take drugs and the other people would take the drugs. I would make sure they were safe. Very different from Ken Kesey [whose leadership of the psychedelic movement is portrayed in Tom Wolfe's *Electric Kool-Aid Acid Test*]. I wanted to make sure that they did not go to any dangerous places, make sure they went to beautiful places with flowers and music and birds" (Seshachari, 18).

After college Kingston stayed in the Bay Area as an English major looking for work. Like Tana in *Tripmaster Monkey* she got a job as an assistant claims adjuster, and like Wittman she "thought about suicide every day" (Vitale). In 1962 she married Earll Kingston, an actor whom she had met when they both had small parts in a Berkeley production of Bertolt Brecht's *Galileo*. Their son, Joseph, was born in 1963. Later both Kingstons taught in a ghetto school in Hayward, California, Maxine teaching high school English and math. Then, in 1967, as the drug culture took a violent turn, as the Vietnam War continued, and as their Berkeley apartment increasingly began to look like a "crash pad" (Saffa), Maxine and Earll Kingston left Berkeley to "drop out" in Hawaii.

When they arrived in Hawaii they did not look for jobs. Kingston explains: "It was the duty of a pacifist in a war economy not to work. When you used plastic wrap or made a phone call or drank grape juice or washed your clothes or drove a car, you ran the assembly line that delivered bombs on Vietnam" (*HS*, 13). Spending money in a supermarket would also support the war economy, so the Kingstons dug for free food in supermarket dumpsters. They lived in a $90 apartment above a grocery story, picked up abandoned furniture off curbs, and foraged for fruits and nuts (*HS*, 13).

But Hawaii was not exactly the peaceful paradise the Kingstons had hoped to find. Rather, it seemed to be serving as a sort of funnel through which soldiers and war hardware passed on their way from the mainland United States to Vietnam. The Kingstons continued their antiwar work by taking part in a sanctuary project for soldiers who were AWOL. Here, however, Kingston witnessed a view of the Vietnam War that differed from the one prevalent in Berkeley. Paradoxically embodied in the immature person of an AWOL soldier is the America Kingston was trying to change: "The soldiers, mere kids, illiterate boys from the poorer states, did not agree that the war was wrong; some went AWOL because they didn't like their officers, or the food was bad, or they wanted a vacation, or they were just fooling around" (*HS*, 15). One young soldier whom Kingston attempted to befriend reminisced about his boyhood pleasure in lining up his model cars, then shooting and burning them. When Kingston asked why he found this so enjoyable, the boy responded: "It felt good—like when I was a door gunner on the chopper in Nam. Thousands of bullets streaming out of my gun." Kingston was silent, thinking, "Don't tell me about the gooks you shot. . . . Don't tell me about the hooches you torched" (*HS*, 15).

Eventually the Kingstons returned to teaching. Her husband worked with a Shakespearean theater group while she took a series of positions: Kahuku High School, Kahaluu Drop-In School, Honolulu Business College, and finally at a private school, the Mid-Pacific Institute, where she was working when her first book, *The Woman Warrior,* was published in 1976.

"Why Must I Represent Anyone but Myself?"

Kingston sent the manuscript for *The Woman Warrior* to agents whose names she found in writer's books. So cold were her leads that two of the envelopes came back stamped "out of business." The third agent was still functioning and took the book, sending it first to a prominent publishing house where an editor returned it saying, "This is a pig in a poke." And Kingston remembers thinking, "Pig in a poke, they called my book a pig in a poke. I'll never forget that" (Simmons). The book was accepted by Knopf, however, and launched by the *New York Times* critic John Leonard, who picked it up because he needed something short to review on deadline. As he recounts in the documentary film *Talking Story,* he read three pages of the unknown author before he found himself asking, "Where does this come from?" The word *genius* had already come to mind (Saffa). In the opening lines of his review of 17 September 1976, Leonard expresses his sense that something unusual has happened in the publishing world, an event that would challenge the white male hold on American letters: "Those rumbles you hear on the horizon are the big guns of autumn lining up, the howitzers of Vonnegut and Updike and Cheever and Mailer, the books that will be making loud noises for the next several months. But listen: this week a remarkable book has been quietly published; it is one of the best I've read for years." Leonard ends his review by asking: "Who is Maxine Hong Kingston? Nobody at Knopf seems to know. They have never laid eyes on her."[29]

In early 1977 *Mademoiselle* magazine sought to solve this mystery by sending Susan Brownmiller to Hawaii to watch the Kingstons make dinner (a Cantonese dish of chicken and sausage) in their "bohemian" apartment and to answer the question being asked in New York publishing circles: "Who *is* Maxine Kingston? . . . Who is this unknown Chinese American woman who has dropped a brilliant, polished gemstone in our midst?" (Brownmiller, 148). Brownmiller reports that the author both is and is not the stereotypical China doll. At four feet, nine inches, Brownmiller notes, the author is "tiny, doll-like in an ankle-length purple and white dress that is minutely patterned. But she is no porcelain China doll. At thirty-six her face is the face of a woman who had known hard work, whose childhood was burdened with grown-up responsibility" (Brownmiller, 148).

Soon the literary world knew—or at least thought it knew—who Kingston was. The woman who had begun writing at 8 was a publishing sensation, an overnight success at 36. The book won the 1976 National Book Critics Circle Award for Nonfiction and was favorably received by reviewers across the United States. Academics began to publish what would become an avalanche of articles and dissertations on an author who, according to the Modern Language Association, would go on to become the most widely taught living American author in American colleges and universities.[30]

Most critics loved the book. But this did not stop them, as Kingston saw to her dismay, from reading it through a haze of cultural and racial stereotypes. In an essay entitled "Cultural Mis-Readings by American Reviewers," Kingston responded to those who both loved the book and at the same time missed its point, those who had read in the light of their own fantasies of China and the Chinese. Although she expected that the book would be read "from the women's lib angle and the Third World angle, the Roots angle," Kingston writes, she had not imagined that critics would measure the book and her "against the stereotype of the exotic, inscrutable, mysterious oriental. About two-thirds of reviewers did this. . . . A year ago I had really believed that the days of gross stereotyping were over. . . . Pridefully enough, I believed that I had written with such power that the reality and humanity of my characters would bust through any stereotypes of them. Simple-mindedly, I wore a sweat-shirt for the dust-jacket photo, to deny the exotic. I had not calculated how blinding stereotyping is, how stupefying."[31]

Repeatedly, Kingston reports, the reviews note a "brooding atmosphere" in the book that is "inscrutably foreign, oriental." And reviewers from such diverse publications as the Chattanooga News-Free Press and Newsweek play on the "stupid Kipling British-colonial cliché" that "East is East and West is West and never the twain shall meet" (Kingston 1982, 61). Although most critics enjoyed what they took to be the book's inscrutable charm, some disapproved of the book because it was not inscrutable enough. Kingston was particularly bothered by the review that took the book to task for the fact that "[t]he background is exotic, but the book is in the mainstream of American feminist literature."[32] What this means, Kingston observes, is that the reviewer "disliked the book because it is part of the mainstream. He is saying, then, that I am not to step out of the 'exotic' role, not to enter the mainstream. One of the most deadly weapons of stereotyping is the double bind, damned-if-you-do-and-damned-if-you-don't" (Kingston 1982, 56).

So completely did reviewers and others trust their own assumptions about the Chinese that they did not hesitate to set the book in San Francisco's famous Chinatown even though it takes place in Stockton. (Stockton is not named in the book, but one passage shows the family driving home from the San Francisco airport "across the Bay Bridge, over the Diablo hills, across the San Joaquin River to the valley" (*WW,* 118). And one could not simply blame the notorious New York provincialism. Not only did *The New Yorker, Newsweek,* and numerous other East Coast publications assume that all Chinese Americans live in San Francisco's Chinatown, but even California's *New West* magazine made the same mistake.

Sometimes, Kingston notes, "you just have to laugh because there really is no malice, and they are trying their best." This was how she felt when she saw that *Viva* magazine had published the "No Name Woman" chapter with "a full-page color illustration of Japanese maidens at the window; they wear kimonos, lacquered hair-dos, and through the window is lovely, snow-capped Mount Fuji. Surprise, Asian brothers and sisters! We may as well think of ourselves as Asian Americans because we are all alike anyway. I did not feel angry until I pointed out the Japanese picture to some Caucasians and they said, 'It doesn't matter' " (Kingston 1982, 61).

While many reviewers found that *The Woman Warrior* could be inserted nicely into their preconceived notions of Chinese Americans, others fretted about whether the story was really "typical," always implying that being "typical" was the book's obvious duty. A reviewer for the *Columbus Dispatch,* in a piece entitled "Rebellious Chinese Girl Rejects Ancient Heritage," found the story to be "atypical of the relationship between Chinese parents and their American Chinese children whom I have known in New York City and in Cincinnati" and also of the "business friends" and "servants" whom the reviewer knew when she lived in China (Kingston 1982, 58). Others, conversely, loved the book because they found it so "ineffably Chinese." Kingston replied: "No. No. No. Don't you hear the American slang? Don't you see the American settings? Don't you see the way the Chinese myths have been transmuted to America?" (Kingston 1982, 58).

A decade later, when *Tripmaster Monkey: His Fake Book* appeared, Kingston's anger at the stereotyping, exoticizing reviewers was still fresh. In the concluding monologue Kingston's protagonist, Wittman Ah Sing, rants in a phrase borrowed from the Civil Rights movement:

> Deep in my heart, I do believe we have to be of further outrage to stop this chanting about us, that "East is east and west is west." . . . We've failed with our magnificence of explosions [i.e., Wittman's theatrical production, but also Kingston's blockbuster book] to bust through their Kipling. . . . I am so fucking offended. Why aren't you offended? Let me help you get offended. Always take offense. . . . Do I have to explain why "exotic" pisses me off, and "not exotic" pisses me off? They've got us in a bag, which we aren't punching our way out of. To be exotic or to be not-exotic is not a question about Americans or about humans.[33]

It wasn't only Caucasians whose responses to the book Kingston found objectionable. She cites a Chinese American reviewer who worried that non-Chinese readers might assume that all Chinese American families had the same conflicts and difficulties as the Hong family. A review in the San Francisco Association of Chinese Teachers newsletter warned: "It must be pointed out that this book is a very personal statement, and is a subjective exposition of one person's reactions to her family background. . . . Especially for students unfamiliar with the Chinese background, it could give an overly negative impression of the Chinese American experience" (Kingston 1982, 62).

The concern over whether Kingston's book is "typical" indicates the special burden placed on all minority writers in the United States, Kingston says. "This is the same thing I have heard so many black writers say—that they have to take the whole responsibility of race. Then, at the same time, there are people of our own community, other Chinese Americans, who will say, 'Well, how dare you speak for us? Who voted for you? How can you make fun of us?' " (Perry, 187). In response Kingston asks:

> Why must I "represent" anyone beside myself? Why should I be denied an individual artistic vision. And I do not think I wrote a "negative" book . . . but suppose I had? Suppose I had been so wonderfully talented that I wrote a tragedy? Are we Chinese Americans to deny ourselves tragedy? If we give up tragedy in order to make a good impression on Caucasians, we have lost the battle. . . . I'm certain that someday when a great body of Chinese American writing becomes published and known, then readers will no longer have to put such a burden on each book that comes out. Readers can see the variety of ways for Chinese Americans to be. (Kingston 1982, 63)

All of her life, Kingston has said, she wanted to push back the black curtains that represented, in part, her own silence "and see what's on the other side" (BC, 5). Like the World War II blackout curtains, a wall of silence had blocked out both the great show of the world and also dangers that might be lurking just beyond. With the publication of *The Woman Warrior*, those curtains had been parted, and on the other side Kingston found national acclaim, publishing hoopla, and the adoration of readers, many of whom felt that she had spoken for them. Chinese American poet Marilyn Chin says, "*The Woman Warrior* was a very important book in my life. . . . I recognized Brave Orchid as my grandmother and Moon Orchid as my sad, sad mother. And my father was Moon Orchid's doctor-bigamist husband. My whole family was in that book. All those faces, with the complete physiognomy of that first generation of Chinese-American chaotic families. But it was wonderful. I think it gave [Asian American young people] permission go on. That book set a precedent" (Marilyn Chin, 62).

But by opening the black curtains, Kingston had, predictably, left herself open to attack. Not only did the very fact of a work by a Chinese American woman provoke an outpouring of ethnic stereotyping, but the work also provoked a flood of criticism and hostility. Although generally favorable to Kingston's work, Berkeley sinologist Frederic Wakeman Jr. complained in the *New York Review of Books* that the myths used in the book "are only remotely connected with the original Chinese legends they invoke; and sometimes they are only spurious folklore, a kind of self-indulgent fantasy that blends extravagant personal imagery with appropriately *volkisch* themes."[34] Wakeman understands that Kingston herself knows that the myths she uses in *The Woman Warrior* and in *China Men,* published two years later, "are largely her own reconstructions" (Wakeman, 42), and he sees that Kingston's intent is to use the myths to "make it possible for her to rediscover an otherwise lost China, and then summoning it, lay that spirit to rest" (Wakeman, 44). Even so, he is troubled by the liberties she takes. It is, he finds, "precisely because the myths are usually so consciously contrived, her pieces of distant China lore often seem jejune and even inauthentic—especially to readers who know a little bit about the original high culture which Kingston claims as a birthright" (Wakeman, 44).

Kingston responded that Wakeman, a history professor and author of such books as *The Fall of Imperial China,* is a scholar "on what he calls the 'high tradition,' and so he sees me as one who doesn't get it right, and who takes liberties with it. In actuality, I am writing in the peasant talk-story Cantonese tradition ('low' if you will), which is the heritage of Chinese Americans. Chinese Americans have changed the stories, but Mr. Wakeman compares our new stories to the ancient scholarly ones from the old country and finds them inauthentic."[35]

Chinese myth, Kingston argues, is a living, changing thing in the United States; the people she grew up with "tell peasant myths to one another, they pass them on and derive their strength from them. They also derive their doubts by comparing themselves to heroes of the past. I know all of these great heroes from the high tradition and they're not helping me in my American life. Such myths need to be changed and integrated into the peasant's life as well as into the Chinese American's life. And don't forget, the myths change from one telling to another."[36]

Rather than intending to "record" myths, Kingston says she set out to use them. Criticized for having "incorrectly" conflated the story of the male Yue Fei, whose mother carved a charge of loyalty on his back, with her woman warrior figure, Kingston says, "I took that and gave it to a woman. . . . I gave the strength of that story to a woman. I see that as an aggressive storytelling act, part of my own freedom" (Bonetti).

Kingston does not accept the notion that these stories are owned by the keepers of the Chinese literary canon. Rather, she says, they "belong to me. They're mine. They are part of my psyche which I inherited. Probably in utero I was hearing these stories. . . . I went with the way the story formed in me." She did research the stories, to see the way they appeared in the classical texts, but decided to go with her own version (Simmons).

Although these stories may have originated in China, Kingston now thinks of them as "American myths. That's where I heard them. It is less important what they have to do with China than what they have to do with America. What interests me is which chants and stories survive in America. . . . Which things die away; which come with us" (Bonetti).

Kingston demonstrates her meaning in *China Men,* showing how scenes from the famed historical epic *Romance of Three Kingdoms,* in which three disenfranchised men swear eternal brotherhood against a common foe, are particularly cherished by the immigrant Chinese men. The immigrants, who are themselves disenfranchised and who face the common foe of American racism, draw strength from this portrayal of loyalty and heroism. Attending a performance of this scene, the immigrant grandfather in *China Men* recognizes the legendary hero, Guan Goong:[37] "The main actor's face was painted red with thick black eyebrows and long black beard, and when he strode onto the stage, [the grandfather] recognized the hero, Guan Goong. . . . [His] heart leapt to recognize hero and horse in the wilds of America. . . . When [attacked] Guan Goong fought the biggest man in one-to-one combat, a twirling, jumping sword dance that strengthened the China Men who watched it. . . . [The Grandfather] felt refreshed and inspired."[38]

Attack

While Kingston was surprised by the stereotyping and exoticizing of reviewers and by the claims of inauthenticity by scholars, she was shocked at the vicious attacks that came from a group of men in the Asian American literary community, a group that Kingston had expected to welcome her as an ally. The attacks were led by playwright Frank Chin who, as founder of the Asian American Theater Company in San Francisco, and as author of the first Chinese American work produced by a major New York theater, was the first Chinese American "to rise to literary stardom" (Iwata, 1). In his work Chin expresses the sense that the Chinese man has been feminized and that he needs to find ways to restore his masculinity. In the introduction to Chin's play *The Chicken-coop Chinaman,* Dorothy Ritsuko McDonald writes that Chin seeks to counter the image of the "effeminate, Christianized Charlie Chan image" and has "restored the immensely masculine [Chinese mythical figure and god] Kwan Kung [Guan Goong], whose strength of mind and body, individuality and loyalty, capacity for revenge and essential aloneness are reminiscent of the rugged Western hero of American myth" (McDonald, xxix). Chin does not only write about the supermasculine, Kwan Kung, McDonald says. He seeks to *be* Kwan Kung: "Chin in his own life and work has maintained the heroic stance of the old Chinaman god" (McDonald, xxix).

Although the two authors have never met, Kingston says she knew of Chin, who was in her class at Berkeley: "I did admire him because I had heard that there was somebody in our department, the English Department, who had written. And I think he was editor of the literary magazine at the same time as Diane Wakoski. I was thinking, Oh my god, they're all doing so well, and I'm not doing anything. I'm on the *Daily Cal.* I'm doing journalism" (Simmons).

Kingston had assumed that her own success would be applauded by Chin and others as another step forward for the Asian American literary movement: "At that time there were some Asian American men who were all we had of our literary community. And I expected, when my book came out, for them to say, welcome. Welcome to the community of artists.

Because there are so few of us. So here's another one to add strength to our numbers" (Marilyn Chin, 67). Instead, she found herself continuously attacked by Frank Chin "in forum after forum, essay after essay" (Iwata, 1). The group accused Kingston of writing "white racist art" that "distorts beloved Asian myths and folk tales to fit her feminist views" (Iwata, 1).

In the summer of 1978 a group of these critics came to Hawaii and attacked Kingston in person at "Talk Story," a literary conference for Asian American and Hawaiian writers. Jeff Paul Chan and Shawn Wong, editors with Chin of *The Big Aiiieeeee!*, an anthology of Asian American writing, claimed that "publishers maintain a ghetto of female ethnic autobiographies and reject the work of male ethnic novelists" (*HS,* 36). (Chin himself had refused to participate in the conference if Kingston were present.) Kingston, according to reports of those present, rose from the floor to defend herself in a "quavering" voice, claiming that her work had been "misread" (Iwata, 9).

In *Hawai'i One Summer,* written during this period, Kingston can be glimpsed attempting to find a silver lining in the controversial conference. She does not express anger or hurt, writing only, "It was embarrassing that we were the only ethnic group that did not show a harmonious face; on the other hand, I felt good about our liveliness" (*HS,* 36). When a "famous writer" walks out on Kingston's reading of "my suspenseful new chapter," Kingston nonetheless allows herself to remember a line from Diana Chang's *Frontiers of Love*: "Nothing but disdain could make some Chinese passionate" (*HS,* 37).

Writing recently of that conference in a re-issued edition of *Hawai'i One Summer*, Kingston recalls a general tone of conflict over the question of who owns stories. Not only has she been criticized for misappropriating Chinese myth, but "the literary community in Hawai'i argues over who owns the myths and stories, whether the local language and writings should be exported to the Mainland, whether or not so-and-so is authentic, is Hawaiian." She notes that at the conference, "[w]e addressed one another with rancor and panic, though some did try for aloha. The name *Asian Pacific American* had barely been thought, and many people denied every term in it. We were divided between those who would give the stories, myths, ceremonies to whoever hears them, and those who would have possession be by blood."[39]

Hawai'i Diary: Solving Life and Suicide

To take a respite from her work on *China Men,* which was nearing completion that summer, and also, Kingston suggests now, to extricate herself from the controversies that swirled over who owned the stories of China and Hawaii, she decided that she would "write personally, about myself." The result was a series of "diary entries" that appeared in the *New York Times,* and which was later collected and published in limited edition accompanied by original woodcuts, as *Hawai'i One Summer.* (The book was reissued in 1999 by the University of Hawaii Press.) It may be here that one can best sense the impact on Kingston of fame and prominence, the payoff and the price of parting the black curtains of silence.

One of the most tangible results is that the Kingstons bought their first house, agonizing over the frightening permanence and finality such a purchase implies. They noted that the root of the word mortgage means death, and they feared that with home ownership they would lose their radical edge, would no longer be willing to say "burn it down to the ground," no longer be able to just pick up and go as the mood strikes (*HS,* 5). At the same time, renting had come to feel "irresponsible," as other counterculture types were buying land and building communes, establishing their own little worlds. Maxine also loved the idea of a place of her own to write, and the house they bought had a real "writer's garret" where she felt she could "brood . . . thick novels with no interrupting chapter breaks," just "one long thought from front to back cover" (*HS,* 5). Finally, the Kingstons reason that their new house can be put to good counterculture use "as a place for meeting when the bombs fall" (*HS,* 5).

We hear in these pieces Kingston's familiar upbeat voice, a voice determined to undermine difficulty by subjecting it to minute and humorous examination; still, there is a wash of fear throughout the book. The successful writer who has finally managed to break silence in a way that fulfills the wildest fantasies of the unpublished and underrated, and who has just purchased her dream garret, frets about going to her high school reunion and realizes that writing, even writing success, does not insulate her from her fears. The swim out to the island, Chinaman's Hat, is full of beauty and interest yet subject to moments of black confusion and the always lurking fear of sharks. And having to face endless stacks of dirty dishes in the sink sets Kingston thinking "about what to write in a suicide note" (*HS,* 17). On the wall beside her sink she has glued a card upon which she has written:

"I have just entered the monastery. Please teach me."
"Have you eaten rice?"
"I have."

"Then you had better wash your bowl."
At that moment the new monk found enlightenment.

"I have a glimmering," Kingston writes, "that if I solve this koan, I can solve dishwashing too, or if I can solve dishwashing, I can solve life and suicide. I haven't solved it but I have a few clues" (*HS*, 19).

In the last two essays of the collection, written at the end of the summer, Kingston describes her visit some years earlier to poet Lew Welch, and her recent morning at the beach with her son, Joseph, a surfing addict. In these pieces Kingston celebrates the transcendent artistry of both the poet and the surfer; at the same time she studies the dangers inherent in such transcendence.

Kingston admires Welch for his ability to integrate poetry and life, and for his refusal to let his art become something rarefied and precious or, conversely, to be turned into a mere commodity. Like Kingston, he believes that life can be changed through art. He is proud that one of his poems "for protecting the town" has been put up in the window of a Sausalito bar and that the owner published the poem, "Sausalito Trash Prayer," by duplicating 40 copies and handing them out. He liked the idea that the poem had been "pasted in a florist's window, . . .that it might remind of love, that it might sell flowers" (*HS*, 47). When one of his young poets cannot make a reading because he has to fix his car, Welch approves. Poets should be car fixers too.

Kingston also admires Welch for the way he nurtures other writers, the counterculture community he supports. He plans a magazine called *Bread* that would "discuss the economics of being a poet in America" (*HS*, 46). Although the magazine never appeared, Kingston still likes the idea. He "comforts and feeds kid writers," worrying over them as she does her own students. And like Kingston—who worries that her students will be paralyzed by the requirement that they master the essay form and thus lose track of what they wanted to say (*HS*, 33)—he urges that poetry is about only truth, saying, "When I write, my only concern is accuracy. I try to write accurately from the poise of mind which lets us see that things are exactly what they seem. I never worry about beauty, if it is accurate there is always beauty. I never worry about form, if it is accurate there is always form" (*HS*, 48). Kingston uses these lines to teach her own students, copying them and handing them out at the beginning of a writing course, telling them she has not much more to teach than this, but "they don't believe me and stay" (*HS*, 48).

But the writer she learned from and identified with, whose purity of purpose she admired, one day disappeared forever. She writes in *Hawai'i One Summer,* "he walked in the woods and has not come back" (*HS,* 48).

Why, at the moment of unimaginable success, when the impact of her own art is being felt in the world, does Kingston return to meditate on Lew Welch? Perhaps there is a clue in *China Men,* the book Kingston is finishing in this summer of 1978. The chapter "The Li Sao: An Elegy," is based on the ancient Chinese poem *Li Sao,* variously translated as *The Lament* or *Encountering Sorrow,* in which the poet Ch'ü Yuan tells of his wanderings in exile. Ch'ü Yuan, who lived in the third and fourth centuries B.C., is banished because he advised his king not to go to war, and, as Kingston recounts the story, "people were so blind, they thought he was a wrongdoer instead of the only righteous man left in the world" (*CM,* 257). In Kingston's portrait Ch'ü Yuan writes a poem with many questions—such as "Can I convince people one by one what is right?"— but no answers, and he yearns for his homeland, realizing that "escape and return were equally impossible" (*CM,* 258). Finally, walking beside a river he meets a fisherman, whom he tells: "The crowd is drunk; I alone am sober. I alone am clean, so I am banished. The world has gone bad. Even the reliable orchid has changed" (*CM,* 259).

But the fisherman doesn't see the problem: " 'Why should you be aloof?' asked the fisherman. 'When the water's clear, I wash my tassels, but when it's too muddy for silk, I can still wash my feet' " (*CM,* 259). Ch'ü, hearing this, decides he too will use the river: "He sang all his poems and his elegy, his requiem. He danced at the edge of the river to make his last moments happier. He threw himself into the water and drowned" (*CM,* 259). The people, now understanding, try to get him to return, but he refuses and is remembered by people all over the world on the fifth day of the fifth month as "Ch'ü Yuan the incorruptible" (*CM,* 260).

Is this, then, the payment for breaking silence, for telling the truth, for urging peace and purity? Are exile, vilification, and martyrdom required before people will understand who you are, what your intentions have been all along?

In "A Sea Worry," the last essay in *Hawai'i One Summer,* Kingston examines another form of discovery and expression: surfing, as practiced by her son and other local "surfing addicts" (*HS,* 49). Here, too, is a life completely devoted—at least for the moment—to a kind of transcendent purity. The surfers' passion for their art is so great that it overrides all fear.

Kingston's son recounts how he saw a huge shark in the waves, but he didn't want to tell the lifeguards so as not to spoil the surfing (HS, 49). Curious about this powerful experience, and apprehensive of more than sharks—"I'm afraid that the boys give themselves up to the ocean's mindlessness" (HS, 49)—Kingston goes early one morning to watch her son ride the waves. Although she does not go out into the water, she can glimpse inside the "tubes" from shore and gets a sense of what the boys are experiencing: "The magic ones . . . were made out of just water, green and turquoise rooms, translucent walls and ceilings. I saw one that was powder blue, perfect, thin; the sun filled it with sky blue and white light" (HS, 51).

When the boys speak of the experience, they describe it as being "about silence, peace, 'no hassles,' and a feeling of being reborn as they shoot out the end of the tube." And as Kingston watches the boys looking toward the sea for the next wave, she is reminded of "altar boys before a great god" (HS, 49).

And so what of this route to purity and transcendence? Will this too lead to death, of the body or the mind? Does the desire to transform life into peace and beauty necessarily lead to exile and death?

Kingston closes Hawai'i One Summer not with dread but with a sense of relief. At breakfast the boys are able to describe their experiences as they eat; the quest for transcendent purity has not resulted in dangerous disconnection. And Kingston is also comforted by "the streams of commuter traffic, cars filled with men, passing Sandy Beach on their way to work" (HS, 52). One can have a pure and powerful experience, she seems to say at the end of her summer's meditations; one can be filled with the desire for peace and transcendence but need not inevitably be exiled from the human community or cut off from the steadying mundanities of human life.

Making American Myth

In 1980 Kingston's second book, China Men, appeared, and this time it was not Mademoiselle but the New York Times that sent a reporter to observe the writer in her Honolulu home. This time there is no reference to Kingston's size, to her dress, or her "doll-like" quality. Rather, the reporter notes the galley proofs lining the dining room walls. Whereas the Mademoiselle reporter described a tiny, "hesitant" woman, who "giggles" her responses, and seems obsessed by themes of "hard work" and "easy guilt when one is not at work" (Brownmiller, 148), the *New York Times* interviewer finds a writer now making "confident, protracted" statements about her work.[40]

Kingston had been stacking up tributes since the appearance of *The Woman Warrior*—The National Book Critics Circle Award for the best nonfiction book of 1976; the *Mademoiselle* Magazine Award, 1977; the National Education Association Award, 1977; and the Anisfield-Wolf Race Relations Award, 1978. *Time* magazine named *The Woman Warrior* one of the top 10 nonfiction books of the decade, and in 1980 the writer who worried that she had been seen as a foreign interloper in Hawaii was given a particularly gratifying award. A Honolulu Buddhist sect named her a Living Treasure of Hawaii "during a chant and incense filled ceremony at Honpa Hongwanj Temple" (Pfaff, 1). The tradition, Kingston says, comes to Hawaii by way of modern Japan, and the honor is usually bestowed on someone much older; in Japan, the recipient must be at least 80. For Kingston, the honor felt as if "the islands are saying, 'You can be a part of Hawaii too.' I think this is a hard place to belong to" (Pfaff, 25).

In interviews Kingston repeatedly emphasizes that she sees *China Men* as quintessentially American, as a reenvisioning and retelling of the American myth, much in the manner of William Carlos Williams's 1925 work *In the American Grain,* which Quentin Anderson calls "an almost frantic burrowing into the past for instances in which heroic figures had achieved an imaginative grasp of the continent."[41] Kingston sees her account taking up where Williams's book, which closes with the Civil War, leaves off. *China Men* spans the period that begins in the mid–nineteenth century with the arrival of large numbers of Chinese immigrants and ends with the Vietnam War, when Kingston's brother is transported to Asia on a troop ship. In creating an American mythology around Chinese men, she argues that she is "claiming America" for the Chinese Americans. Williams "retold the American myth, which I think is exactly the right way to write American history. His book starts with Leif Ericsson and ends with Abraham Lincoln, but his Lincoln is a woman, a feminine force in American history. . . . Williams has told American history poetically and, it seems to me, truly" (Pfaff, 25).

Kingston, who dresses a woman as a man (the woman warrior) and a man as a woman (Tang Ao in *China Men*), particularly likes the way Williams collapses gender boundaries by making Abraham Lincoln the "mother" of the country: "He talks about this wonderful woman walking through the [Civil War] battlefields with a beard and a shawl. I find that so freeing, that we don't have to be constrained to being just one ethnic group or one gender. [He makes] me feel that I can now write as a man, I can write as a black person, as a white person; I don't have to be restricted by time and physicality" (Fishkin, 784).

Kingston not only see herself as building on Williams's project to remythologize America and to break down rigid ethnic and gender boundaries, but she also sees herself in a long tradition of writers who have felt the newness of American culture and sought to create a correspondingly new literature: "I am in the tradition of . . . Mark Twain, Walt Whitman, Gertrude Stein, the Beats. [They] all developed ears for dialect, street language, and experimented with how to make the written language sound like spoken language. The content of that language is the ever-changing mythology. I am writing American mythology in American language."[42]

Even though she had originally conceived of the two books as part of one big project, Kingston sees *China Men* as a significant departure from *The Woman Warrior*. She decided to separate the two, she explains, because the men's stories were "weakening the feminist point of view. . . . The women had their own time and place and their lives were coherent; there was a woman's way of thinking. The men's stories seemed to interfere. So I took all the men's stories out, and then I had *Woman Warrior*."[43]

The two ways of thinking couldn't go together, she says, because of history. The lives of Chinese American men and women have been very different:

> Historically, of course the men went to a different country without their families, and so they had their adventures by themselves. It was as if they went to a men's country and they had men's stories. This is hindsight now; but it does seem as if the women's stories have a convolution and the men's stories have more of a linear passage through time. The men's myths and memories are not as integrated into their present-day lives, and that influences the structure of both of those books. In *The Woman Warrior*, when the girls and women draw on mythology for their strength, the myth becomes part of the women's lives and the structure of the stories. In the men's stories, I tell a myth and then I tell a present-day story, a myth, and then another present-day adventure story; they are separate narratives. The reason I think that happened was that those men went to a place where they didn't know whether their mythology was giving them any strength or not. They were getting very broken off from their background. They might not have even been drawing any

strength or they may have gone against the teaching of the myth. They
were so caught up in the adventure of the new land that they thought,
'What good are memories and the past?' Memory just hurts them,
because they can't go home. So, the myth story and the present story
became separated. . . .

Those men were making history. They were making a new myth too.
They were not so caught up in old myths as the women were. . . . In fact,
I wrote the characters so that the women have memories and the men
don't have memories. They don't remember anything. The character of
my father for example, has no memory. He has no stories of the past. He
is an American and even his memories are provided by the mother. She
says that he went dancing, or whatever; he is so busy making up the present, which he has to build, that he has no time for the continuity from
the past. (Rabinowitz, 180)

Besides showing men who were "making up the present," as well as
helping to build a country, Kingston felt she was forced to create figures
that were intended to break the stereotype of the Chinese American
man: "As much as you would like to ignore the stereotype, saying it's
totally irrelevant, actually you can't. It impinges on your life a lot, it
impacts on your work, and I know that quite often I write against the
stereotype and I react against the stereotype. One stereotype of Asian
Americans is that we're really serious, and we never have any fun, and
we have no sense of humor" (Fishkin, 788). As a result, in *China Men*
Kingston wanted to show how "Chinese and Chinese Americans are the
most raucous people; they laugh so much, they're telling jokes and
they're always standing up and performing for one another. They are *so*
outgoing. . . . I also think that being able to laugh and to be funny—
those are really important *human* characteristics, and when we say that
people don't have those characteristics, then we deny them their
humanity" (Fishkin, 788).

By grasping the difference between the experiences and stories of
men and women, Kingston feels she is winning her struggle to escape
the domination of the first-person narrator, which she finds to be "an
artistic as well as a psychological improvement on my part" (Marilyn
Chin, 59). *The Woman Warrior,* Kingston explains, "was the story of a
young woman . . . still creating herself. She only knows her self and
knows women." She has "little sympathy or interest in knowing what
men are like." But with *China Men* Kingston believes she is a "mature
grown person able to look at the opposite sex and know them for themselves." Opening *China Men* with the myth of the Tang Ao, who goes to

the land of the women, is Kingston's way of saying, "I am a woman going into the land of men; what will become of me? I became the kind of woman who loves men, and I can tell their story without judging them or showing them just in relation to myself" (Bonetti).

Roots

In 1984, after a lifetime of imagining China, Kingston finally had the chance to see the real thing when she, along with authors Toni Morrison, Leslie Marmon Silko, and Francine du Plessix Gray, was invited to China as a guest of the Chinese Writers' Association. A part of Kingston was afraid to make the trip, asking herself, "What if China invalidated everything that I was thinking and writing?" Kingston's mother was afraid for her to make the trip for a more concrete reason: "You have written some very bad things about the regime," her mother told her. "Tell them you didn't mean it. Tell them you take it back.' "[44]

But Kingston's dread that she would find she had gotten China all wrong was unfounded: "One of the great thrills was to see how well I had imagined it. Many of the colors, and the smells, the people, the faces, the incidents, were much as I imagined. Many people said to me, 'Welcome home.' I did feel that I was going back to a place I had never been" (Rabinowitz, 181).

One thing that did surprise Kingston, however, something she wished she had known before writing about China, was how tightly packed together people were:

> The tight quarters of the rooms and of the villages. If I had been in those rooms earlier, I would have understood even better the sense of a village and how each person's drama reverberates through the village. I would have seen that people did not have to walk as far as I said to go from one place to another. At my father's village, the well where the aunt drowned herself was right next to the Hong family temple. My mother said that the guys used to hang around on the steps of the temple and make remarks at the girls to try to get them to drop and break their water jars. That is so real to everyone of all cultures. You know, guys whistling at girls, and, also, it's so sexy. I wish I had had it in the book. I saw small things like that that I wished I had had earlier, but nothing large that invalidated the whole work. (Rabinowitz, 181)

The China visit also gave Kingston a stronger sense of the importance of theater to Chinese life. In America she had grasped that theater was central: "Talk-stories and letters that came from China were often about what happened at the theater, how the theater became Communist, how theaters went dark." In China Kingston saw the physical presence of theater: "The first time I crossed the border from Hong Kong into a village in China, I saw that the only large building was the theater, which had the face of a monkey-clown on the wall. On my second, longer trip, I visited my parents' villages. . . . [T]he largest structure in my mother's village is the music hall" (BC, 6).

Kingston found her roots in China, meeting relatives, seeing home villages and ancestral tablets and relics that were being rebuilt after the destruction of the Cultural Revolution. But the other writers, she said, found their roots as well. Buddhists Allen Ginsberg and Gary Snyder went to the temples. Silko, a Native American writer, saw familiar woven patterns in Mongolian fabrics. Later, Kingston was amazed to see motifs in Toni Morrison's Beloved, which Morrison was working on at the time of the China trip, resembling those in Kingston's own work. The symbols carved in the back of Morrison's escaped slave woman, Sethe, are similar to those carved on the back of Kingston's woman warrior. Further, Kingston noticed, the silence enforced on cane field workers in Morrison's book is "the same silence that Chinese workers, my great-grandfathers had enforced on them in the fields of Hawaii while they worked in the cane fields." She also noted that Beloved, like The Woman Warrior, was told as a ghost story. Of the similarities she says:

> I was so thrilled that there was this connection with African Americans and Asians and Native Americans and Asians. It affirmed the connection of all people—that our myths break across all kinds of barriers and then it makes me wonder about the connection with working sugar cane. What is it about physical labor and silence? Why do we have to be silent as we work like animals? That is a human question, not just an African American question or a Native American question, or a Chinese question. I see us all working toward breaking this silence. It is not white masters that stick a muzzle on us, it is something larger than that. There is a universal struggle between silence and speech.[45]

Kingston also found the trip to be a "linguistic adventure" as she traveled south through China, realizing that the closer she got to her home village in Canton the better she could communicate. Asked to speak for the writers' group on formal occasions, Kingston was initially at a loss, knowing neither Mandarin nor formal Cantonese. Finally, she spoke in the only Chinese language she knew, her "peasant village

dialect," a strategy that worked well for the veteran of the antiestablish-
ment, power-to-the-people 1960s:

> It occurred to me, I'll just do it in village speech. And so I did, and I
> translated myself. I would say a sentence and then I'd translate it into
> English. And I realized that no one there understood me because the
> Chinese there wouldn't either. And it felt really good when I realized that
> I was being more politically correct than anybody else because my class
> credentials were impeccable! I bet no Communist did this because they
> would do whatever the official national language was. Or, if they were
> really feeling peasant, they would do Cantonese, but they wouldn't do
> this peasant dialect. I just got such a kick out of it. I felt so at home.
> (Perry, 191)

Her mother's fears that her writing would anger Chinese Communists did not materialize. Journalist Harrison Salisbury, who accompanied the writers on their trip through China, reported:

> When Kingston reached Canton, everyone seemed to know her writing.
> She was picked up by local writers and whisked off to the village of
> Gongzhou where her family came from—a two or three day round trip
> into the interior of Guangdong province. Her cousins stood beside the
> road all day waiting for her to arrive. Her visit to the village was one long
> feast. She was put up in not one of the simple plaster-and-wattle houses
> but a new three story hotel, in the best corner room. Everyone claimed to
> be a relative. No one complained about what she had written about the
> Communists. (Salisbury, 25)

By her second trip to China, Kingston found that she had an extensive
reading public. She had been published in China in many different translations, Hong Kong pirated editions, Taiwan pirated, Taiwan legal, and
Beijing Language Institute, who did a "very careful Mandarin transla-
tion" (Marilyn Chin, 790). In some of the pirated editions, the translators
fit the work into ready-made forms, often a kind of soap opera genre
(Perry, 181). Initially the Chinese were more inclined to translate the
realistic stories; by her second trip Kingston found them willing to translate the surrealist aspects of her work as well. Kingston was told by a
Chinese poet that parts of *Tripmaster Monkey*, which she read in an early
draft version, were in the tradition of the Chinese classic *Dream of the Red
Chamber*, because "Wittman as the effete young man [is] battling to keep
his manhood among the matriarchy, the twelve women of that book"
(Marilyn Chin, 64). Kingston was also surprised to find herself claimed as

part of a Chinese "roots literature" movement that was undertaking to rework connections to the classical past severed during the Cultural Revolution. She notes that the radicals of the Cultural Revolution

> had cut off their ties to the West, and cut off the bindings of feudalism, the imperial arts and all that. But then they weren't left with anything. So, as I came to the end of the trip, when we got to Shanghai, they were crying and talking about all this Cultural Revolution stuff. Then I thought, I know why they invited us American writers there, especially me, because they felt that I was working in free conditions. Here I was in America, where I had free speech and free press. And I spent this lifetime working on roots. So what they were saying was that I was their continuity. And they wanted help in figuring out where to go. . . . It felt so terrific. Because they were telling me I was part of the Chinese canon. And here I was writing in English!" (Marilyn Chin, 65)

Monkey Spirit

In 1989, nine years after the appearance of *China Men*, Kingston published her third book, and first novel, *Tripmaster Monkey: His Fake Book*. With this book Kingston departs from the memoir form of her first two works, which were dominated by coming-of-age questions and which sought answers by examining her own and her parents' lives. In the new book Kingston turns away from the girl Maxine, the angry Tom Hong, and the domineering Brave Orchid. Rather, in a work that is, she says, influenced by the avant-garde theater of the 1960s (Saffa), she turns her attention to an angry, young, motor-mouthed Chinese American English major, the beatnik poet Wittman Ah Sing, whose struggle against racism and fight to find his place, to make his contribution as a Chinese American, are given form by the counterculture attitudes of the early 1960s. Just speaking the language of the 1960s seems to make Wittman freer: "What I like about [Wittman] best," Kingston says, "is that he's got this wild, inventive sixties language. . . . There was this new language that people were inventing for new psychedelic states, and spiritual states, and for political activities" (Fishkin, 789).

Like the African Americans he sees around him in the 1960s, Wittman, says his creator, "wants to be bad, to do heroic things" (Moyers). In her interview with Bill Moyers, Kingston acknowledges that many readers don't like the enraged, endlessly rapping Wittman, but she explains: "He's responding to racism. This is why he's not likable. Minority people know how to be charming. There are charming stereotypes." But this presents a dilemma: "If he puts on a likable style, he plays into the hands of an emasculating America" (Moyers).

In her portrait of Wittman Kingston creates a character who is angry, who refuses to be emasculated by racism, but who, at the same time, manages to transform his anger, depression, and loneliness into the positive energy of inclusion and community building through the transformative magic of theater. Of his anger Kingston says,

> Even though Wittman is ranting and raving and is verbally violent, he doesn't do anything about it. His explosions aren't even explosions—he implodes quite often. He cuts his own hair. He burns his own socks. But he never hurts other people. And I'm very aware that he never does racist name-calling. . . .
>
> I'm working with [the question], Is it possible to get all the anger and hate out verbally? And, if so, does that turn a person more peaceful? It's the same question that Wittman asks at the beginning, 'Does playing football make you more violent or less violent?' Does it mean that you get all your violence out, and football players then become the most peaceful of men because they realize that the violence is just a game and they are not out there to kill anybody, and then it's over with and everybody goes home? Or does it aggravate it, and then you become more and more violent? What does letting the anger out do? (Perry, 174)

Besides being full of the protest spirit of the early 1960s, Wittman is also full of the spirit of play, like the Monkey King, a mischievous, irreverent figure in Chinese literature who, in *The Journey to the West*, guides a Buddhist monk on his trip to India to take possession of sacred Buddhist texts. Monkey, who is almost always in defiance of established authority, has the power to get out of trouble through endless transformations. Although he undertakes a "quest for spiritual understanding," he also is involved in "a quest for magical power."[46] C. T. Hsia notes that, unlike other rebels such as Satan in Milton's *Paradise Lost,* Monkey never loses "his ability to view himself in a humorous light. . . . He is never too solemn even when fighting a whole battalion of heavenly troops. Without his sense of humor, Monkey would have become a tragic hero or else shared the fate of the other monsters. With his sense of humor, he can turn from rebel to Buddha's obedient servant without forfeiting our sympathy" (Hsia, 135).

It is this spirit of play, and a sense of the magically liberating power of humor and knowledge, that Kingston relies on to transform the angry young Wittman Ah Sing. Monkey, Kingston observes,

> was always looking for the elixir of Life. And the gods in heaven put him through so many trials. But he always bounced back; no matter how the evil prince and his army chased after him and so forth, he always bounced back. . . . His bouncing back has to do with irrepressible joy and his spirit of fun. Somehow we are going to solve the world's problems with fun and theater. And with laughter. The reason this is all set in the Sixties, too, is that the monkey was here in the Sixties. Abby Hoffman, Allen Ginsberg. . . . They were trying to change the world with costumes and street theater. . . . The monkey's task was to bring chaos to established order. So Wittman has that also. (Marilyn Chin, 61)

"The King of the Monkeys leads his people," Kingston writes. "They find a land where they cavort and parade and tell jokes. The Monkey King has seventy-two transformations, and of course, he changes into an American, a Californian, a North Beach-Chinatown cat. He does stand-up comedy and stand-up tragedy" (BC, 6).

By wedding the angry protester of the 1960s to the mischievous, unquenchable trickster Monkey, Kingston suggests that his involvement with the theater is a way for him to avoid being "brutalized" by his anger; through theater he can transform his anger into something positive. Like Kingston, Wittman originally views himself as a poet; like her, he switches to a genre that will, Kingston says, have a better chance of "making a difference, socially. And he wants to form a community. His being a playwright would do that better than being a poet. So he picks a more social art" (Marilyn Chin, 61).

According to Kingston, Wittman puts on a theatrical performance to create a new vision of why the Chinese Americans came to America in the first place, what fired their ambition to seek a new world. In doing so she transforms the image of the Chinese immigrant from dehumanized work machine to rollicking hero of an extended road show. As *Tripmaster Monkey* was in progress, she wrote: "As I write further into [the new book], I learn a new view of human nature and why we migrate— we didn't go looking for the Gold Mountain in order to plunder it, nor to find something more to eat. I had thought after writing *China Men* that curiosity and adventure were high-minded enough purposes. But out-on-the-road and off-the-boat, we made theater. The songs and myths and dances changed to fit circumstances in the new world. . . . The pioneers built the West by putting on shows" (BC, 6, 11).

Finally, through the transformative art of theater, Wittman must find a way to use the energy of his anger to produce a new inclusive vision, one in which there is a place for everyone, including himself. For, Kingston suggests in the book, there exists to date no workable vision of identity and community for the Chinese American. These will only be achieved through an act of improvisation, which brings together a variety of influences, melding them through performance into a new whole.

Although most reviewers praised the book overall, there was some sense of disappointment that Kingston had not continued in the memoiristic vein so many readers had come to love. LeAnne Schreiber, writing in the *New York Times Book Review*, is one of those who seems to regret the new direction Kingston has taken. She finds Wittman "at times compelling, touching, wildly imaginative." Still, the reviewer expresses a longing for the "less fevered but more exciting voice of Maxine Hong Kingston speaking for herself as she did in *The Woman Warrior* and *China Men*. In *Tripmaster Monkey* the ventriloquism is too complete."[47] Critic John Leonard, who launched Kingston's first book, *The Woman Warrior*, summarizes the problem some readers were having: "What everybody seems to have wanted from Kingston, after a decade of silence, is another dreambook, like *The Woman Warrior*. Or another history lesson like *China Men*. Anyway: more magic, ghosts, dragonboats, flute music from the savage lands. Never mind that she's earned the right to write about whatever she chooses, and if she chooses to write about looking for Buddha in the wild, wild West, we'd better pay attention because she's smarter than we are. Nevertheless, the reviewers are demanding more memoir. Where's the female avenger?"[48]

But Leonard does not believe that the "real" Maxine Hong Kingston has been lost in the voice of Wittman Ah Sing. Rather, he hears the voice of Kingston as a grown up, no longer buried under the stories of her mother and the anger of her father. "The grown-up Maxine," Leonard argues, "after all was a Cal English major just like Wittman." From the "slang of be-ins and love-ins and trippings-out in the psychedelic 1960s, from radical chitchat and the calisthenics of Left Coast Zen, an adult Kingston had fashioned a language of her own," Leonard finds. "But she'd no place to put it in her first two books. Like Bak Goong in *China Men*, forbidden to talk on the Hawaii sugar cane plantation, she shouted into a hole in the ground. To sing herself, she needed someone like the unbuttoned Wittman" (Leonard, 769).

If the novel was seen by some reviewers as too great a departure from the more accessible memoir form her readers had grown to love, others struggled with the manic energy and complexity of the novel. Anne

Tyler, who pronounced *Tripmaster Monkey* a work of "satisfying complexity and bite and verve," admitted that she also found it "exhausting," a
novel of "excesses—both the hero's and the author's."[49] She is worn out
with Wittman's "exuberance" and finds the numerous references to Chinese stories "particularly tiring." Wittman, she finds, "loves to tell
lengthy stories that possess the grandiosity and the meandering formlessness common to folk legends. It's hard to believe that his friends,
who tend to be as frenetic as Wittman himself, would sit still for what
amounts to hours of this. Certainly the reader has trouble doing so.
After a while, the merest mention of Liu Pei[50] or Sun Wu Kong, the
Monkey King, is enough to make our eyes glaze over" (Tyler, 46).

But Wittman himself has a response to Tyler and others who yearn
for the relative simplicity of Kingston's first memoir, and whose eyes
cross at the mention of one more Chinese name and the telling of one
more Chinese myth: "No more accessible girls and unspeakable men,"
Wittman declares, apparently referring to characters found in Kingston's
first two books: "Let the gringo Anglos do some hard hearing for a
change" (*TM*, 138).

Still others who had claimed the author's earliest work as a pioneering feminist project have, Kingston acknowledges, expressed "disappointment" with a book that had an angry young man—whom the
author describes as "macho"—as its protagonist (Saffa). But Kingston
contends readers are wrong to believe that she has lessened her commit-
ment to the cause of feminism:

> I think to be a good feminist first you realize who you are yourself as a
> woman and, when you become a strong woman, then you face the Other.
> Whatever the Other is, whether it's men, the rest of the world, people of
> other races—whatever to you, in your psyche, the Other is. And so,
> when you become a strong woman, you also face the yang, and so, of
> course the next book has to be about men, that's the other half of the
> universe. So to me it's profoundly feminist to write about men, to be able
> to create men characters, and to understand what I previously could not
> understand. (Perry, 180)

Furthermore, Kingston points out something many of her feminist readers seem to have missed: The book's omniscient narrator is in fact a
woman and a goddess, Kuan Yin, the goddess of mercy, who in *Journey to
the West* oversees Monkey's progress, repeatedly intervening to keep the
impetuous Monkey on his road to spiritual enlightenment.[51] For
Kingston, Kuan Yin is the one who is really in charge: "She is actually

pushing Wittman Ah Sing around, telling him to shut up. She gives him various girlfriends; she gives him different difficult human situations to contend with. . . . She is sometimes very tough on Wittman." In *The Journey to the West,* Kuan Yin pins Monkey under a rock for 500 years. Similarly, Kingston says, "I felt that as narrator I took a rock and threw it on top of the protagonist and captured him. And kept him in place. So I was beginning to see that my narrator is Kuan Yin, and she is very merciful. I mean, nobody is going to get killed or hurt. She keeps giving people wonderful opportunities" (Marilyn Chin, 59).

Although Kingston sees the book as an effort to understand men, it may still be seen as a struggle between the male and female, which is quite reminiscent of her earlier work. "His struggle is . . . with the society around him," Kingston says. "It's also with women. He's a very macho spirit. The narrator is the great female, so he struggles with her and fights with her and refuses to accept reality. He has to learn to be one with the female principles of the world" (Marilyn Chin, 60).

According to Kingston, the struggle between Wittman and his goddess narrator has no definitive outcome. She is not certain that Wittman has become a pacifist through the act of letting his anger out, even though she allows her narrator to "come in" and "say that Wittman is a pacifist. . . . It's more like her hope and her blessing for him rather than truly knowing that it would happen" (Perry, 175).

Indeed, Kingston's title suggests that readers will have to work at making the book meaningful. The term *fake book,* borrowed from the world of jazz, is used to describe a book of basic melodies, which a group of musicians can use as a basis for improvisation. Kingston's idea, she says, is that "I'll throw out a few things, and you improvise and finish it in your mind and imagination and life, and then also I, myself, will finish it in a sequel" (Perry, 175).

The term *fake book* surely also refers to the charge against Kingston that she has "faked" Chinese myth in her first two books by departing from canonical versions.[52] For Kingston, however, identity and community, which cannot rest on or be confined to the usual monologic categories (Chinese, American) must be invented, improvised, or, in the term of jazz musicians, faked.

Although Leonard and others see Kingston's protagonist as the voice of the adult Kingston, it is also frequently suggested that Wittman, with his angry response to racism and his verbal fireworks, is a portrait of Kingston's nemesis, playwright Frank Chin. Amy Ling argues, "It is immediately clear to anyone who knows him and his work that Wittman

Ah Sing is modeled after Frank Chin."[53] Chin himself has accused Kingston of "ripping off" his personality, according to the narrator of the film *Maxine Hong Kingston: Talking Story* (Saffa). According to Kingston, however, many men have claimed to the inspiration for Wittman: "Frank plus three other people plus my husband have told me they are Wittman" (Saffa). The actor Victor Wong, who starred in Wayne Wang's movies, *Dim Sum* and *Eat a Bowl of Tea,* and was once "the only beatnik in Chinatown," has also seen himself as the model for Wittman. In fact, Kingston says, so many men have told her they are Wittman Ah Sing, she feels that she has written an archetype "in which many Bay Area poet-rebels, including herself, see their own reflections" (Saffa).

There are other links between Wittman and Frank Chin, beyond the beatnik slang. In *Tripmaster Monkey* the angry male protagonist studies and then puts on the "mightiest war epic of all time," the Chinese classic *Romance of Three Kingdoms.* It is not difficult to see in this a reflection of Chin, who has frequently expressed his powerful identification with one of the epic's heroes, Kwan Kung (Guan Goong). So central is this "national epic," Chin has said, that it dominates not only his own imagination but that of all Cantonese immigrants in the United States, a "Kwan Kung happy race of people who wanted to hear, read, and rewrite, only one story and sing and sit through and pass with one opera only." In the nineteenth century, Chin writes, some of these immigrants "traveled by wagon from camp to camp selling tonic, breaking chains, and doing flash versions of *Three Kingdoms*" (quoted in McDonald, xxvii).

But while Wittman Ah Sing resembles Chin in that he is a Bay Area beatnik poet who is angry about continued racism in American society, and who is a devotee of the great Chinese war epic, it is clear that Wittman, despite superficial resemblances, is not Frank Chin but Maxine Hong Kingston herself. Chin's concerns, as demonstrated through his writing, are almost exclusively with the construction of Asian manhood. And manhood, Chin asserts, is created and defined by warfare: "We are born to fight to maintain our personal integrity," he contends. "All art is martial art. Writing is fighting. . . . Living is fighting. Life is war" (Frank Chin, 35). Chin's outlook also seems to include the sense that the fighter is fundamentally on his own. His affection for the "immensely masculine Kwan Kung," McDonald writes, stems in part from his "essential aloneness" that is "reminiscent of the rugged hero of American myth," the cowboy of the American frontier (McDonald, xxviii).

But while Kingston, too, focuses on Guan Goong and the great war classic *Romance of Three Kingdoms,* she uses them to quite different ends. Wittman prizes Guan Goong not for his "essential aloneness" but for a completely opposite quality, his ability to inspire a sense of brotherhood. Intent as he is on his vision of synthesis and inclusion, Wittman seems very little like Frank Chin, for whom these are not important themes, and very much like Maxine Hong Kingston, for whom they are everything.

Furthermore, Kingston uses Wittman's involvement with the war epic not to extol the masculine virtues that are so important to Chin or to teach that life is war, but on the contrary, to teach her young protagonist the ultimate futility of war, a view that Kingston strongly holds. After involving all of his friends in a production of *Romance of Three Kingdoms,* Wittman, noting that the heroes of this war epic actually lost in the end, announces himself a convert to pacifism:

> He had made up his mind: he will not go to Viet Nam or to any war. He had staged the War of the Three Kingdoms as heroically as he could, which made him start to understand: The three brothers and Cho Cho[54] [their arch rival] were masters of war; they had worked out strategies and justifications for war so brilliantly that their policies and their tactics are used today, even by governments with nuclear-powered weapons. And they *lost.* The clanging and banging fooled us, but now we know—they lost. Studying the mightiest war epic of all time, Wittman changed— beeen!—into a pacifist. (*TM,* 340)

The last word goes to the female, and now maternal narrator, who says to him: "Dear American monkey, don't be afraid. Here, let us tweak your ear, and kiss your other ear" (*TM,* 340).

In interviews Kingston has hinted that she sees *Tripmaster Monkey* as a response to Chin's attacks, as a way of showing her respect for his anger and his fight against racism, as well as her appreciation for his pioneering work in reenvisioning the Chinese American experience. If Wittman has some resemblance to Chin, it is a Chin whom Kingston vigorously attempts to transform by offering him a different avenue for venting his feelings than through attacks on her. Of *Tripmaster Monkey* and its possible connection to Chin she has said: "I see this book as a kind of big love letter. If it is answering—if it is—then it's like him sending me hate mail, and I send him love letters, it's like that. I sure hope his soul is big enough to understand that."[55]

Despite her "love letter," however, Chin's attacks keep coming. Recently, Kingston commented:

> When Frank Chin was writing all this horrible stuff, he was also sending me voluminous letters which were really terrible. He talked about beating me up. They were threat letters. And so I answered a couple of his letters directly because I didn't want to do it publicly but I answered him directly. All I got back was more horrible stuff. Then I thought I do not want to waste any more of my energy in confrontations with Frank Chin. I was thinking, he was writing on a low karma level and if I write back to him, I'm not getting a worthy enough opponent in order to write great literature. I'm not going to honor him by making him my selected enemy and I'm not going to get good writing out of it. (Simmons)

Kingston seems increasingly to see Chin as the model of the oppressed minority man, in that "racism has messed with his manhood really badly": "[I]nstead of understanding he's got to go out and change the world, he has it all wrong, who the enemy is—so he hits his wife. It's appalling, that it takes place on that level of people who solve problems with their fists. We're doing the same thing. It's so sick. And it's all because we're buckling under the racism" (Marilyn Chin, 67).

Comparing the attacks of Frank Chin on her with those of Ishmael Reed against Alice Walker and her novel *The Color Purple,* Kingston says: "It's the same thing. And Ishmael and Frank are friends. The guys are doing all this criticizing and the women are just going about creating. In general, also, the women don't answer the critics. . . . Sometimes people see this as weakness and say, 'See, these women don't have an answer.' But we don't want to answer, because any little thing we do to them will destroy their manhood even worse because they are already so fragile" (Perry, 188).

Kingston was recently asked if she was ever shaken by the attacks on her work, whether all the patronizing, exoticizing reviews made her wonder if there was some justice to the claims made by Chin and others that she had given the mainstream a tool with which to stereotype the Chinese and Chinese Americans further. Kingston responded:

> I would feel bad about [both the reviewers and the critics] but I never took them seriously. I think I never believed them. I always saw it as a smallness in those critics, a small mindedness that they would use me politically. It never occurred to me that they were right. . . . I felt that I had broken stereotypes and that I was writing really human characters.

And I felt that the people who said I was writing stereotypes were really a lost cause because they themselves were not able to see through stereotypes. (Simmons)

Frank Chin declined to be interviewed for this book. But in a December 1996 letter to the author he reiterated his charge that Kingston's work was tainted with Christianity and served only to gratify white racists.[56]

In a paper entitled "The Woman Warrior versus the Chinaman Pacific," given at the 1989 Modern Language Association convention, King-Kok Cheung addresses Chin's repeated claim that autobiography is a "Christian" confessional form, and one that is antithetical to the Chinese heroic tradition, noting: "Feminist critics, many of whom are skeptical of either/or dichotomies (in this case fighting vs. feeling) and are impatient with normative definitions of genre, . . . believe that women have always appropriated autobiography as a vehicle for *asserting,* however tentatively, their subjectivity" (Cheung 1990, 239).

Cheung writes that she understands Chin's desire to combat white attitudes toward Asians, which have included a "historically enforced 'feminization' of Chinese men" (Cheung 1990, 234). And she notes that white feminists are "often oblivious to the fact that there are other groups besides women who have been 'feminized' and puzzled when women of color do not readily rally to their camp" (Cheung 1990, 245). But she is disturbed that in "taking whites to task for demeaning Asians," Chin "seems nevertheless to be buttressing patriarchy by invoking gender stereotypes, by disparaging domestic efficiency as 'feminine,' and by slotting desirable traits such as originality, daring, physical courage, and creativity under the rubric of masculinity" (Cheung 1990, 237). The Asian American men, she argues, "need to be wary of certain pitfalls in using what Foucault calls 'reverse discourse,' in demanding legitimacy in the same vocabulary, using the same categories by which [they were] disqualified." And, she contends, "women of color should not have to undergo a self-division resulting from having to choose between female and ethnic identities" (Cheung 1990, 246).

"You'll Just Have to Speak Up If I've Got It Wrong"

If there has been no rapprochement with Frank Chin, Kingston seems to be at peace with the first man in her life, her father, Tom Hong. Asked to name the good things that have come to her as a result of literary success, she first mentions her father, himself a poet and a scholar, who had spent his life as a laundry worker, but who, at least, lived to see his daughter pursuing the interests he had been forced to give up (Perry, 192). In her interview with Bill Moyers, Kingston says she felt that in his life her father had "died" as a poet but that now, as a result of her writing, poetry had returned to him. She challenged her silent father, as she writes in *China Men:* "I'll tell you what I suppose from your silences and few words, and you can tell me that I'm mistaken. You'll just have to speak up with the real stories if I've got you wrong" (*CM*, 15). Taking up the challenge, Tom Hong read both *The Woman Warrior* and *China Men* in pirated Chinese versions. Then he wrote in the margins "all these poems and responses and commentary. . . . I've had critics and readers tell me, people who read Chinese very well, that his writing style is incredible. He can write classical poetry; have a classical poem memorized and he'll quote it" (Simmons). Not all of Tom Hong's comments were allusions to great literature. He also responded to his daughter's portrait of him by making "conciliatory" remarks in the vernacular. "He would say, like when I was writing [in *China Men*] about the gypsies, these horrible gypsies who came in and cheated him, he wrote something about there being good in all human beings. These gypsies had to do what they had to do" (Simmons).

Finally, Kingston says, she feels that she and her father "communicated in the ultimate way that he could and that I could. . . . I think that my father and I are both very similar in that both of us feel the height of communication is when we write it down." Kingston is looking forward to new Chinese editions of *The Woman Warrior* and *China Men,* as editors have promised that they will also publish Tom Hong's poems in the margins. This, she says, would be in the "classical Chinese tradition of the poets and the scholars and the monks writing their thoughts to one another, so I think that he responded to *China Men* in the very best way that he could" (Kingston 1990).

"What If You Let Your Guard Down?"

Both of Kingston's parents are dead now, her father dying in 1991, her mother in 1997. But although Kingston appears to be very much at peace with her father, she seems still to contend with her domineering mother, Brave Orchid: "I think I put it in a very nice way in *Woman Warrior* that she was this amazing storyteller. Well, she was, but I think I was [also] verbally assaulted by her." And Kingston compares Brave Orchid with her aunt Moon Orchid, a figure similar to the one portrayed in *Woman Warrior.* Although Brave Orchid had what it took to survive and Moon Orchid did not, still Moon Orchid had qualities that one could yearn for in a mother. Of Brave Orchid, Kingston says: "She survives, she survives, but, can one survive gracefully? Moon Orchid is the way Brave Orchid could have been. She's softer, she's got toys, she takes it easy, she lightens up, she doesn't have a sense of mission. What if you let your guard down, relaxed?" (Simmons).

One senses that Kingston is speaking here not only of Brave Orchid but also of herself. As Brave Orchid never allowed herself to relax, she kept the pressure up on her daughter. "The way I was raised," Kingston says,

> you were never good enough. No matter what I did I was criticized, had to be better, had to be better. Writing these two books it was my way of doing better, and they had to be big books. They had to have these huge mythic worlds and they had to contain continents because it had to be better. It had to be bigger and better, better, better. And it was this tremendous push which I could never do right. Even right at the end, after doing all these books, it's like, is it better yet? My mother at one point did say *Women Warrior* is accurate, and I thought, 'Oh boy, that's the highest praise,' because to me accuracy—that's the same word as truth. (Simmons)

Even death has not caused Brave Orchid to "lighten up," for she appears to her daughter in recurring dreams: "When she comes to me, she is a mid-age woman, at the height of her powers, and she says to me, What have you done to educate the world? Have you finished educating the world yet? That's what I have to do. . . . There's a review somewhere that said the flaw in my writing is that I'm so educational, and I think, of course! I'm a teacher. I go out there and I educate 'em and that's what I have to do" (Simmons).

The relationship between mother and daughter can be glimpsed in the documentary *Maxine Hong Kingston: Talking Story,* which was filmed in 1990 when both of Kingston's parents were still alive. Both were in their late 80s and despite their children's efforts to move them to a better house in a better area, still living in the tough Stockton neighborhood where Maxine had grown up. Kingston's mother refused to move, so her children had to settle for putting up a Cyclone fence and installing an alarm system. While the film crew sets up in the Kingstons' home, writer Stephen Talbot describes the scene: Tom Hong sits with his Chinese-language newspaper, "shrewd, scrawny and silent, except for a hacking, rumbling cough that can wake the dead" (Talbot, 9).

Kingston's mother strikes Talbot as "so old now, so diminished" that she could not be the same imposing, dominating woman of *Woman Warrior.*" But he soon takes back this assessment: Brave Orchid, apparently unimpressed by the presence of the film crew or the injunction to keep quiet while her daughter is being interviewed, goes about her business as usual. "Briefly silenced by the lights and the bustle and the strangeness of it all," Brave Orchid "quickly regained her voice. She managed to position herself in front of the camera whenever possible and to inform us, repeatedly, that the Hong family included 'seven Ph.D.s' which—although her children are certainly intelligent and well-educated—is not exactly factual" (Talbot, 11). As Kingston speaks for the camera, her mother—"precariously carrying a pot of tea and several cups on a tray—shuffles into the room, right through the interview and starts serving. The cameraman is aghast. Kingston apologizes for the interruption and reminds her mother of the important business at hand. But this bent, white-haired, deceptively frail-looking woman is implacable. Nothing Kingston says can prevent her from dispensing tea. Only after she pours a second round does she relinquish center stage and accept our offer to sit down beside the camera to watch the rest of the interview" (Talbot, 10).

It is clear to Talbot that Brave Orchid still sees herself as very much in control of both her environment and her world-famous daughter: "She grips her daughter's shoulder firmly and starts talking and doesn't stop. Sometimes Kingston squirms, or even escapes, but she mainly seems to listen" (Talbot, 10). In the film the 50-year-old, gray-haired celebrity looks young and subdued as the mother talks; the daughter watches the mother cautiously, head a little tilted, listening carefully.

The Next Step

In 1989, two years after *Tripmaster Monkey* was published, Kingston wrote an article for *Mother Jones* magazine entitled "The Novel's Next Step," in which she indicated the direction her work was now taking. Wittman, she said, needs to grow up. Maybe then, she says, other American heroes like Huck Finn and Holden Caulfield will be able to grow up too: "We need a sequel to adolescence—an idea of the humane beings that we may become."[57]

She not only intended to break the rule that says our heroes and heroines must be young, Kingston explains, but she also intended to break the rule that says we can be interested in only a plot that has lots of violent action: "How to write a novel that uses nonviolent means to get to nonviolent ends? We are addicted to excitement and crises. We confuse 'pacific' and 'passive,' and are afraid that a world without war is a place where we'll die of boredom. A tale about society in which characters deal with one another nonviolently seems so anomalous that we've hardly begun to invent its tactics, its drama" (Kingston 1989, 37).

For this book Kingston said she was imagining Wittman and his Caucasian wife, Tana, going someplace to start a commune, maybe Hawaii where they—rather like Maxine and Earll Kingston in Vietnam-era Hawaii—will work for peace. There, too, the compulsive talker Wittman will come to appreciate for the first time the need for silence, understanding that "the universe is made up of more silence than words. All he need do is stop talking, and he becomes one with everything and everybody else." In this new understanding of the silent unity of the universe, Kingston will say to her hero: "Forget territory. Let's make love, mate and mix with exotic peoples, and create the new human being." Wittman, she predicts, "who invents philosophies to catch up with his actions as well as vice versa, recommends interracial marriage as the way to integrate the planet" (Kingston 1989, 38).

In addition to trying to find a way to write about maturity, and to find a style that is both nonviolent and dramatic, Kingston also wanted to write a global novel, for "the dream of the great American novel is past." Kingston imagines the setting of this global novel to be the United States because it is the

> destination of journeys from everywhere. Wittman and Tana cut out of California only to find themselves among more Americans. Everybody gathers and regathers, unable to get away from one another until we work out how to live peacefully together. . . . We shut the borders, migrants drop from the sky, as in [Salman Rushdie's] *The Satanic Verses,* a pioneer Global novel for which the author has risked life and art. The danger is that the Global novel has to imitate chaos: loaded guns, bombs, leaking boats, broken-down civilizations, a hole in the sky, broken English, people who refuse connections with others. How to stretch the novel to comprehend our times—no guarantees of inherent or eventual order—without it falling apart? How to integrate the surreal, society, our psyches? (Kingston 1989, 39–40)

For Wittman (and, presumably, for the author herself) the task will be to "break open the Chinese American consciousness that he built with such difficulty and be a world citizen" (Kingston 1989, 40).

As she imagined this new approach to the novel, however, Kingston was apprehensive about whether such a project could work:

> I have never tried writing a novel by looking at it as a whole first. I've never before given away the ending and the effects—how I want readers to react. Ideas for a global novel are rushing in to fill some empty sets that have been tantalizing me for a long time. William Burroughs said, "There's no such thing as a great Buddhist novel." Kurosawa tried making a great Buddhist movie, *Kagemusha,* which is about sitting still as war strategy. Pauline Kael said that even Kurosawa can't make a good movie about not moving. (Kingston 1989, 41)

Kingston has sought to "stretch [her] form" by considering a mix of journalism and fiction, as she told Bill Moyers, by doing "field work" for the next book with Vietnam veterans. On a leave from her teaching job at the University of California at Berkeley, Kingston set up a series of writing and meditation workshops for war veterans:

> I first started thinking about the veterans' workshop . . . when I attended one of the retreats that Thick Nhat Hanh had for veterans of war. We called these workshops, "Healing the Wounds of War." Most of the people who attended were Vietnam veterans from America and from Vietnam. They'd get together for meditation and discussions. At the time I thought, "They need one more component; they need an art. And specifically writing." So I asked to give a writing workshop during one of these Thick Nhat Hanh retreats. I incorporated writing into a Buddhist day of meditation.[58]

When the Lila Wallace Fund gave Kingston a fellowship to do a community project, she decided to hold more writing workshops, including "veterans of all wars" (Schroeder, 93). Her challenge to the veterans was, "Let's get together and figure out how to express ourselves in art. Let's make an art out of this war that we were all in" (Schroeder, 94).

Kingston followed this advice in her own writing and was at the time working on a novel set during the Vietnam War. It was to be, she has said, a sequel to *Tripmaster Monkey,* with Wittman involved in the peace movement in Hawaii (Schroeder, 90). The manuscript was lost, however, in the 1991 wildfire that raged over the Oakland hills, taking several dozen lives and destroying hundreds of homes. Kingston's house was completely destroyed and along with it the entire manuscript and computer disks for her fourth book. She received word of the fire while she was away at a memorial service for her father, who had recently died. She rushed back to Oakland to try to save the 200-page manuscript. Even though there were police lines around the hundreds of burning houses, and helicopters hovered above, from which loud speakers warned that it was a crime to enter the fire area, she was determined to retrieve the book. By the time she arrived, however, the entire house had gone up in flames (Simmons).

In the immediate wake of the disaster, Kingston has said, she realized that "the only things that remained after the fire were the things I gave away." And in speeches, she asked listeners to return the favor:

> I asked people to give me things. I asked them to give me titles or ideas on *The Book of Peace.* I asked them to find Hemingway manuscripts, Anais Nin pictures, Vietnam war stories, World War II stories. . . . Right after the fire I gave speeches asking people to give me things. What I was doing was saying, You are my community. I'm not going to write your book all by myself! Will you help me write it? You help me with the research and just send me all this material. (Seshachari, 14)

The call produced an outpouring of gifts, from teddy bears and underwear to audio- and videotapes of Kingston's readings of works in progress. She plans, she has said, to use it all in the next book, which she has tentatively entitled *Another Book of Peace* or *The Fifth Book of Peace.* Three ancient "books of peace," Kingston says, once existed but were destroyed by Chinese authorities; the fourth, her novel, which she had titled *The Book of Peace* was burned in Oakland (Simmons).

Chapter Two

Kingston's Swordswoman:
A Ballad of Belonging

The Ballad of Mulan[1]

A sigh sounds and a sough replies,
Mulan must be at the window weaving.
You can't tell the sounds of the loom
From the sighs of the girl.
Ask her whom she's longing for!
Ask her whom she's thinking of!
She's longing for no one at all,
She's thinking of no one special:

"Last night I saw the draft list—
The Khan's mustering a great army;
The armies' rosters ran many rolls,
Roll after roll held my father's name!
And Father has no grown-up son,
And I've no elder brother!
So I offered to buy a saddle and a horse
And campaign from now on for Father."

In the eastern market she bought a steed,
At the western a saddle and cloth;
In the southern market she bought a bridle
At the northern a long whip;
At sunrise she bade her parents farewell,
At sunset she camped by the Yellow River;

She couldn't hear her parents calling her,
She heard only the Yellow River's flow surge and splash.

Dawn she took leave of the Yellow River,
Evening she was atop the Black Mountains;
She couldn't hear her parents calling her,
She heard only the Tartar horse on Swallow Mountain
whinny and blow.

Hastening thousands of miles to decisive battles,
Crossing mountains and passes as if flying!
The northern air carries the sentry's drum,
A wintry sun glints off her coat of mail.

After a hundred battles the generals are dead,
Ten years now, and the brave soldiers are returning!

Returning to audience with the Son of Heaven,
The Sun of Heaven, sitting in his Luminous Hall.
Their merits quickly moved them up the ranks,
And rewards, more than a hundred thousand cash!
Then the Khan asked what Mulan desired:
"I have no use for a minister's post,
Just lend me a famous fleet-footed camel
To send me back to my village."

"When my parents heard I was coming,
They helped each other to the edge of town.
When my big sister heard I was coming,
She stood at the door, putting on her face.
When my little brother heard I was coming,
he ground his knife in a lash and went for a pig and a sheep.

"I opened myself the east chamber door,
And sat myself down on the west chamber bed;

Took off my wartime cloaks,
And draped myself in my robes of old.
At the window I put up my cloudy black tresses,
Before the mirror I powdered my face,
Came out the door to see my camp mates,
My camp mates so shocked at first!
They'd traveled together for many a year
Without knowing Mulan was a girl!"

The hare draws in his feet to sit,
His mate has eyes that gleam,
But when the two run side by side,
How much alike they seem![2]

Throughout Kingston's work there is the desire to transform fear into bold and beautiful action and the insistence that one can survive brutality without being brutalized, that one can endure abuse but keep one's gentleness and tenderness, one's humanity intact. Kingston's first such transformation, in *The Woman Warrior,* is of Chinese women and is spurred by the story told of an aunt in China, the No Name Woman, who has experienced the ultimate brutality. The aunt, as a female in the male-dominated Chinese kinship system, appears to exist only to serve that system. When she fails in her central duty—to guard her reproductive powers for the service of her husband's male line—she is wiped out. She is not only driven to suicide and to kill her child, but she is erased from memory, destroyed in the most complete way the human mind can imagine. The response of the family and community to the improper pregnancy demonstrates how completely the aunt, in their view, exists only to serve the male-dominant system. In the story told to the young Maxine by her mother, the aunt has no subjectivity, is granted no emotions, and is accorded no sympathy. It does not matter whether the pregnancy was the result of adultery or rape; the pollution has occurred all the same. Defined entirely by the needs of the male order, No Name, once she fails to meet those needs, becomes, quite literally, nothing.

The mother's story concentrates on the actions of the villagers, who wreak havoc upon No Name and her family to demonstrate the way in which the aunt has violated the proper order of things. But whereas the

villagers and the family are portrayed in vivid detail, the aunt's suffering
and death is alluded to in only one sentence. Even in this single reference the emphasis is on the insult to established order rather than on the
agony of the aunt: "The next morning when I went for water, I found
her and the baby plugging up the family well" (WW, 5). In Kingston's
first act of transformation, she reimagines No Name Woman, attributing to her subjectivity, pain, and even desire. In this Kingston takes the
first step of a long and continuing journey, as she uncovers throughout
her literary works stories by which the identities of the powerless are
defined in such a way to reflect the needs of the powerful. Once she has
identified these stories, she retells them so that those who have been
entirely defined by the needs of others are now granted a rich, complex
subjectivity.

Although Kingston's first work, *The Woman Warrior*, concentrates on
the subjectivity of once-subjugated women, and although she is frequently identified as a feminist writer, the author throughout her work
links gender and racial oppression. She underlines the similarity
between the oppression of women in the male-dominated Chinese kinship system and the oppression of Chinese men in the United States,
where a dominant culture has sought to define the immigrant Chinese
according to its needs.

Kingston's focus on the way in which the powerless are defined by
the controlling narratives of the powerful appears to anticipate the work
of postcolonial theorists such as Edward Said, who has examined the
way in which these master narratives work. Writing of European colo-
nial power and the narratives developed to explain and justify that
power, Said describes a system whereby "it is Europe that articulates the
Orient; this articulation is the prerogative, not of a puppet master, but
of a genuine creator, whose life-giving power represents, animates, con-
stitutes the otherwise silent and dangerous space beyond familiar
boundaries. . . . [T]he Oriental is *contained* and *represented* by dominating
frameworks."[3]

In her comparison between the plight of the Chinese woman and that
of the Chinese man in the United States, Kingston also seems to anticipate the work of critics such as Françoise Lionnet, who see a similarity
between the task of women and of those marginalized by colonialism to
rewrite the stories that have defined them. Lionnet observes: "Since history and memory have to be reclaimed either in the absence of hard
copy or in full acknowledgment of the ideological distortions that have
colored whatever written documents and archival materials do exist,

contemporary women writers especially have been interested in reappro-
priating the past so as to transform our understanding of ourselves. . . .
They rewrite the 'feminine' by showing the arbitrary nature of the
images and values which Western culture constructs, distorts, and
encodes as inferior by feminizing them."[4]

In Kingston's work not only Western power but also the male Chinese system is guilty of constructing a distorted identity for those whom
it controls; and, as is apparent in *China Men,* not only women but also
subjugated Chinese men may be "feminized."

Kingston's first act, then, is to retell the story of No Name Woman,
giving her subjectivity and even suggesting a hint of subversion, casting
her as a "spite suicide" who intentionally pollutes the drinking water.
But having established the need to retell the stories of the subjugated,
Kingston moves, with an audacity many have considered shocking,
from a family tale to a myth known to most Chinese for centuries, the
story of the woman warrior Fa Mu Lan. By examining the woman warrior, a figure that appears in a number of guises in Chinese literature, we
may consider how even this story—apparently an account of female
empowerment—reinforces the male-dominant system. And we can see
how Kingston's revision subverts that order.

In this order, based on an ideology of patrilineal patriarchal kinship,
women tend to be viewed as outsiders, either "potential deserters" of
their birth families or "stranger intruders" in their husbands' families
(Johnson, 9). Young girls, who will inevitably leave their families to
help build another family, may be despised as useless, parasites, or
"maggots in the rice" (*WW,* 43), in a phrase used repeatedly in
Kingston's family; in nurturing them one nurtures only a valuable property that will ultimately belong to and enrich another family. In times of
economic dislocation, particularly the warlord period of the 1920s during which Kingston's parents came of age, the perceived expendability
of girls could lead families to kill their girl babies or to sell girl children
into slavery.[5]

Against this background the figure of the woman warrior represents
a striking transformation of the despised and useless female. Here, as in
the case of the mythical Mulan, woman is moral, noble, and heroic—the
opposite of a despised parasite; she saves the very system that does not
recognize her as a member. Through her heroic defense of patriarchy—
family and emperor—she is transformed from the eternal outsider in a
male system to the glorious savior of that system, a feat for which she is
recognized and accorded honors usually reserved for men. The young

Maxine, protagonist of *The Woman Warrior*, whose mother tells her stories of both No Name Woman and the Woman Warrior, sees that she has two options—parasite-slave or hero—and knows that she must choose the latter: "It was important that I do something big and fine, or else my parents would sell me when we made our way back to China" (*WW*, 46).

Although Kingston is intent on bringing about this transformation, thereby ennobling and empowering the lowly and despised, she is not free of the burden imposed on her by cultural assumptions of female inferiority and destructiveness. She must still grapple with the ambiguous nature of woman as portrayed in the Chinese stories she hears. Can the Chinese girl be both a useless, destructive parasite and a potentially heroic and moral savior of her people? What is the nature of the alchemy that turns slave into swordswoman?

Woman as Outsider

Although an Orientalist scenario of submissive females and cruel mandarins has undoubtedly been embroidered in part for the gratification of Western observers, one cannot deny the male dominance at the heart of traditional Chinese society, where "Chinese women were imbedded in perhaps the oldest, most highly developed, male kinship system in history" (Johnson, 24). In this system women were not a recognized part of society. Rather, "society was composed of male groups and women existed in the interstices between these groups, not fully belonging to either the group in which they originated or the one into which they moved at marriage" (Johnson, 23). Thus, "women were subordinate and held to be inferior to men not only because of misogynous cultural values and attitudes of disdain, but also by structural patterns inherent in marriage and kinship, patterns that made men the rooted basis of community networks and made each new generation of women 'outsiders' to social organization" (Johnson, 25).

The image of women as chattel, as reflected in the saying "A woman is married like a horse is bought; you can ride them or flog them as you like" (Johnson, 12), is reinforced by both the bride price and the tradition of foot binding. In many parts of traditional China a woman was not considered suitable for marriage unless her feet had been bound—broken at the age of six, bent under, and tied. The result was a three-inch foot upon which the woman could not walk unaided. The custom was not simply a result of attitudes about female beauty; it also served to control women and underline their dependence on males by literally prohibiting their ability to move. One manual on foot binding states: "Feet are bound not to make them beautiful as a curved bow, but to restrain women when they go outdoors" (quoted in Johnson, 16). In a second-century poem, Fu Xuan described the position of women: "How sad it is to be a woman / Nothing on earth is held so cheap." The poem goes on:

> When she grows up
> she hides in a room
> Afraid to look a man in the face.
> No one cries when she leaves home.[6]

As the pressure of Western incursion increasingly disrupted China's economy in the nineteenth century, women, by virtue of their place at the bottom of the hierarchical scale, were often made to absorb increased economic pain. With the arrival of European and American capitalism to south China, where Kingston's family lived, "the pattern of exploitation and erasure" of women was only made worse: "The opium trade and the introduction of cheap manufactures, war taxes, and reparations brought about severe inflation and economic dislocation. For poor families, who bear the heaviest burden of taxation, usury, and crushing land rents, surplus value extracted from the labor of women and their sons was often the margin of survival, while the presence of more women than required for labor and reproduction threatened the survival of such families" (Lee, 56).

The potentially hellish existence of women in China in the early modern period has been acknowledged in the literature of China's first reform-minded writers. For example, Liu T'ieh Yun's *The Travels of Lao Ts'an*[7] (1904–1907) portrays the daughter of a starving family that has been ruined by a flood caused when callous and inept officials knocked down community dykes. The girl is sold by her desperate mother into a brothel where the treatment is such that she will not long survive.[8] In the story "The New Year's Sacrifice" by Lu Xun, generally considered China's most influential early-twentieth-century writer, a poor woman, Sister Xianglin, is treated with increasing cruelty by an entire community as her troubles mount and her usefulness declines. But even death cannot free the woman from the abuse that all are free to heap on her. She stands accused of the sin of remarriage, an act that confuses patriarchal lineage. She is considered guilty of this sin even though she was sold into the second marriage by her grasping first mother-in-law who tied the unwilling young woman to the bridal chair and even though she tried to kill herself before the marriage could be consummated. For this "sin," she is told she will be tortured in the afterlife. "Just think," she is warned by a mocking neighbor, "When you go down to the lower world in future, these two men's ghosts will still fight over you. To which will you go? The King of Hell will have no choice but to cut you in two and divide you between them."[9] Somewhat like Kingston's No Name Woman, Sister Xianglin stands guilty of damaging the all-important patriarchal line through a connection with a second man, even if that connection is forced upon her. The cruelty of marriage practices is also at the heart of Ye Weilin's story "Five Girls and One Rope," in which five young women, horrified by the conditions they observe in marriage, plot to hang themselves before they can become the property of a husband and his family.[10]

Although the descriptions of subjugation and frequent ill-treatment of the Chinese female are based on fact, this is not a simple story of victimization, as is sometimes assumed by Kingston's Western feminist readers. The view of Chinese women as "purely passive victims of Chinese history," Kay Johnson observes, that "has characterized many of the contemporary portrayals of women in traditional Chinese society, including those of Chinese revolutionaries and many Western feminists . . . has merit, but alone is too superficial and static" (Johnson, 20). At the same time that Chinese women are portrayed as weak and submissive, possessions to be used and disciplined as one would a domestic animal, they are also portrayed as sources of potentially great power. Images of female power are widespread in several classic Chinese novels, where women are given surprisingly prominent roles. In *Flowers in the Mirror,* a novel by Li Ju-chen that appeared in 1828, 100 flower fairies descend to earth, where they become women warriors. One daughter sets off to rescue a disappeared father, Tang Ao, a story referred to in Kingston's *China Men.* These magical young women are also allowed to study and become successful scholars.[11] In the 1792 novel *The Dream of the Red Chamber* by Tsao Hsueh-chin, the young hero Pao Yu lives in a world almost entirely dominated by females, from his grandmother, the powerful matriarch, to his girl cousins and even to the ubiquitous female maids. In this setting Pao Yu is the prize over which women battle.[12] And in *Journey to the West* the trickster Monkey and other pilgrims are kept on the right track in their quest toward enlightenment by a loving and merciful, though sometimes scolding, female goddess, Kuan Yin, who will reappear as the narrator of Kingston's *Tripmaster Monkey*.[13]

How has this portrait of female power emerged, if women in Chinese culture are so thoroughly disenfranchised? One answer may be that Chinese women have always found ways to subtly subvert their society's rules. Women in male-dominated family structures, Johnson contends, "are rarely as passive as norms dictate. Rather, women often actively attempt in patterned ways to influence their own lives and others even as they overtly accept the broad restrictions on formal rights and authority imposed on them by the system." Women cannot seek power overtly, so they must "work in informal, indirect or concealed ways, often relying on the development and manipulation of interpersonal relationships to influence men" (Johnson, 18). The primary way that Chinese women achieve power is through the development of what Margery Wolf and Roxanne Witke have termed the "uterine family," created within the alien territory of the husband's family and based on emotional ties between a woman and her children.[14] Mother-child relationships are not formally recognized in the Confucian system. Still, influence over children becomes one of the main paths to female power. Particularly through a loyal son, who could serve as a "political front man," the Chinese mother could hope to influence "domestic and even public affairs" (Johnson, 18).

Although the uterine family is not a recognized social entity, it offers women an avenue to power, a power that is often seen as a threat to the male-dominated family unit. This power can be seen as

> subverting and disrupting the family form that most Chinese men hold dear—the family that grows from generation to generation without interruption and without division. Sons, their wives and their children should live in harmony under the guidance of the eldest male. The goals and desires of young married women conflict with this ideal, and it is largely their machinations that prevent its attainment. The *power* women have is their capacity to alter a family's form by adding members to it, dividing it, and disturbing male authority; the *danger* they pose is their capacity to break up what men consider the ideal family.[15]

In addition, although women in traditional Chinese society were in some sense permanent "outsiders" with no recognized mode of group action, they often established informal social networks outside the family, particularly in peasant societies. Through the agency of gossip, women could gain a weapon over men. When women gathered to wash clothes or do other chores together, "much information was exchanged about the affairs of men." Thus, women, whose gossip could cause men to lose face, could affect men's behavior "merely by talking about them. . . . No matter how well ensconced men are in the established positions of power, the surreptitious influence of women remains beyond their capacity to control" (Ahern, 201).

One further means by which women can exert influence, that taken by Kingston's No Name Woman, is suicide. This act, Margery Wolf notes, is not especially "exotic" among Chinese peasant women. Rather, "it is part of their repertoire of threats, a conceivable course of action, and for some the pathetic finale of their existence" (Wolf and Witke, 112). By the time a girl is of marriageable age, she has probably "heard the details of a suicide in a friend's family or even been privy to the personal misery that led to suicide" (Wolf and Witke, 112). But according to Wolf, suicide in China is not seen in the Western sense as principally a gesture of individual despair; it is, instead, an act "that implicates others" and is for a young woman "the ultimate rebellion in a society that requires respectful submission to the will of one's seniors, and for a woman it is the most damning public accusation she can make against her mother-in-law, her husband, or her son" (Wolf and Witke, 112). Indeed, as Wolf observes:

> Suicide may be the purest act of revenge a woman can undertake. Through suicide, the woman intends that her mother-in-law, or other offender shall be brought to terms, shall be made to repent keenly of her cruelty to her. She gloats upon thoughts of what a disturbance her death will create, pictures to herself the consternation that will fill all hearts, when they enter her room and find her dead, the stern anger of her own fathers and brothers, the settlement that will ensue, the lawsuit her tormentor will be obliged to bear the heavy expenses of, the grand funeral that will be exacted for the repose of her soul, the probability that her mother-in-law or the whole family will be compelled to follow her coffin as mourners, and the opportunity her ghost will have of inflicting all imaginable evils! Yes, she who has always been despised will now be felt as a power for once, and the deed is done, she commits suicide. (Wolf and Witke, 114)

Woman as Savior

As illustrated above, the ambiguity toward women with which Kingston's young Maxine must grapple is seen throughout Chinese culture and complicates the picture of the submissive Oriental female that has often been drawn in the West. Although woman is theoretically the eternal outsider in the patrilinear Confucian order, she has in fact developed numerous strategies for asserting herself within that order. This contradiction may be best embodied in the numerous depictions of the female warrior, a figure that is not an isolated phenomenon in Chinese culture but which is visible in both history and literature through a "plethora of tales which relate the deeds of such strong and exceptional women."[16]

Louise Edwards finds that the woman warrior figures have generally been misunderstood by Western readers, who assume that the fighting women are using the guise of "patriotism or wifely devotion" as a cover for the true nature of their warfare, which is a rebellion against "restraints imposed upon their sex" by patriarchal society (Edwards, 225). These figures are not the same as the female figures of Western literature of the early modern period, in which women who go out into the world dressed as men usually are pursuing clearly individualistic desires. In Western narratives "from the eighteenth through to the twentieth centuries women dressed as men to embark upon adventures as an escape from domestic boredom or to gain employment in spheres normally denied women" (Edwards, 238). In these stories women long for male privilege to escape a confined and powerless domestic life, or they are led on by a love interest that results, finally, in marriage. But, Edwards writes, "this self-indulgent realization of fantasy lifestyles or attainment of romantic desires is absent in the women warriors of the Chinese tradition," who almost always fight to defend patriarchal power (Edwards, 238).

While Chinese fighting women defend authority, they do not support the patriarchy unambiguously; their very existence implies a potent criticism of male-dominated society. The woman warrior's emergence implies not only that something is deeply wrong and that the proper order has broken down but also that men have not fulfilled their duty: The woman warrior "shames the menfolk by her depth of loyalty and devotion to her patriarch. The woman warrior is thereby a moral mirror for the degenerating menfolk. When the women are more moral than the men a strong condemnation of the depths of depravity into which society has sunk is implied" (Edwards, 244).

Finally, Edwards seems to suggest, the woman warrior both upholds the principles of patriarchy and at the same time indicts individual men for their failure to properly uphold it themselves. Although these stories in no way suggest that female power should be part of any normal order, they still hint of a sense of submerged female power, always there, ready to surface when the men slip up, a power that is both supportive and disruptive of the patriarchy.

In choosing the woman warrior motif, then, Kingston has not chosen a figure who is a Western-style individualist, but one who exists in a complex relationship to traditional authority, simultaneously supporting and shaming. An examination of the ballad of Mulan allows us to look more closely at Kingston's use and revision of this central motif.

The Ballad of Mulan

In a traditional version of "The Ballad of Mulan" given at the beginning of this chapter, the heroine is presented to the reader in distinctly girlish terms as she sits at her window, weaving and sighing.[17] The last lines of the first stanza play on the reader's assumptions about the preoccupations of such a figure: we are expected to assume that the young woman is longing for a lover and that her life is to be one of emotional dependence on a husband. But her sighs do not reflect her longing to be chosen and protected by a husband; as the second stanza reveals, the normal order of things has broken down. The emperor's armies are under attack; the father, it is implied, is too old to fight; and the family has failed in its duty to produce young men. In this emergency the daughter rises to the task—and, it seems, in the absence of other champions, the duty—of saving her father's family.

Beyond her sighs, which indicate that she greets the task before her with apprehension rather than with a rebel's joyful anticipation, Mulan is not granted an inner life; there is no attempt to explain how it feels for a young girl to go from her weaving to a 10-year military campaign. Nothing explains how the girl is able to undergo such a transformation, how and when she masters a warrior's skills. All we are given is the moment when she realizes that she must fight in place of incapacitated or missing men. She moves instantly upon this realization, seemingly without a thought of herself, outfitting herself for battle in a process reported by the poet.

Through the eyes of the poet, Mulan now takes on all the trappings of heroic and even mythical warfare as she "flies" over difficult terrain, drums beating, armor gleaming. All we have to remind us that she is not the typical fighter are the repeated calls of her parents, which she for once does not heed. Here we see her complicated relationship to patriarchal authority; her defiance of the patriarchal order can take place only in the cause of defending that order.

Although we see Mulan hastening off to battle in her coat of mail, we see nothing of the actual battle itself, suggesting that the point of the story is not woman's ability or experience as warrior—it may be that such a thing simply cannot be imagined—but her heroic and selfless devotion to both family and emperor. After dispensing with 10 years of warfare in one line—"After a hundred battles the generals are dead"— the poem returns to its preoccupation with her sense of filial duty. When the emperor, who, like everyone else, apparently believes that she is a man, offers her high office, Mulan declines, wanting only to return home to her village and her family.

Returning, she regains the voice she lost upon leaving home, as if on some level a woman can be imagined reporting only on family and home life, not on the manly rigors of battle. What she reports, again, are not her own sensations. Rather, she describes the activities of her family, their ritual expressions of appreciation for her devotion. This, the ballad indicates, is what is important. The young woman's actions have not been an exercise in personal power and independence but an act of filial duty. Now Mulan, her mission accomplished, has nothing more pressing to do than to change back into her women's clothes, arrange her hair, and powder her face. Her only observation of herself is to note her womanly beauty, her "cloudy black tresses."

In closing, however, she is allowed one sensation, the first since we have seen her weaving and sighing in the first stanza. This sensation is one of somewhat wry amusement at the shock her comrades-in-arms express upon discovering that she is a woman. This is followed by the poet's observation in a similar vein that the male and female of the species may seem very different at rest but when pursuing the same action are nearly indistinguishable. Mulan seems perfectly content to be prized once again mainly for her beauty. Still, the ballad leaves us with this potentially disruptive question: Are men and women really so fundamentally different?

In this version of the woman warrior, then, we have a portrait of filial devotion and the implication that only devotion to the system, paradoxically, could cause one to go against its central tenets. The portrait does not suggest any change or desire for change in the traditional status of the girl; rather, the transformation from submissive girl to heroic defender of empire takes place only because—and only as long as—it is necessary to save the patriarchy. Once the emergency is over the girl wants only to return to her former state. The ballad reinforces the sense of devotion that all must feel to the patriarchal order, and there is nothing to suggest anything even faintly resembling rebelliousness on the part of Mulan. At the same time, however, the ballad must pay for its reinforcement of ideas of filial devotion by imagining a potentially dangerous instability in the Confucian system. If sheltered young girls can be imagined rising to defend the system, then the system can also be imagined to be in such profound disarray as to need their defense. Further, though the portrait of the filial Mulan dwells as little as possible on the actual actions of the woman warrior, there is the sense that her transformation from girl to warrior, then back again, must be addressed in some way. The ballad does this by leaving the world of Confucian hierarchy and drawing on an image from the animal kingdom. One knows that male and female are different, the last stanza seems to say: "The hare draws in his feet to sit, / His mate has eyes that gleam." Yet they may also be indistinguishable: "But when the two run side by side, / How much alike they seem." Are the genders fundamentally different though they may sometimes look the same, or fundamentally the same though they may sometimes look different? The riddle is not solved, as if the ballad is subversive enough just in allowing the question to be posed.

Fa Mu Lan in America

For the protagonist of Kingston's *The Woman Warrior,* there was no choice but to take the swordswoman as the central motif of her life; not surprisingly, however, this inevitability is couched in paradox. As a Chinese girl she is taught that she will grow up to be a wife and a slave, but also that her life will be a failure if this is all she achieves. Maxine and her sister, who are humiliated by misogynist expressions of female uselessness, are also taught the chant of Fa Mu Lan, "the girl who took her father's place in battle," who "fought gloriously and returned alive from war to settle in the village" (*WW,* 26). The chant is the gift of the mother, Brave Orchid, who "said I would grow up a wife and a slave, but she taught me the song of the warrior woman, Fa Mu Lan. I would have to grow up a warrior woman" (*WW,* 26).

But in facing this inevitability, Kingston must confront the ambiguity implied by the swordswoman figure, in respect both to Chinese culture and to the Chinese American culture in which she is born. In Chinese tradition it is the swordswoman's mission to uphold a patriarchy within which she will never be accorded a place; she will be granted a major role in this system only when its male members are temporarily incapacitated. When the crisis is over she is expected to return to her former insignificant role, to her face powder and hair arrangement. In Chinese American tradition, as received by Kingston and as described in her memoir, woman's place in the Confucian system is unchanged. From her parents and others who have emigrated from the same Cantonese village, Maxine hears the maxims that portray girls as parasites ("feeding girls is feeding cowbirds"), deserters of their families ("when you raise girls, you are raising children for strangers"), whose achievements would only be "for the good of [a] future husband's family" (*WW,* 46–47).

But while the Chinese immigrants to the United States repeat the maxims and the attitudes of the Confucian system, that system is, in their own time, in profound disarray. The Confucian order dominant in the Imperial China of the Fa Mu Lan ballad may have had its contretemps, but it could always be counted on to right itself and regain control. For thousands of years Imperial and Confucian China had survived more or less intact, despite dynastic decay and even foreign invasion, and the Chinese were comfortable with the view that their culture was the unquestioned parent of world civilization. Since the nineteenth century, however, the Chinese have been faced with a patriarchy not in temporary disarray but apparently permanently shattered. The Chinese empire, increasingly undermined by the West from the middle of the nineteenth century, collapsed completely in 1911. In the 1920s and 1930s, the period during which Kingston's parents emigrated to the United States, empire was replaced by the chaos of feuding warlords and by a brutal Japanese occupation. Civil war between Chiang Kai-shek's Kuomintang and Mao Tse-tung's Chinese Communist Party caused further confusion as the Communists were bent on toppling the Confucian system, inveighing against evils of patriarchy.

Although the Mulan of the ballad could count on the male order eventually righting itself, this expectation became less and less reliable during the early twentieth century. Not only did foreign domination and invasion, civil war, and the ideology of Communism conspire to shatter the Confucian order, but for many women, particularly those in the Canton of Kingston's family, men were often missing entirely, having left China's chaotic conditions to seek work in America and elsewhere. Women were left behind to wait for their men, to hope for their letters, their remittances, their return, but also—as does Brave Orchid when her husband goes to America—to build lives of their own in the vacuum that was left.

Nor could the Confucian hierarchy order fully reassert itself in the United States, where Chinese men were themselves treated as useless and despised outsiders. Once Chinese labor was no longer needed on the railroads, Chinese men were driven out, lynched, or deported, as Kingston has detailed in *China Men*. If allowed to stay in the United States, Chinese men were often relegated to the lowliest tasks of cooking and laundry, jobs that were particularly galling to the men, as they were traditional woman's work. Furthermore, immigration laws keeping out Chinese women and other laws forbidding miscegenation denied to Chinese men the essential male prerogative of establishing a family descent line. Indeed in America, as Kingston has suggested, Chinese men were accorded a treatment strikingly similar to that traditionally accorded Chinese women in China.

For the Chinese American girl, then, the figure of the woman warrior, contradictory even within the traditional context, rises to an even higher level of paradox in this country. In China, Mulan's task was to take her father's place and to come to the defense of a system in temporary disarray that would, once back on its feet, never recognize her as an important member of that system. In America Kingston's revised Fa Mu Lan must still take her father's place to defend a system that shows no signs of ever accepting her as a full member. But an immense change has taken place, for now the disarray of the traditional Chinese order appears to be permanent. The American swordswoman cannot count on ever going back to her makeup table, leaving the world to the men, for in America Chinese men have been disenfranchised and disempowered. In America, then, it is her perplexing filial duty to defend her family and village, even though they actually no longer exist in any traditional sense. Paradoxically, she must defend an order the central tenets of which she, as an individualistic American and a 1960s feminist, cannot possibly support.

By comparing Kingston's swordswoman to the traditional ballad of Mulan, we may try to understand the transformation Kingston works on this well-known figure and how, in rewriting the swordswoman to the new world, Kingston fundamentally alters the vision of the Chinese woman.

The first thing to note about Kingston's woman warrior figure is not that she is a rebel but that she, like her traditional forebearer, is profoundly filial. She fights to "get even with anybody who hurt her fam-

ily" (*WW,* 19), "avenge [her] village," and to be "remembered by the
Han people for [her] dutifulness" (*WW,* 23). Kingston's woman warrior
is not simply a Western feminist, as she has often been read, determined
to break out of a confining cultural script into individualistic self-
determination. For her, the family and the village are everything.
Although she has been called away to train as a hero, the girl does not
forget her family even for a moment, interrupting her adventures to
gaze yearningly at images of family life that are displayed in the water of
a magic drinking gourd. She strengthens her resolve to train for battle
by reminding herself of their need. Lonely and afraid, despite the thrills
of adventure, she dreams of her mother's cooking, and her longing is so
intense that, warrior or not, she cries (*WW,* 26). She watches the New
Year festivities in the magic gourd, remembering the holidays of her
childhood, how she had felt "love pouring from their fingers when the
adults tucked red money in our pockets" (*WW,* 30). Kingston even
allows her swordswoman to look with approval upon the marriage that
has been arranged for her by her family. When her son is born she seems
to accept that he belongs to her husband's family and sends the child to
them. When she wins riches she sends these to her own family, as if
accepting the charge that families make a bad bargain in raising girls
and that they should be repaid. Triumphantly returning from war she
does not signal that her status has been changed; on the contrary, she
seems bent upon assuring her relatives that she will resume her previous
position. She kneels at the feet of her parents-in-law, promising, "I will
stay with you doing farmwork and housework, and giving you more
sons" (*WW,* 45).

Only once does Kingston seem to be in danger of being pulled away
from her filial stance. This occurs when her heroine comes across a
roomful of weak, cowering women, who have been kept like pets and
who cannot walk on their bound feet. This barbarity seems to demand a
more enraged response than filial devotion would allow. Still, Kingston
protects her swordswoman's filiality, for it is not the woman warrior who
will avenge these women, but the victims themselves as Kingston transforms the pathetic creatures into bloodthirsty Furies who declare war on
the entire patriarchal system. In black and red dresses they ride the
land, protecting and avenging women and killing men and boys
because, it is implied, they are male. This is a fantasy that Kingston
seems unable to avoid, but which she separates from her filial swordswoman. And Kingston's narrator, who never questions the "reality" of
the woman warrior, backs away from the image of murderous, avenging

women, as if it has be created by someone else, protesting that she cannot "vouch for [their] reality" (*WW,* 45).

Kingston, then, clearly intends that her swordswoman be seen as devoted to her family and to the traditional order within which the family lives. Never is the swordswoman granted a moment of personal pleasure in her power or her achievements; never does she act out of personal rage—it is all for the family. Like the Mulan of the ballad, she willingly returns to a woman's subservient role once her "public duties" are done. At the same time Kingston destabilizes this picture, creating a figure and a context that give rise to the questions: Will the public duties ever be completed? Will the swordswoman really be able to replace her battle dress, as does Mulan, for her "robes of old"? The woman warrior is filial, but what does that mean in the vastly changed environment of twentieth-century America?

As Kingston changes the impetus for the girl to become a warrior, she also reimagines the process, asking questions that do not interest the balladeer, who is primarily intent on producing a parable of extreme filiality. In this the version of "The Ballad of Mulan" reproduced in this chapter resembles Brave Orchid's rendering of the No Name Woman story. Both accounts are intended to reinforce patriarchal values, and in both the subjectivity of the young female protagonist is deemed unimportant, seeming not even to exist. The focus of the Mulan ballad is on the glory of warfare and the filial actions of the daughter, not on how it feels to be a young girl masquerading as a warrior. Similarly, the focus of Brave Orchid's account of No Name Woman is on the rage of the villagers and the humiliation of the family at the illicit pregnancy. No Name's feelings during this ordeal are not the point.

In retelling the stories of No Name Woman and Mulan, Kingston adds what the traditional storytellers left out: imagining the inner lives, the passions, fears, and desires of both young women. In rewriting No Name Woman, Kingston imagines the aunt giving birth alone under a huge and terrifying sky, lapsing in her pain into hallucinations of the family circle from which she is now outcast. And in rewriting Mulan, Kingston imagines the inner life of the girl who will become the swordswoman: What does she have to go through to prepare herself for warfare? How does it feel? And we are shown the long, lonely agony of training. Kingston appears to draw from various sources to imagine this experience. Part of the girl's training taps the sense of magical power seen in kung fu movies as the girl learns to "survive barehanded," "jump twenty feet in the air from a standstill," and fight by kicking backward

(*WW,* 23–26). Another part of the training seems to replicate an LSD vision of the sort Kingston describes in *Tripmaster Monkey,* as the fighter seeks to enlarge herself and her understanding of her world by grasping the mystical unity connecting all things. In all of this we see not only a figure who is training for physical battle but one who seeks to understand nature and the order of things, "to make [the] mind large, as the universe is large, so that there is room for paradoxes" (*WW,* 29). Through this imaginative creation of the swordswoman's inner life, Kingston revises the filial daughter of legend, creating a woman who is no longer a simple placeholder in the pageant of patriarchy. If the new woman warrior devotes herself to her family, she does so as an individual who is strong enough to contain the paradox that stance entails.

To understand how Kingston both uses and transforms the woman warrior figure, we may look first at what occasions a young girl to take on the challenge of saving her people. In the traditional ballad the girl's actions are the result of an emergency: the Tartars are attacking, the emperor needs soldiers, Mulan's father is too old to fight. In Kingston's revised story there is no triggering emergency that calls the girl to action. Rather, there is a simple recognition—by the girl and by her parents—that it is her destiny to be a swordswoman, to defend her people not in a particular fight but in an ongoing struggle in a world that is veering into chaos. The girl always knows that this is her destiny, declaring: "I would have to grow up a warrior woman" (*WW,* 20). The parents also recognize that this is and has always been the girl's destiny. When the mother laments losing the daughter so soon, the father replies, " 'You knew from her birth she would be taken' " (*WW,* 22). Only after the girl has been in training for years does an event take place that causes her to take action.

But why is this the girl's destiny? The traditional Mulan is called to service because men are temporarily incapacitated. In Kingston's story, by contrast, the swordswoman is apparently called because the men are permanently incapacitated; there seems to be no expectation that men will undertake the task of defense. In the Mulan ballad—and in the historical account it embroiders upon—the father's old age is the reason that the girl must fight in his place. But in Kingston's story there is no such explanation for the failure of men to ensure safety and order. Our first glimpse of the swordswoman's father does not suggest warrior potential; he is engaged in the lowly task of digging potatoes with his wife, a task from which the warrior-in-training has been relieved. The next time we see the father, armed men menace a family gathering.

Others take up weapons, but the father declares it useless to fight—
" 'There are too many of them' "—and the family waits passively for the
marauders "as if for guests" (*WW*, 31). Required to contribute men to
the baron's army, the father declares he will go, but he is "held back" by
women and allows two young boys to go in his place (*WW*, 32). In the
next challenge the father again says he will go but does not do so;
instead, the woman warrior hurriedly leaves the mountain where she has
trained to take his place, as if there is no real expectation that he would
fight. In this version Kingston may reflect a sense of the powerlessness,
even the feminization, of Chinese men as the traditional Chinese order
has disappeared, existing in neither China nor America. This seems to be
borne out by Kingston's portraits of men. In *China Men* Kingston paints
her immigrant father, Ed, as overcome by frivolous fantasies; his failures
later cause him to succumb to depression. In both cases his solid, well-
grounded wife snaps him out of it. If, as Edwards claims, the woman
warrior exists to critique male society, functioning as a "moral mirror" of
male degeneration (Edwards, 244), we see in *The Woman Warrior* that
the reflection in the mirror has changed. In China men could fail to
uphold responsibilities. In the United States men seem to have no
responsibilities.

Filial Fighter, Secret Rebel

Filial though she may be, then, in dedicating herself to the defense of
her people and putting this before individualistic self-actualization,
Kingston's woman warrior is also subtly subversive: she assumes that
women, not men, save the world, implying that women are actually
better equipped for warfare than men. "Even when you fight against
soldiers trained as you are," her old woman mentor tells her, "most of
them will be men, heavy footed and rough. You will have the advan-
tage" (*WW*, 32). Even the appearance of the menstrual period is read as a
symbol of power rather than of feminine incapacitation; the menstrual
blood is shown to look just like the blood received from a sword wound
and is equated to the blood of heroism (*WW*, 31). Nor does pregnancy
slow the woman warrior down; it only makes her look bigger and more
powerful as her armor accommodates her swelling belly. And while she
is capable of fighting like a man, she nurtures her troops in a way, it is
implied, that is both feminine and superior: "I inspired my army, and I
fed them. At night I sang to them glorious songs that came out of the
sky and into my own head." Unlike armies headed by men, this is an

army that does not rape or pillage. Rather, the woman warrior reports, "we brought order wherever we went" (*WW,* 37).

And whereas both the traditional Mulan and Kingston's swordswoman fight enemies of their people, the enemies differ. Mulan's fight is clear-cut; she has one enemy: the aggressive Tartars who challenge the imperial order. When they are defeated, empire and family are restored. But Kingston's swordswoman must fight on many fronts, and her enemies are not barbarian but Chinese. In a chaotic situation, reminiscent of the confusion into which China was plunged with the collapse of empire in the early twentieth century, the woman warrior must fight evil barons and bandits who are intent on terrorizing and plundering the common people. Furthermore, she must march on Peking to replace the emperor himself, facing him "personally" and beheading him (*WW,* 42). This done, she returns to behead an evil baron who still thinks it is permissible to abuse women.

As all of these activities show, Kingston's woman warrior does not simply take her father's place in battle. Her task is much more vast, for it is up to her to fix everything that is wrong, to quite literally clean house, as her forces "clean out" the emperor's palace and put a new emperor on the throne, beginning a "new order." And although Kingston's swordswoman does express her willingness to return to women's work, it is not until after she has defeated all foes and arranged for an improved village life of "meetings," "operas," group singing, and talk story. It is year one, she declares, of a new order of community, justice, and perhaps women's good sense.

As the traditional Mulan does not "clean house" all over China, she also does not undergo any personal change. She wears a coat of mail and is away for 10 years, but when she returns she goes to her room, takes off her "wartime cloaks," and "drapes [herself] in [her] robes of old." She powders her face, does her hair, and is so completely the girl she used to be that those who have fought and lived with her for 10 years do not recognize her. In Kingston's version, however, the swordswoman's fight to save the world is an ongoing responsibility; she can never go back to being a helpless "little sister." To signal that there is no going back, Kingston reaches beyond the ballad of Mulan to the traditional story of General Yue Fei,[18] whose parents carve characters of revenge on his back. This act, more than anything else in the story, represents a reversal of the attitude, hateful to Kingston, that women are eternal outsiders, parasites on their own families, strange interlopers in the families of their husbands. For unlike the traditional Mulan, Kingston's swordswoman cannot ever shed her battle garb, returning to her prescribed female life as if nothing had happened, as if she had not been called on to save the world, as if her experiences had not hinted of the breakdown of patriarchal order. To make sure that her own heroine never falls back into her previous insignificant state, that neither she nor anyone else forgets the important role she has to play, Kingston causes the record of "sacrifice" to be carved on the swordswoman's body in a ceremony of filiality, undertaken kneeling before the pictures of the ancestors. The carving is intensely painful, but it is also a moment of great tenderness, as though the young woman's act of supreme devotion makes her even more beloved to her family. The mother washes the swordswoman's back gently, as if, the young woman reports, "I had left for only a day and were her baby yet" (WW, 34). The carving also reinforces the inherent power of women: the blood that is shed is caught in a basin, the sacred blood of sacrifice, which also suggests the blood of menstruation and childbirth, the blood of women's suffering, their devotion, and their life-giving power.[19]

Finally, it is clear that it is because of her carved back that the swordswoman's value to her family can never be overlooked or denied: " 'Wherever you go, whatever happens to you, people will know our sacrifice,' my mother said. 'And you'll never forget either.' She meant that even if I got killed the people could use my dead body for a weapon" (WW, 34). Even in death her position will be secure. And what if the skin is removed, if the swordswoman is "flayed" by torturing enemies? The record will still be clear; indeed, her sacrifice will be a thing of beauty, as "the light would shine through my skin like lace" (WW, 35). If she is not killed or tortured, she will still belong to the family, for they "have carved their names and addresses" on her. Having undergone this ordeal the swordswoman is treated like a wounded but victorious hero, "nursed . . . just as if I had fallen in battle after many victories." And the pain she has suffered has not weakened her; if anything, it has strengthened her as she rides once again to battle on a "kingly white horse" (WW, 35).

The heroine is now honored, not as a returning son, as was the case before the carving, but as a bride, with cousins and villagers bearing traditional gifts. With this portrayal Kingston reverses the traditional bridal ceremony, during which the bride is put in a palanquin and carried away from her family forever. This time, the young woman, rather than being a "deserter" of her own family or an "intruder" in the family of her husband, is recognized as a full and valued member of the social network. In the traditional Mulan ballad, the swordswoman is only a temporary aberration, a blip on the screen of patriarchy; in Kingston's revised story the woman warrior has the ongoing responsibility of saving the world. In rewriting the Mulan story, and in reversing the defining ceremony in a young woman's life, Kingston replaces woman's outsider status with eternal, if painful, belonging.

Chapter Three

Fighting Ghosts in a
World Turned Upside Down

With the "Shaman" section of *The Woman Warrior,* Maxine Hong Kingston continues her search for ancestral help, for models who can show how the powerless—particularly the powerless and often placeless Chinese women—can be transformed into heroes, saving themselves and others. Here, the author, whose family emigrated from Canton, uses a powerful female figure well known in Cantonese culture, the village shaman. Like the woman warrior who saves the world in the "White Tigers" section, the shaman must venture out against fearsome foes that threaten her people. Unlike the woman warrior, however, the shaman's enemies are not Tartars, bandits, evil barons, or ineffectual emperors. Indeed, they are not human at all, but the malevolent spirits who inhabit a hellish underworld and who prey on the living, stealing their souls and causing sickness and death. It is the shaman's duty—and a task that falls only to a certain kind of woman—to identify these evil ghosts, to discover how they may be placated, and when necessary, to battle them for a human soul. If Kingston casts herself as the woman warrior, whose duty it is to battle across the world to save her people, she casts her mother, Brave Orchid, as the shaman, for whom life is one long face-down with the magical forces of fear and evil, and whose motto is always "Act unafraid. Ghost chasers have to be brave" (*WW,* 74).

Here, Kingston examines the ambiguities of woman's place both in the traditional Chinese culture that is her inheritance, and in the Chinese American culture to which she is born. Although women in general have no recognized role in the patriarchal, patrilinear Confucian power structure, and although shamans in particular are accorded low status,[1] these women are nonetheless entrusted with the essential task of mediating between human life and the all-powerful spirit world, of saving souls and saving lives, especially those of children, who are particularly vulnerable to spirits and whose sicknesses are usually attributed to supernatural evildoing. In the same way that Kingston's swordswoman can be seen as the woman who comes in to clean house, imposing a woman's order on physical and moral chaos, so the shaman may be seen as the woman who comes in to clean, straightening out in the afterlife the mess created by men who run the world of the living.

The very existence of these evil spirits suggests a hidden dysfunction and chaos lurking behind the male-ordered world, and also the hidden, dangerous power of women, the ability of women—both the shaman and the angry revengeful, usually female ghosts—to use the spirit world as an arena of psychic control, to take power not granted them in the Confucian system. For the angry ghosts are those with a grudge, those who were ill-served by the earthly system, those who cannot rest because in life they were the "unsuccessful, the unfulfilled, the jealous, the angry" (Potter, 228). Although in life they were not strong enough to retaliate against those who caused their suffering, it is believed that they do so in death, haunting those who have harmed them, turning the tables on the earthly power structure. It may not, then, be surprising that most of these malevolent hosts are female. In his study of shamanism in the Cantonese village, Jack M. Potter writes:

> Ground down by the lineage and family system, women may not join the competition for power, wealth, and prestige except vicariously, through their husbands and sons. They are the most downtrodden group in village society. When they marry they leave their parents' home and all their friends in the village of their birth. In their husband's village they must defer to their mother-in-law, to their husband, and to their husband's family. In many cases they are mistreated. Often they must endure the humiliation of seeing their husband take a mistress or a second wife. The frustration of Cantonese women from one village could supply enough discontented, angry, revengeful ghosts to populate ten village hells. (Potter, 229)

The spirits of young women who died unmarried are particularly angry ghosts who present a special problem because they have no resting place. Because a daughter is not granted a place in her father's lineage but must be attached to her husband's family line, a girl who dies unmarried has no lineage, and thus no one to honor and placate her spirit after death. The village shaman has a particular responsibility to these unhappy spirits. Often, Potter notes, the spirits of these girls are entrusted to the shaman, who will hang one of the young woman's garments near her altar so the girl's spirit will know that this is now her home (Potter, 217).

A World in Disarray

Through her use of the shaman figure, and her interest in the Cantonese view of the spirit world, Kingston examines the role of women in Chinese culture. And she studies further how this role has changed as the traditional Chinese system has been challenged in the early modern period by the forces of rebellion, Western economic imperialism, the chaos and banditry of warlordism, the suffering of Japanese occupation, and finally the dislocation of emigration, as experienced by Kingston's own emigrant parents and grandparents.

As the traditional woman warrior figure takes on new power against Kingston's American background, so the traditional shaman figure becomes even more important when translated to the new world. If the power of the female shaman is derived from dysfunction, this figure becomes even more important in a world in disarray, as suggested by the character Brave Orchid in "Shaman." In a world in which the power of the Chinese patriarchal system is in chaos, the ghostly mirror image of that system may also have become more chaotic and less easily managed. Now, Brave Orchid suggests, ghosts might be "an entirely different species of creature" (*WW,* 66), as they reflect a different kind of disfunction. No longer testaments to flaws in the patriarchal system, the ghosts are now symptoms of a system that has broken. The ghosts whom Brave Orchid fights in her role as shaman are not the rather "playful" ghosts of tradition, who "twirl incense sticks or throw shoes and dishes." Nor are the present ghosts content, as were traditional ghosts, to only take the lives of babies. The new type of ghost, Brave Orchid says, who is more serious, is "surfeited with babies and is now coming after adults" (*WW,* 74). Kingston's figure, Brave Orchid, is in China as she speaks these words, but she seems to be looking forward to the United States she will find herself in, itself a "terrible ghost country" (*WW,* 104). Now the ghosts are not confined to a shadowy hell, but as teacher ghosts, scientist ghosts, newsboy ghosts, and garbage man ghosts, have taken over the world. In this new environment there can be no more important figure than the shaman, the woman who can face down ghosts again and again, who takes ghost fighting as her mission in life.

Women Hold the World Together

Kingston here again suggests that the job of holding the world together has passed from men to women. That this is true in the world of

Kingston's immediate family is suggested by Kingston's study of her parents' photographs, with which she opens the "Shaman" section. In the photographs of the father, we are shown a man who has no thought of anything but his own frivolous pleasures, no connection to the China he has left behind, no notion that it could be his obligation to put a broken world back together. Unlike Brave Orchid, who stares gravely into the future, the father lives only for the moment, connected only to his frivolous bachelor friends, who "took pictures of one another in bathing suits at Coney Island beach, the salt wind from the Atlantic blowing their hair. He's the one in the middle with his arm about the necks of his buddies. They pose in the cockpit of a biplane, on a motorcycle, and on a lawn beside the 'Keep Off the Grass' sign. They are always laughing" (*WW,* 59). These are not the photos of warriors who will put the world back together; they show no signs of even remembering the world and the family they have left behind.

In contrast, Brave Orchid in her photograph looks at the camera with the gravity of an idol, staring straight ahead, it seems to the daughter, "as if she could see me and past me to her grandchildren and grandchildren's grandchildren" (*WW,* 58). It is a photograph to "command relatives" in foreign countries and "posterity forever" to honor the ancestors and support ancestors and family members, to keep the line intact. The photograph also shows her awareness of how vast and changing is the world she will have to comprehend and encompass, her eyes "big with what they held—reaches of oceans beyond China, land beyond oceans" (*WW,* 59).

The portrait of Brave Orchid shows her to be a woman who can take responsibility for those around her. But a sense of responsibility is not the only requirement for a shaman, Potter suggests. For the shaman is chosen, called to her duties, in somewhat the same way the woman warrior is called, as a result of a loss or a dislocation so intense it cannot be handled in any ordinary way. In the traditional "Ballad of Mulan," a girl becomes a woman warrior because the male order has broken down; the emperor is under attack by barbarians and the men in her family are unable to fight. In Kingston's "White Tigers" section of *The Woman Warrior,* the same girl is destined to serve in a world in confusion where men simply do not step up to their responsibilities to protect their people. According to Potter's study of Cantonese village society, shamans are believed to be called—even coerced—to their ghost-hunting duties only after traumatic loss, usually the death of children, whose spirits urge the mother to become a shaman. Indeed, Potter says, deceased children "who mediate between their mother and the supernatural world, are essential to a career as spirit medium" (Potter, 226). The spirits of the children facilitate the woman's rule as medium, as they have connections with "spirits and deities" and may "use their influence to help [the woman] deal with the supernatural world." Usually, women struggle against the fate of becoming a shaman, and husbands often forbid wives from engaging in this lowly and mistrusted occupation. But the spirits of the dead children are believed to possess such a woman, causing her to become ill and to choose between dying or becoming a shaman. Once she chooses to become a shaman, the villagers, hearing of her vocation, begin to bring her their sick, particularly children whose illness is believed to be caused by spirit possession (Potter, 227).

Brave Orchid as Village Shaman

In Kingston's story Brave Orchid is given many of the characteristics of the typical village shaman. Although we are not shown that she has been possessed by the souls of her dead children, we know that she has experienced the loss of two small children, and also that her husband too is gone, emigrated to America, where "year after year [he] did not come home and did not send for her" (*WW*, 60). If he does not return she will have no more children; the dead children will be her only children. That there is a connection between Brave Orchid's losses and her vocation as a shaman is clear; when Brave Orchid goes into her seance and temporarily "dies," we are told that her soul has gone traveling to "where her children were not" and also to America to be with her husband (*WW*, 72). Although this is the story of Brave Orchid's audacity in facing down ghosts and in making a life as a "new woman," the specter of loss and fear always floats just below the surface. Kingston's narrator senses this, studying her mother's photograph, "looking to see whether she is afraid" (*WW*, 60).

Childless, with her husband gone and China in upheaval, Brave Orchid, like the traditional shaman, is compelled by her losses to take up the task of curing others. She does so by studying to become a medical doctor, the modern, Western equivalent of the shaman, one who has the ability to diagnose and then eliminate the cause of sickness and death. For Brave Orchid and the other women who are training to become doctors, modern medicine is only a continuation of the ancient practice of shamanism, not a replacement for it. Their studies embody the old and the new, both "up to date western discoveries," and "ancient cures" (*WW*, 63).

Thus Brave Orchid fights the Sitting Ghost, a figure who terrorizes the young female medical students, even as she declares "there are no such things as ghosts." For Brave Orchid, whose mind, like that of Kingston's woman warrior, has "room . . . for paradox" (*WW,* 29), ghosts and germs coexist easily and are probably more or less the same. In urging her fellow students to help battle ghosts, she describes the spirits in terms of modern medicine: "You have to help me rid the world of this disease, as invisible and deadly as bacteria" (*WW,* 74).

With both the woman warrior and the shaman, then, Kingston creates female figures who have taken the responsibility of saving the world. In many ways they are the same figure, women forced to step outside their traditionally submissive role to cure, clean, and save. Like Kingston's woman warrior, Brave Orchid leaves the safety of home, traveling alone, following a bird. As the woman warrior follows a bird into the mountains, Brave Orchid follows the sea bird painted on the prow of the ship she takes on her journey to medical school. Both undertake a course of training that will allow them to become fighters, leaving the traditional female occupations of home. The swordswoman leaves her tasks of digging potatoes and feeding chickens; Brave Orchid leaves her life of running errands for her "tyrant" mother-in-law. Both are shown to subtly relish the freedom from the hierarchy of home and from the menial women's tasks, and both appreciate the way in which their training strips their lives down to the essentials. The woman warrior has learned to "survive bare-handed" (*WW,* 24). Brave Orchid revels in the simplicity and orderliness with which she may arrange the few possessions she has brought. (Both the woman warrior and Brave Orchid are careful to pack their silver chopsticks.) Although both are, for this time of training, "free of families" (*WW,* 62), they also both have moments of intense longing for the well-known structure of home. The woman warrior gazes yearningly into a magic gourd, watching the beloved family activities that go on in her absence; Brave Orchid is conscious that, in addition to leaving the tyrannical mother-in-law, she also leaves the "slaves and nieces [who] wait on her" (*WW,* 62).

In addition, Kingston sees in the training of both figures a kind of exaltation and temporary transcendence of the mundane cares of ordinary life. Both figures face a rigorous course of training; both study self-control; both so thoroughly master the difficult as to make it look easy. The swordswoman, in the tradition of the intensely controlled kung fu fighter, learns in her solitary training to control the space around her, see in all directions, and fight all comers at once. Similarly, Brave Orchid, in her solitary training, controls her studies in such a way as to make herself appear omniscient to her fellow students. Although she is not, like the swordswoman, trained by immortals, she knows that the true warrior must somehow gain an aura of mythical inevitability: " 'I studied far in advance,' says my mother. 'I studied when the breathing coming from the beds and coming through the wood walls was deep and even. The night before the exams, when the other students stayed up, I went to bed early. They would say, 'Aren't you going to study?' and I'd say, 'No, I'm going to do some mending,' or 'I want to write some letters tonight.' The sweat of hard work is not to be displayed. It is much more graceful to appear favored by the gods" (*WW*, 64).

Setting the Psychic World Right

While Kingston's swordswoman has the task of righting a world in physical chaos, fighting bandits, evil barons, and even beheading and replacing an emperor, Brave Orchid has the task of righting the psychic world, fighting the ghosts that embody chaos. In the battles they undertake, both women fighters protect their people in general, and protect and avenge women in particular. The woman warrior beheads an evil baron who captures and uses women. And as the traditional shaman has the particular responsibility for the souls of unmarried girls, so Brave Orchid seems to undertake the task of looking after the spiritual well-being of the young women in her medical school dormitory, most of whom are young enough to be her daughters. Indeed, as she goes to confront the ghost who bedevils them, she sees the young women as babies, whose souls go traveling when they sleep.

Traditionally, the souls of babies and small children are seen as "loosely attached" in life and thus "easily frightened out of the child's body, making the child ill" (Potter, 222). The young medical students, too, are particularly vulnerable to psychic trauma, to ghost sickness. In their untraditional lives as women, the medical students are far from home and family and have lost their attachment to life as it has always been known. As a result they may not be able to rely on traditional means of protection. Fear, Kingston notes, which is equated with soul loss, is traditionally counteracted by linking the person to his or her place in the Confucian system. When, for example, Brave Orchid was afraid as a child, one of her "three mothers" would "chant their descent line, reeling the frightened spirit back from the farthest deserts. A relative would know personal names and secrets about husbands, babies, renegades and decide which ones were lucky to chant" (*WW,* 75). But the young women medical students, who have left their homes, and those who would know the intimate details of family descent, are especially vulnerable; Brave Orchid must mediate directly between them and the ghost that is haunting them.

Similar to the traditional shaman, Brave Orchid undergoes the ordeal of an all-night seance in which she searches out the identity of the ghost and wrestles from it the ability to sicken with fear. As in the traditional seance, in which the shaman, in a state of trance, leaves her body to search for the lost soul, Brave Orchid also leaves her body, and her spirit goes wandering. As she reports to the young women later, "For ten years I lost my way. I almost forgot about you; there was so much work leading to other work and another life" (*WW,* 72).

Women Clean Up

Like the woman warrior, who does not fight for personal gain or revenge, Brave Orchid does not fight for herself alone but against a generalized fear and dislocation that seems to be in danger of taking over everything. The ghost, if it were allowed, would "suck in" and then "begin on the rest of the dormitory. It would eat us up" (*WW,* 73). In the ghost sounds, intended to drive the ghost fighter crazy, are the power and horror of the modern world, the sound of "electric wires" heard in the city, the sound of "energy amassing." There is also the sound of a civilization breaking down, of "babies crying," and of "tortured people screaming, and the cries of their relatives who had to watch" (*WW,* 73). As the woman warrior loses her magic beads to an enemy fighter and must win further victories "on my own, slow, and without shortcuts" (*WW,* 42), Brave Orchid too suffers reverses, losing her way in the underworld for 10 years. During the ordeal she is afraid and in danger that the fear "may have driven [her] out of her body and mind" (*WW,* 71). And like the woman warrior, Brave Orchid must prevail not only because she is strong, but because she is righteous. She has "bodily strength and control," but she is also "brave and good," and, she tells herself, "Good people do not lose to ghosts" (*WW,* 73).

As does the woman warrior, Brave Orchid finally returns in triumph, to be welcomed as a hero and reintegrated into the kinship system from which her heroic activities have taken her. The swordswoman is welcomed home with sacrifices and celebration, and public acknowledgment of her "perfect filiality" (*WW,* 45). Having radically redefined the nature of woman's power and devotion, having demolished the view that women are useless outsiders with no real place in either their own families or their husbands', the woman warrior can put on traditional wedding attire, kneeling at the feet of her parents-in-law "as [she] would have done as a bride" (*WW,* 45). Paradoxically, she must be—she yearns to be—both: heroine and submissive daughter.

Similarly, Brave Orchid, having defeated the Sitting Ghost, may now drop the pose of careless fearlessness she has cultivated earlier for the benefit of her dorm mates. In triumph, she may accept the paradox of her situation: she is both bold heroine and vulnerable young woman, who, though she can face down every fear, still desires to be herself saved from fear. She too yearns to be both welcomed as a hero and returned to her prehero status. Thus, although she has fought and triumphed over the ghost, she asks her fearful fellow students to chant back home her soul, which may have been lost. And so her friends call her back home, even though "home" for these new women has become a problematic concept: "Come home, come home, Brave Orchid," they chant, "who has fought the ghosts and won. Return to To Keung School, Kwangtung City, Kwangtung Province. Your classmates are waiting for you, scholarly Brave Orchid. Come home. Come home. . . . We need you. Return to us" (*WW,* 71). Simultaneously valued as a hero and restored to her prehero place in the system, Brave Orchid allows herself, at least temporarily, to relax: "Abundant comfort in long restoring waves warmed my mother. Her soul returned fully to her and nestled happily inside her skin, for this moment not traveling in the past where her children were nor to America to be with my father. She was back among many people. She rested after battle. She let friends watch out for her" (*WW,* 72).

As the woman warrior not only fights enemies but also establishes a new order, "cleaning out" the palace of the corrupt emperor, declaring her new day "year one" (*WW,* 45), Brave Orchid leads her fellow medical students in a campaign to clean out the ghosts that are symptoms of a system that is sick, to reestablish a woman's order. The young women, all of whom are themselves learning to embrace paradox, use both science and magic to dispel the ghost, which is "as invisible and deadly as bacteria," cleansing with alcohol but also with dog's blood. As they clean out ghosts, Kingston creates a tableau of women's resolve to give no quarter in wiping out the forces of fear, sickness, and evil. These young women are not posing on Coney Island or dancing with Fred Astaire. Rather, "in their scholars' black gowns" they "walked the ghost room, this circle of little black women, lifting smoke and fire up to the ceiling corners, down to the floor corners, moving clouds across the walls and floors, under the bed, around one another" (*WW*, 75). Such a force cannot be withstood, and the women know they are winning. Secure in this knowledge, the fighters can for a moment revert to the traditional roles that events have forced them to leave behind. The ghost is vanquished, and there is nothing left of it but a blood-soaked piece of wood, which the young women burn, laughing merrily like the girls they still—on some level—are.

When Brave Orchid's studies are complete, she returns to her village as a doctor and is once again welcomed as a hero with "garlands and cymbals" (*WW*, 76). Like the woman warrior, she is elevated beyond the status usually accorded a woman, as was the woman warrior, having "gone away ordinary and come back miraculous, like the ancient magicians who came down from the mountains" (WW, 76). And although Brave Orchid does not avenge the denigration of women by lopping off heads, as does the swordswoman, she does, in purchasing and training a slave, prove the worth of such a girl, despite the low value placed on her by society. For the girl she buys is very much like Brave Orchid herself, possessing a "strong heart" that "sounded like thunder" with a beat that "matched" Brave Orchid's own (*WW*, 80). Like Brave Orchid, the slave girl enfolds within herself both an ancient and a modern worldview. When asked how she would find a gold watch lost in a field, she outlines a strategy that is both magical ("I know a chant on the finger bones") and logical ("I would go the middle of the field and search in a spiral moving outward"). She will believe what the chant tells her, especially if it is backed up by empirical evidence (*WW*, 81). As has Brave Orchid, and the "new women" medical students, the slave girl has been transformed by her own loss into a strong-hearted female of wit and skill.

With this portrait of Brave Orchid, Kingston studies the nature of women's transformative power. Although women are outsiders in the Confucian system, frequently portrayed as useless, even parasites on the male body of the family, in Kingston's vision it is these very "maggots in the rice" who must, in the face of male failure or absence, transform themselves into heroes of the people. And, Kingston implies, the more complete the rupture in the male order, the more entrenched is woman's power.[2] American life, itself a symptom of the collapse of empire and the Confucian order, allows and forces the ghost-fighting woman to achieve a permanent position of power. The United States is not a real place but a kind of underworld, "thick with ghosts," as Brave Orchid puts it: "Taxi Ghosts, Bus Ghosts, Police Ghosts, Fire Ghosts, Meter Reader Ghosts, Tree Trimming Ghosts, Five-and-Dime Ghosts" (*WW*, 97). Indeed, her life in the United States seems to be one long seance. In a seance, time is altered, and the spirit can wander for 10 years in the course of an hour. In the United States, too, time behaves differently: "Time was different in China," Brave Orchid laments. "One year lasted as long as my total time here; one so long you could visit your women friends, drink tea, and play cards at each house, and it would still be twilight. . . . I would still be young if we lived in China" (*WW*, 106).

While women rise to the challenge posed by the breakdown of order, Kingston suggests, changing themselves into fighters, this is more of a duty than an opportunity. The work of heroism is onerous and never ending: In this "terrible ghost country," where time races, "a human being works her life away," Brave Orchid says. "I didn't need muscles in China. I was small in China" (*WW*, 104). But she had no choice but to come to America. She could not have stayed in China, she tells her daughter, because her family couldn't have gotten along without her in America: "[Y]our father couldn't have supported you without me. I'm the one with big muscles" (*WW*, 104). Of course, the daughter points out, there would have been no child if Brave Orchid had not rejoined her husband. But that is actually Brave Orchid's point; without her, the father would not have had children to support, and Tom Hong, susceptible to the lure of American fantasies, would have, like one bewitched, lost his grip on the thread of life.

In the "White Tigers" section of *The Woman Warrior*, Kingston transforms the victimized, helpless No Name Woman into an avenging swordswoman, a role in which Kingston casts herself, though she acknowledges that in the United States the task of saving one's people is much more complex than it was for Mulan in ancient China. With the portrait of Brave Orchid as ghost-fighting shaman, Kingston creates another heroic woman figure, but one who faces an even more overwhelming challenge. For this fighter the world has turned upside down, and her life is a constant battle against the "ghosts" of confusion, loss, and change. Women, as Kingston defines them, have the power to change the world. Ironically, their very power is a symptom of dislocation, the world gone wrong.

Chapter Four

The Lady in the Moon

Maxine Hong Kingston has sought to transform the identity of the Chinese woman from useless, often destructive, outsider to heroine and savior of her people, with the ability to clean and restore order. These are not simple acts of rebellion. Rather, they are based on a sense of responsibility, and an understanding that the male order has permanently failed; women must now step forward and save the world. Although necessary, this act of transformation is not without its price. While Kingston's swordswoman manages to be a warrior as well as a gentle wife and mother, the shaman, Brave Orchid, seldom drops her ferocious vigilance. With the figure of another female relative, Moon Orchid, the aunt who comes from Hong Kong and who is decidedly not a warrior, Kingston explores the ambivalence that women fighters invite, even in the author herself.

Kingston begins this transformation in the "No Name Woman" section of *The Woman Warrior* by reimagining the narrator's aunt in China. The aunt is married, then abandoned, and becomes pregnant either through rape or by yielding to the desire for love. Willing or forced, she is understood by her community and even her family to have jeopardized the stability of her absent husband's line. For this she must be punished and destroyed, as support of this male line is seen as her only legitimate function in life. No Name is a victim, not a savior; she cannot save even herself. As a spite suicide, however, she takes one of the few forms of assertive action available to such a woman (Wolf and Witke, 112), transforming herself from helpless human into a potentially raging ghost. Such ghosts, it is believed in Cantonese village culture, turn the tables of power, taking revenge on those who have harmed them, stealing their victims' souls, causing them sickness and even death. Such afterlife revenge is not seen as an indictment of the male-dominated Confucian system in general; rather, it reflects conflicts between individuals who have caused the spirit's anger or grief. Still, afterlife revenge is a particular province of women; the power to oppress and destroy exercised by the usually male human power structure appears in mirror reversal as the power of the usually female spirit underworld to haunt and destroy (Potter, 229).

But No Name Woman in the end does not make the kind of transformation Kingston seeks. For this ghost is dangerous to anyone who gets close to her; she does not necessarily limit her vengeance to her persecutors. Vengeful spirits of the drowned are also known, as Kingston notes, to seek to change places with a human who gets too close; the drowned one "wait[ing] silently by the water to pull down a substitute" (*WW,* 16). And so Kingston moves beyond No Name Woman, looking for other, healthier, models of female action, other ways to transform the identity of the Chinese woman. But she does not completely free herself from the fear that the vengeful woman may present a danger, even to those she purportedly saves.

In "White Tigers" the woman warrior, with whom the narrator Maxine identifies, is a fantasy heroine, saving family, village, and empire, thereby winning the acceptance and acclaim usually reserved for males. Now that she has demonstrated her worth and restored order to the world, she can return to the female role of submissive daughter-in-law; no one will mistake her submission for a sign of weakness or inferiority. In "Shaman" the exorcist figure with whom Maxine's mother, Brave Orchid, is identified, fights not human but ghost enemies. Both the swordsman and the shaman figures reflect Kingston's sense of widespread disarray. The woman warrior confronts a chaotic world, resembling the chaos in the China of the early twentieth century experienced by Kingston's parents. The shaman confronts a spirit world in which ghosts are no longer merely angry family members, but are an "entirely different species," reflecting a wider spectrum of grief and dislocation. As traditional ghosts represented the pain or anger experienced by individuals in the Confucian system, now ghosts are everywhere, representing the agony of those who find themselves in a world that seems to be disintegrating. When Brave Orchid gets to America, she finds herself in a land of ghosts, a place where the proper order of things has entirely broken down, and where she must dedicate herself to a life of constant ghost fighting. She is a successful ghost fighter, her daughter tells us, because she "can eat anything" (*WW,* 88), overcoming and devouring anything that stands in her way.

Both the woman warrior and the shaman figures provide models for transforming the identity of Chinese women from slave to hero; both undergo arduous training, both face fear boldly and cheerfully, both fight to fix and save a broken world. But while Kingston imagines the swordswoman being welcomed back into her family after her exploits, a trusted, gentle daughter, despite the words of revenge carved on her back, the shaman figure is more problematic. Although the shaman of Cantonese village culture is a valued figure, depended upon to exorcise the sick, especially sick children, she is relegated to a low status in the community, regarded with suspicion, even feared for her connection to the underworld and her capacity to wreak vengeance (Potter, 227). Kingston's protagonist, Maxine, regarding the character Brave Orchid, expresses a similar distrust and fear. Understanding the mother's ability to "eat anything," to crush anything that stands in her way, and also, when necessary, to cut her losses—as a doctor she treats only those she can cure—the daughter wonders how a less-than-perfect girl like herself fits into the mother's economy of survival. On one hand Brave Orchid defends and rescues girls, exorcising the dormitory for the younger women students, buying and caring for a girl slave, then finding her a husband. But the young medical students and the girl slave whose "strong heart sounded like thunder in the earth" (*WW,* 80) all stood a good chance of survival. How did Brave Orchid react, her daughter wonders, when confronted with imperfect females such as herself? Did she kill girl babies when their families didn't want them? Would she sell her own troublesome daughter if given the chance? How far will Brave Orchid go in refusing to let anything weaken her ability to dominate her world? Brave Orchid is a powerful, often heroic figure, but she is also a frightening one, and it is not clear whether her daughter ultimately profits or suffers by being close to such ferocious energy. And so, it seems, Kingston turns with some yearning to examine the figure of Moon Orchid, the aunt from Hong Kong, who is gentle, lovely, weak, useless and accustomed to being pampered—in short, the opposite of her indomitable sister. With this figure, Kingston seems to pause in her project of transforming women from victims to fighters to study the costs of such a stance. In creating a new identity for Chinese women, Kingston stops to speculate: Does one really want to identity with such a frightening figure as Brave Orchid? Are there other options?

Indeed, for all her attention to female figures who have escaped from woman's traditional role, Kingston's protagonist harbors some yearning for that traditional role—although she does not really approve of herself for this. In some respect she envies the submissive, helpless, often pampered female that is also part of Chinese tradition. Congratulating herself at the end of "White Tigers" that she can take care of herself, that no man must support her "at the expense of his own adventure," she instantly becomes bitter. Although she does not approve of such dependence, a part of her yearns for it just the same: "Nobody supports me; I am not loved enough to be supported. That I am not a burden has to compensate for the sad envy when I look at women loved enough to be supported" (*WW*, 48).

Lovely and Useless

The combination of distrust of Brave Orchid's ferocious power and the guilty yearning to be one of the women who does not have to be a hero to be accepted and loved seems to produce Kingston's portrait of Moon Orchid, as the author tests whether the work of transformation, with all of its frightening ramifications, really need be done after all. By putting the "lovely, useless" Moon Orchid into a contest of attitudes with the ferocious shaman, Brave Orchid, Kingston seems to ask—though probably already knowing the answer—which way is really best? Who will come out on top?

In her portrayals of the woman warrior and shaman, Kingston has drawn on well-known figures in Chinese culture. With the figure of Moon Orchid, Kingston suggests yet another female image from Chinese culture, that of Ch'ang-o, the Moon Goddess, the female figure who lives in the moon. According to myth, Ch'ang-o was the wife of the Divine Archer, who, in a time when there were 10 suns, saved the earth from scorching by shooting down all but one. As a reward for his feat, he was given the elixir of immortality, but this was stolen from him by his wife, who, to escape punishment, fled with her treasure to the moon where she continues to live.[1] Her husband lives in the sun and continues to shoot arrows at her, a relationship that is seen as symbolizing the interplay of the negative female principle of yin and the positive male principle of yang. The story of Ch'ang-o further represents "woman's eternal separation from her husband," as well as her life as a reflection of her husband's light.[2]

While the Moon Goddess suggests a life lived in the reflection of another, the monthly cycles of the moon also suggest woman's power to give birth, constantly renewing life. The story of Ch'ang-o is told during the Moon Festival, a harvest celebration, which occurs when the moon is full in autumn and which, tied to the cycles of the moon, is seen as a time of rebirth and settling accounts. In ceremonies carried out primarily by women, sacrifices are made to the Moon Goddess. Cosmetics

blessed by the Moon Goddess are said to have special beautifying powers, and the moon is believed to "bless the female devotees with hand-
some, robust and intelligent offspring."³ A reminder of woman's creative power, the moon is also a reminder of woman's sometimes
dangerous beauty: The poet Li Po is said to have drowned leaning too
far out of a boat during a moon-viewing cruise as he drunkenly tried to
embrace the moon (*Cycle,* 145).

A familiar figure in Chinese culture, the moon lady is a figure in Amy
Tan's *Joy Luck Club,* where the Moon Festival occasions a lesson for a
young girl on the proper nature of female desire.⁵ The girl also learns of
the punishment for improper desire, which, it is implied, women
inevitably harbor. She is told by her nurse that during the Moon Festival
Ch'ang-o will grant a secret wish, which the nurse defines as "what you
want but cannot ask" because asking would turn the wish into a "selfish
desire" (Tan, 68). During the festival the girl sees a performance in
which an actor representing Ch'ang-o, upon tasting the forbidden fruit
of immortality, begins to rise into the air "like a dragonfly with broken
wings." She knows she has been banished for this overweening desire,
crying out, " 'Flung from this by my own wantonness!' " just as her
husband discovers what she has done, crying, " 'Thief! Life-stealing-
wife!' He picked up his bow, aimed an arrow at his wife and—with the
rumblings of a gong, the sky went black." Ch'ang-o then laments her
fate, "to stay lost on the moon, forever seeking her own selfish wishes.
'For woman is yin,' she cried sadly, 'the darkness within, where untem-
pered passions lie. And man is yang, bright truth lighting our minds' "
(Tan, 82).

In "At the Western Palace," Kingston casts her aunt as the Moon
Goddess and then, bringing her to America, tests the power of the beautiful, eternal, and eternally punished moon lady to survive against the
power of Brave Orchid, the ferocious, ghost-eating shaman. As has the
Moon Goddess, Moon Orchid has been banished from her husband's
life. Both are punished, at root, for being women. The Moon Goddess's
real crime is having seized the gift of immortality, which can be read as
woman's hold on the ability to perpetuate human life. Moon Orchid's
crime is that she could not accompany her husband to the United
States, as American law did not allow most Chinese wives to be brought
to this country until 1952. Although Moon Orchid is blameless—just as
No Name Woman was probably blameless—she is still guilty of failing
to contribute to her husband's line, and he is within his rights to start a
new family in the United States. Separated from her husband—she in

Hong Kong, he in California—she still lives her life in his reflected light, well cared for by the checks he sends. Although she is, like the Moon Goddess, banished and eternally punished for the essential crime of femininity, she is also lovely and adored, as everything about Moon Orchid bespeaks a life of pampered luxury, and one that she has apparently been comfortable in accepting.

The contrast between the moon lady and the shaman is clearly drawn as Brave Orchid, after years of battle with immigration officials, has finally managed to get permission for her sister to come to the United States, a project Moon Orchid would never have undertaken on her own. Brave Orchid does not let down her guard during any part of the immigration process. As Moon Orchid's plane takes off from Hong Kong, Brave Orchid goes to the airport to protect her sister in flight, adding "her will power to the forces that keep an airplane up" (*WW*, 113). Brave Orchid is alert to the dangers immigrants face and is wary of the benign appearance of the "new plastic" airport setting, which, apparently more welcoming than the wood and iron of Ellis Island, could be "a ghost trick to lure immigrants into feeling safe and spilling their secrets" that could get them sent back to China (*WW*, 115).

When Moon Orchid finally arrives, she is the opposite of the tough, practical Brave Orchid, who has come to the airport armed with the necessities of food, drink, and blankets. Not only is Moon Orchid a "tiny, tiny lady, very thin, with little fluttering hands, and her hair . . . in a gray knot," she is dressed elegantly, even wearing expensive jewelry (*WW*, 117). Brave Orchid entirely disapproves of her sister's attire, taking it as a sign that she does not appreciate the gravity of the situation. Arriving at customs, Moon Orchid does not immediately take control of her new situation as Brave Orchid would have done, does not go at once to the glass that separates arrivees from those meeting them, making sure that her family is there, that everything is in order. Instead, Moon Orchid acts as if she were at a festivity of some sort, smiling at the customs inspector as her boxes with their frivolous "puffs of tissue" are examined, "hover[ing] over the unwrapping, surprised at each reappearance as if she were opening presents after a birthday party" (*WW*, 117).

As they drive home to Stockton from San Francisco, under a white moon (*WW*, 118), the aunt continues to betray her "silliness" and her inability to understand that she is no longer in a world of pampered, decorative, passive women who have nothing to do but entertain themselves. Although Moon Orchid does not seem to take the challenge of America seriously, Brave Orchid does, and on arriving home takes control by "hav[ing] a luck ceremony and then [putting] things away where they belonged." But Moon Orchid creates more frivolous disarray with her pretty but useless presents. Even the woman warrior, Fa Mu Lan, has become, in Moon Orchid's hands, a fragile, beautiful paper doll, one of a number of delicate, intricate "paper people" that she strews all over Brave Orchid's house (*WW,* 121). Moon Orchid presents her sister with a silk dress, which Brave Orchid instantly rejects. Once, in China, Brave Orchid was elegant in silk; now that world is gone, replaced with one of ceaseless work and clothes to match. Brave Orchid asks her sister, "What were you doing carrying these scraps across the ocean?" (*WW,* 122).

Moon Lady in the Wilderness

As she begins her stay in California, it is increasingly apparent that Moon Orchid, inept and helpless, will not become the sort of fighter who is able to impose order on the chaos that is American life. Rather, her attitude is that of the tourist, "roughing it in the wilderness" (*WW,* 135), as she studies with fascination the children "raised away from civilization" (*WW,* 134), always assuming that civilization still exists. She attempts to work but is utterly inept, worn out by the slightest effort. So thoroughly does she misunderstand the ghostly nature of the new world that she mistakes the immigrant Chinese she sees in Stockton's Chinatown for native Americans and is gratified that these barbarians are not so terribly different from real people; at least they speak an intelligible language (*WW,* 136). Finally, Moon Orchid seems prepared to resume her life of passively living in the light of others, allowing her husband to be replaced by her sister and her sister's family. As Brave Orchid tries to force her sister to go to Los Angeles to reclaim her husband, who has married again, Moon Orchid protests: "But I'm happy here with you and all your children. . . . I want to see how this girl's sewing turns out. I want to see your son come back from Vietnam. I want to see if this one gets good grades. There's so much to do" (*WW,* 143).

But Brave Orchid will not let her sister shirk her obligation to take her rightful position in her husband's home. Forcing her sister to drive to Los Angeles to meet her husband, Brave Orchid casts the conflict as a battle in which Moon Orchid is actually coming to the defense of her husband, who has been led astray by evil magic. Brave Orchid assigns her sister the role of Empress of the East, "good and kind and full of light," who is trying to save her husband from the "strong spell" cast by the Empress of the West—here the husband's Chinese American second wife—which has "lost him the East" (*WW*, 143). Much as the woman warrior fights to protect her people when the men in her family cannot, Moon Orchid must restore her own marriage to its proper place, as her husband, who has "learned ghost ways," is incapable of maintaining order (*WW*, 143). As Brave Orchid puts it, "That is what a wife is for— to scold her husband into becoming a good man" (*WW*, 130). As the woman warrior figure in Chinese literature is often seen as one who "shames" men into doing their proper duty (Edwards, 244), Moon Orchid, in her sister's view, ought to shame her husband by showing him how he has violated his own beliefs: "You have to ask him why he didn't come home. Why he turned into a barbarian. Make him feel bad about leaving his mother and father. Scare him" (*WW*, 126).

Neither woman, it should be noted, express the outrage a Western feminist would be expected to feel when a husband has taken a second wife. Nor do they exhibit any fellow feeling for the woman who has also, in a Western sense, been betrayed. Rather, they seek to restore traditional order, objecting to the fact that Moon Orchid has been denied her proper privileges as first wife, which include the right to dominate the second wife. Brave Orchid advises her sister: "Walk right into his house with your suitcases and boxes. Move right into the bedroom. Throw her stuff out of the drawers and put yours in" (*WW*, 126). Brave Orchid suggests that her sister make life unbearable for the second wife so that the husband has to build a second house for her, but Moon Orchid thinks it would be better to have the second wife as a servant: "She can comb my hair and keep house. She can wash dishes and serve our meals" (*WW*, 130).

When the sisters arrive at the husband's place of work, however, they find that the ghost magic has been stronger than even Brave Orchid has feared, that the husband has been changed into a ghost, an American, who looks, smells, and talks like someone born in this country. And although he has fulfilled his obligation to support his wife financially, he has entirely lost his sense of the proper way of things, particularly the sacredness of kinship relationships, and cannot be shamed back; he appears to be genuinely mystified as to why his wife would come to him in the United States. As he himself acknowledges, he has "turned into a different person. The new life around me was so complete; it pulled me away. You became people in a book I had read a long time ago" (*WW*, 154).

With this, Moon Orchid's identity collapses. Even the image of herself as the banished wife, who could at least live in the reflected light of her husband, has been forfeited, and order has broken down completely.

As, in Cantonese society, ghosts are the manifestation of dysfunction; here, in a world in complete breakdown, there are only ghosts—everyone is a ghost, even oneself. To Moon Orchid, "her husband looked like one of the ghosts passing the car windows, and she must look like a ghost from China. They had indeed entered the land of ghosts, and they had become ghosts" (*WW*, 153). Ferocious though Brave Orchid's efforts have been, this is ghost magic too big even for her, and she does not manage to engineer the reclamation of Moon Orchid's husband, having to settle for being treated to a meal at a good restaurant. And Moon Orchid, her identity shattered, loses her mind. She grows afraid of everything around her, fearing that the whole family will be taken to Washington, D.C., the capital of the ghost country. In an era in which the bombings of Hiroshima and Nagasaki are fresh in memory, she fears her family will be spiritually destroyed by American power, completely obliterated, turned into ashes, "leaving no evidence" that they ever existed (*WW*, 159).

Through this encounter between Brave Orchid and Moon Orchid, then, Kingston examines the dangers inherent in her mother's determination to "eat" everything that stands in her way. In her will to restore order, focusing so ferociously on her sister's proper role as first wife, she loses sight of the woman herself. Rather than taking Moon Orchid home, she has taken anything resembling home from her, and her sister is so thoroughly alienated that she goes mad, then dies. Brave Orchid understands what has happened, sees that her sister has been taken too far from home and that her spirit is lost. She tries valiantly to chant her sister's spirit back, caring for her tenderly. But it is too late, and finally Brave Orchid must let the sister go. Fearing that the madness is casting a pall on her children's lives, that Moon Orchid's body may now be inhabited by an evil ghost, Brave Orchid has her sister institutionalized. As she did years earlier in her medical career, Brave Orchid once again gives up on an impossible case.

Despite her assault on Moon Orchid's husband, Brave Orchid has failed to put things right. The man was too far gone into ghost ways to be shamed back into traditional customs. Although Brave Orchid has not won this fight, however, her daring raid on the husband's stronghold—the fancy medical office in Los Angeles—allows her to retain her identity as a fighter. Indeed, the hopelessness of the cause, as signaled by the rolling eyes of Brave Orchid's American-born children, suggests that the goal all along may have been primarily to allow Brave Orchid to keep her own self-image intact. Her own sanity, it seems, depends on her ability to keep fighting. But Brave Orchid has retained her self-image as a fighter at great cost: the sanity of her sister. The bold actions that helped Brave Orchid continue to see herself as female avenger have destroyed Moon Orchid's self-image as a lovely, passive, pampered traditional Chinese wife, living in the reflected light of her husband.

After creating the bold, avenging heroes of the swordswoman and shaman, and thereby creating a new model of identity for herself, Kingston seems to pause, as if these figures have worn her out, as if she shrinks, just a little, from the specter of eternal warfare. With the portrait of Moon Orchid, the author looks somewhat yearningly at a female figure who is not a fighter, has no notion of saving the world, but rather enjoys life, as if it were a party, not a battle. Describing the actual aunt upon whom this character is based, Kingston observes, "She is softer; she's got toys; she takes it easy; she lightens up; she doesn't have a sense of mission." Such a figure, Kingston says, invites a question that Brave Orchid would never entertain: "What if you let down your guard, relaxed?" (Simmons).

Sadly, that question is answered by Moon Orchid's madness. Pulled into the maelstrom of the new world, Moon Orchid must, as Brave Orchid understands, fight or go under. Gone is the time in which women could be passive, protected by their men in a system no one could imagine violating. And the words spoken by Kingston's young protagonist in "White Tigers" echo here: "I would have to grow up a warrior woman" (WW, 20).

Chapter Five

In Search of Sanity

Kingston began *The Woman Warrior* with an examination of woman subjugated by male authority, woman as eternal outsider in the system of Confucian values, a figure who, like No Name Woman, will be obliterated if she steps—intentionally or unintentionally—outside that value system. But as she brings her female characters from China to America, the nature of the threat faced by women shifts. Still seen as inferior to men, outsiders in the male order, the women are now doubly marginalized as inferiors and outsiders in American culture. This situation is complicated further by the fact that in the United States the Chinese men too are seen as inferior Others. Now women are placed in the ironic position of continuing to be subservient to men who have lost much of their power to actually control and protect.

It is clear to Kingston that women have to fight in this new setting both to protect themselves from male oppression and to combat the forces of fear and destruction, restore order, and save their men, their families, and the world. And it is Kingston's project to study how women fight. Thus, her young protagonist in *The Woman Warrior* identifies with the traditional swordswoman figure Fa Mu Lan, who takes her father's place in battle, fighting to cleanse the land and restore it to a proper—and it is implied—woman's order. But as she identifies with Fa Mu Lan, Kingston's protagonist also acknowledges the limitations of the woman warrior model in the American context. The mythical swordswoman had to fight only one set of barbarian invaders; when they were defeated life could return to normal. The young Maxine realizes that to truly emulate the swordswoman she must not only "storm across China to take back our farm from the Communists" but she will also have to right injustices to her family by "rag[ing] across America" (*WW,* 49). For the Chinese in America, she suggests, the challenges are nearly overwhelming, and life will never really return to normal. The young Maxine also knows she cannot count on as much ancestral spirit help as the mythical swordswoman probably received, for she suspects that these spirits may not be present in force in America, but are back in China, "dispersed among the real Chinese" (*WW,* 49).

From the woman warrior Kingston turns to another sort of heroine, the shaman, personified by Maxine's mother, Brave Orchid, who battles the forces of the underworld, the ghosts that are the symbol and symptom of a world in disarray. Brave Orchid's tactic, which preserves her own strength and power, is to deny the reality of the "barbarian" American world, to view it as a ghost world, to be constantly exorcised. But Brave Orchid, for all her courage, is a frightening figure. In "Shaman," Brave Orchid is powerful and triumphant, saving people, and particularly women, from ghosts and disease. But in "At the Western Palace," in which Brave Orchid brings her sister Moon Orchid to America and then sets out to reorganize her sister's life, we see that Brave Orchid's ferocity does not always save and reorder; it may actually destroy those whom she intends to champion. Here, it is suggested, Brave Orchid's actions may have more to do with her need to preserve her self-image as a fighter than with a realistic assessment of her sister's situation or a coherent plan to improve her lot. Forced out of her passive but comfortable traditional identity, unable to form a new identity in America, Moon Orchid is lost to herself, goes mad, and dies.

The madness of Moon Orchid, and the destructive irrationality of Brave Orchid that has driven the sister to insanity, suggests a question that is central, though submerged, throughout the book: Does a sane identity exist in America for a woman who is the child of Chinese culture? The two women, apparently so different, are actually two sides of the same coin. One survives and one succumbs, but both live with the fearsome sense that life has come loose from its moorings. Neither can develop a rational, functional relationship with America. Although Kingston began the book as a search for "ancestral help" for the young Maxine, she has not yet found an acceptable model. Neither the bold fighter nor the gentle traditionalist has managed to embrace the contradictions of American and Chinese life in order to form a sane identity in the new environment.

In the final chapter of The Woman Warrior, "A Song for a Barbarian Reed Pipe," Kingston explores the phenomenon of madness among the immigrant Chinese women and girls, including, potentially, herself. It is a condition that is widespread. Not only has Maxine's family experienced the madness of Moon Orchid, but, Kingston observes, "Within a few blocks of our house were half a dozen crazy women and girls, all belonging to village families" (WW, 186). So prevalent is female madness that the young Maxine "thought every house had to have its crazy woman or crazy girl, every village its idiot. Who would be it at our house? Probably me" (WW, 189).

The female insanity that is all around her takes many forms, both passive and aggressive. One of the mad women is a seemingly normal, talkative immigrant who goes into sudden strange silences. Another is a girl who was left behind in China as a toddler and who is crazy when she is finally sent for at age 20. She "seems cheerful" but has lost touch with reality, "point[ing] at things that weren't there" (*WW,* 187). A third is the "witchwoman" of the swamp, a fierce crazy woman who, the children fear, will transform them so that they won't be themselves any more (*WW,* 188).

And Maxine, who dreads that she may go mad like the passive Moon Orchid, also fears the madness of aggression, afraid on some level that she, like Brave Orchid, who can eat anything, will be forced to eat others to survive: "I had vampire nightmares; every night the fangs grew longer, and my angel wings turned pointed and black. I hunted humans down in the long woods and shadowed them with my blackness. Tears dripped from my eyes, but blood dripped from my fangs, blood of the people I was supposed to love" (*WW,* 190).

The Way to Madness

By setting up parallels between Moon Orchid and the young Maxine, Kingston examines the possibility that she will follow Moon Orchid's passive path to madness, that she will lose her voice and sense of self as she too becomes a weapon in Brave Orchid's war on ghosts. Both Moon Orchid and Maxine, we see, are dangerously "liberated" by Brave Orchid. Although Brave Orchid's energy and persistence have freed her sister from her passive, grass-widow's life in Hong Kong, bringing her to the United States and to her long absent husband, this liberation is also Moon Orchid's destruction. Similarly, Brave Orchid liberates her daughter through the "powerful act" of cutting the frenum of her tongue, so that she will not be "tongue-tied," so that she can move easily in any language (*WW,* 164). As Moon Orchid is dragged by her sister into a confrontation with America in the form of her Americanized husband, so Maxine will be dragged into multilingualism. But as Moon Orchid did not survive her liberation, it appears that Maxine's tongue may have been destroyed by the wound intended to free it. By "tampering with [her daughter's] speech," Brave Orchid may have confused the girl's sense of self, rendering her mute. For a time this seems to be the case, as Maxine, faced for the first time in kindergarten with the requirement to speak English, goes into a "thick" silence, a silence that lies like a blanket over her vivid imagination, as her black crayoned curtains cover the flowers and suns of school drawings (*WW,* 165).

It must be noted here that the silence drawn by Kingston is not, as has often been assumed in critiques of Kingston's work, an essential quality of demure Chinese femininity or the result of male domination. As King-Kok Cheung points out, Kingston's emigrant Chinese women have voices that are "strong and bossy." And in the Chinese school as drawn by Kingston the girls are loud and rowdy, fighting and yelling during unsupervised recesses. Nor are the Cantonese, who make up much of Stockton's immigrant community, a quiet people. They are, Cheung notes, a particularly noisy group, shouting at one another over the "wailing" and drumming of a Chinese opera.[1]

The silence that overcomes Maxine and the other Chinese girls is not an essential aspect of Asian or Asian American femininity but, as Kingston shows, a function of identity confusion. The Chinese girls in general are rendered mute by the contrast between a Chinese feminine voice, "strong and bossy," and an American feminine voice, which Kingston portrays as both softer and also, confusingly, more individualistic and self-assertive. As the girls attempt to switch from Chinese feminine to American feminine, they are in danger of losing their power of speech entirely in the transition. Like Moon Orchid, they lose their voices and their sense of self as the old rules are turned upside down. Urged to arrange herself for a confrontation with her husband and his new wife in their Los Angeles medical office—the kind of action an American woman might take—Moon Orchid shivers and shrinks: " 'Oh, I'm so scared. I can't move. . . . I won't be able to talk.' And sure enough her voice was fading into a whisper" (*WW,* 150). Confronted with her husband she can only "open and shut her mouth without any words coming out" (*WW,* 152). Similarly, the Chinese American girls, called on to switch from Chinese to American speech, were reduced to whispers that trailed off into silence. "We American-Chinese girls," Kingston says, "had to whisper to make ourselves American-feminine. Apparently we whispered even more softly than the Americans" (*WW,* 172).

But it is not only the transition from Chinese to American that silences the girls. It is also, as Maxine's cut tongue suggests, the result of the attempts by Chinese parental or authority figures to take control of their American children's voices, to use them for their own purposes, and in so doing to deprive them of the very opportunity to build the sense of identity that they so profoundly need to cope with change: "You can't trust your voice to the Chinese," Kingston writes. "They want to capture your voice for their own use. They want to fix up your tongue to speak for them" (*WW,* 169). The young Maxine is in danger of being shoved, a helpless, voiceless puppet, into a world of change, and finally, lost from herself, transformed, like Moon Orchid, into a ghost and a madwoman.

Through an episode involving the neighborhood pharmacy, Kingston explores further the parallels between her own relationship with her mother, and the relationship between her mother and the aunt. As Moon Orchid is forced to participate in her sister's plan to reinstate traditional Chinese values by reclaiming her Americanized husband, Maxine is similarly made to take part in her mother's plan to restore health to the family after the local pharmacist has brought down a "curse" on their house by mistakenly sending a medicine intended for someone else. Not only must the druggist be made to pay for this insult, but a Chinese reading of the incident must be forced on him, in place of the American interpretation that the medicine was misdelivered as a result of an innocent mistake and that such a mishap could not curse a family. To this end, the young Maxine is forced to go to the drugstore and demand that restitution for the curse be made in the form of free candy, even though she knows the druggist won't understand and will think she is simply begging. If she does not want to risk destroying her own family—"If you don't go, I'm holding you responsible for bringing a plague on this family" (*WW,* 170)—Maxine must comply. She goes, even though she hates her mother's methods of fighting evil spirits. She says, "I felt sick already. She'd make me swing stinky censers around the counter, at the druggist, at the customers. Throw dog blood on the druggist. I couldn't stand her plans" (*WW,* 170). Like her aunt before her, the girl is dragged into Brave Orchid's scheme, even though in doing so she will be forced to abandon her own sense of how things work and who she is. Carrying out this plan will cause her to feel sick and ashamed, will turn her into something she is not—a beggar—and will make her want to simply disappear whenever she comes near the pharmacy. Moon Orchid, too, forced to confront her husband, tries to vanish, hiding her face with her hands, wishing she could hide her hands as well, wanting to disappear and at the same time feeling that she *has* disappeared, becoming a ghost herself, so that she herself is a symptom of a broken world.

The Silent Girl

So threatening to Maxine is the prospect of becoming another Moon Orchid, of losing herself or going mad, that she desperately attempts to destroy everything that resembles her delicate, passive aunt, even though a part of herself is drawn to those same qualities, wishing that she too could be gentle and playful, pampered and protected, rather than always called on to fight (*WW*, 48). As a sixth grader, "arrogant with talk," Maxine tries to toughen up an especially silent Chinese girl and stamp out her own delicate passivity. In doing so Maxine seems to betray the wish that she may stamp the delicacy out of herself, thus saving her own sanity (*WW*, 173). She finds herself, however, emulating the irrationality of Brave Orchid, who, as we have seen, shores up her own self-image as a fighter by forcing others into an unwanted and unwinnable fight. Maxine tries to curb her own fear and undo her own silence by forcing the girl to speak, by taking over her voice. It is as if Maxine has split in two, as the loud, bossy Brave Orchid part of herself tries to stamp out the silent, gentle Moon Orchid part. In her fear of the madness that the passivity displayed by her aunt can lead to, Maxine emulates the madness of Brave Orchid, plunging into a frenzy of insane aggression.

It is clear that the silent girl, like Moon Orchid, is cast in the role of the passive female, prized and shielded even as she is banished from an active participation in life. She is pink and white, "baby soft," always dressed in delicate pastels; she seems to lack both bone and muscle. And like Moon Orchid, she has delicate, graceful, seemingly helpless hands. Her response to abuse is only to suffer; she cannot fight back. Finally, Maxine imagines the girl as the ultimate in helplessness, one of the women crippled by her "little bound feet." And Maxine must smash this soft helplessness, juxtaposing it to her own desired toughness and ferocity, envisioning herself stamping on the little crippled feet, imagining that she "jumped up and landed on them—crunch!—stomped on them with my iron shoes" (*WW*, 178).

But although she sobs in a seemingly helpless misery, the silent girl cannot be forced to speak, cannot be forced to be someone she is not. She is cast in the image of Moon Orchid, but, unlike the latter, she is not able or willing to be pulled into someone else's schemes. Nor is Maxine able, like Brave Orchid, to take over the girl's identity. Unable to dominate the girl, Maxine herself begins to cry. So agonizing and seemingly endless is Maxine's effort to stamp out this unexpectedly hardy aspect of traditional Chinese femininity and replace it with the qualities of a fighter, that it seems to Maxine as if she has "spent [her] life" in the basement (*WW,* 181). In a way, of course, she has, spending her life in a struggle to find a sane, workable identity.

In the end it is not the quiet girl who changes but Maxine, who, apparently as a result of her attempt to destroy the softness of both the girl and herself, is taken with a "mysterious illness," her mind and body overwhelmed by the war that is going on between the two parts of herself. The illness keeps her home in bed for a year and a half. At home, cared for carefully by her family, freed from the contradictory demands of the outer world, both American and Chinese, Maxine for a time *becomes* that girl, shielded from the world by her family as that girl is shielded, "protected by her family, as they would normally have done in China if they could have afforded it, not sent off to school with strangers, ghosts, boys" (*WW,* 182).

The time in bed also, paradoxically, resembles the early training of the swordswoman, a time during which the girl is allowed to develop her identity in peace, momentarily freed from the pressures of the world. Kingston links Maxine's period of sickness to the swordswoman through the symbol of the peach, which represents immortality. The old couple, who train the swordswoman to transcend petty concerns so that the mind has "room for paradoxes," ate "very little except for peaches," the fruit of immortality (*WW,* 21); similarly, Maxine achieves, if not immortality, a kind of transcendence from the confusing, maddening demands of both China and America as she watches the seasons change the peach tree outside her window. Even when she is able to get out of bed, she holds onto the sense of transcendence, using a staff from the peach tree to help keep her balance.

Paradoxically, when the long illness is over silence appears in a different light from before. It is not, as Maxine seems to have believed in her encounter with the quiet girl, the automatic opposite of identity; the quiet girl's silence *is* her identity, and by refusing to relinquish it she remains herself and does not, like Moon Orchid, go insane. Symbolically, she is also part of Maxine's identity, the part that is weak and fearful but also gentle and sensitive. In the end it is not the girl's silence that is defeated; rather, it is Maxine's attempt to conquer silence that is vanquished. Here, Kingston puts a final building block into place, as she struggles to fashion a sane, Chinese female identity in America, and at the same time tries to understand how to integrate the parts of herself:

the bold and aggressive, the silent and delicate, and even the fearful. When she emerges from her sickness, Maxine knows she can not stamp out any part of herself. Rather, sanity and an acceptable identity require an active, vigilant, and even defiant embrace of the contradictions which face her.

But Kingston has one more examination to make as she studies the dangers and the possible appeal and uses of female insanity. For she seems to question whether she might have to use the American illness of insanity to protect herself from another sort of loss of self, the chance that she could be somehow returned to the traditional role of wife and/or slave.

Although she does not "want to be our crazy one," she finds herself "getting stranger every day. I affected a limp" (WW, 190). The "strangeness" seems to be both conscious and unconscious; seeing it in herself she realizes that it has its uses. It might prevent her parents from selling her once they return to China. Too, her strangeness might protect her from a more imminent danger, that her parents might marry her to a "funny looking FOB," Fresh Off the Boat Chinese immigrant looking for a wife (WW, 193). There is a link between insanity and marriage, at least the kind of arranged marriages the villagers contemplate, for marriage is shown as the ultimate loss of identity and thus is similar to insanity as Kingston has begun to define it. Girls are not seen as individuals whose wishes should be considered, but as burdens to be unloaded. As if to underline this denial of female subjectivity, the helplessness and suffering of women in marriage are taken as a great joke. This is evidenced by the scenes Kingston describes from Chinese opera where men and women alike laugh helplessly at the plight of a new wife who, apparently having internalized the view that she is a possession, existing only to gratify her owners, begs to be beaten. To ward off the danger of this form of insanity, Maxine acts out another form, dropping dishes, limping, making faces, spilling soup, and raising dust as she sweeps under the FOB's feet, thus unleashing bad spirits (WW, 194). And while insanity is something to be feared, something Maxine knows she doesn't want, Kingston also suggests that it may sometimes be a woman's only option, the only way to protect herself from the dangers of the world, be they abuses of marriage or the wrenching contradictions of immigrant life.

But Maxine's "strange" behavior does not protect her from the possibility of an arranged marriage; in fact, it seems to draw an "enormous" "growling" "mentally retarded boy" to her, he "probably believing [that

he and Maxine] were two of a kind" (*WW,* 194). A caricature representing both the horrors of arranged marriage and the sense of obligation
women are bred to feel toward such arrangements, the boy, who is said
by the women to be "stupid but rich," is allowed to come to the laundry
to sit. He apparently continues to be acceptable to Maxine's parents
even when the boxes he lugs around prove to be full of pornographic
magazines.

Like the sitting ghost confronted in "Shaman," who represented the
smothering fear that assaulted the "new women" in Brave Orchid's
medical school, this "sitter" represents the assault on another form of
"new woman." Although she is Chinese, Maxine is also an American and
has breathed in notions of American individualism, unable to embrace
the view that it is a woman's duty to free her family of herself and willingly go where she is sent to further a male line. And so this "sitter" has
come to combat Maxine's ability to reenvision herself, to sicken her, to
suck away her will and strength. Maxine reports: "His lumpishness was
sending out germs that would lower my IQ. His leechiness was drawing
IQ points out of the back of my head" (*WW,* 196). And like the Sitting
Ghost he brings fear to the night, a fear that one must face alone. Maxine, afraid that she hears the "monster's" heavy feet dragging around the
house, still "could not ask for help" (*WW,* 196).

Telling the Self

Like Brave Orchid, Maxine must battle this monster on her own, and
her weapon likewise is speech. But the nature of the battle has changed.
Brave Orchid fought the Sitting Ghost by haranguing, belittling, and
finally denying the ghost's existence altogether. But Maxine has seen the
danger of such denial, the harshness that results from the determination
to devour all that is in one's path, and the destruction this attitude may
cause. Insanity, she has seen, is the result of paralysis in the face of fear,
but it is also caused by the denial of fear. Both attitudes represent a loss
of the self. The only course of action, then, is to know the self, to bring it
out into the world where, made visible, it cannot be secretly stolen or
magically siphoned off. And so Maxine, sensing that she must find a
form that will communicate across cultural boundaries, will recount a
list of her inner feelings, appropriating both the forms of Catholic confession and Chinese opera. This synthesis is appropriate, as the desires,
weaknesses, and crimes confessed express all the ambivalence of being
Chinese and American.

As Maxine begins to tell her feelings, she makes her subjectivity visible in the world so it can not be stolen or lost. Like Wittman Ah Sing, the protagonist of her later book, *Tripmaster Monkey: His Fake Book,* who also tells a list of grievances, she seeks to know the self by performing it. She tells to protect herself, and also, like the swordswoman, who is still a part of her personality, to reorder the world: "If only I could let my mother know the list [of secrets], she—and the world—would become more like me, and I would never be alone again" (*WW,* 198). The confessions reveal a consciousness of ambivalence and the ongoing necessity of mediating between Chinese and American values. She confesses her desire to own a white horse, her guilt at this desire—white is a "bad, mournful" color for the Chinese. She confesses her theft of money from the cash register and the further crime of buying candy for "ghost children," which, because the children lack reality in Brave Orchid cosmology, was an utter waste of family resources. She tells of acknowledging the reality and even desirability of the non-Chinese world by coveting a "ghost girl's" doll, hinting her desire so shamelessly that she is finally given a broken doll to repair and keep (*WW,* 197–99).

But these revelations do not cause Maxine and the mother to become more alike. Ironically, the mother sees the confessions, which are designed to preserve identity and thus sanity, as "craziness," for she is committed to denying the claims of the "barbarian" reality, denying the paradox the daughter knows she must embrace. Nor does Maxine's outburst drive off the "hunching sitter" who returns to the laundry with yet another box of pornography (*WW,* 200).

Kingston, who throughout the book has explored a variety of roles for Chinese and Chinese American woman, moves beyond the available identities to forge something new. In her diatribe at the family dinner table, Maxine sounds a new identity for the Chinese American female, one that denies neither the reality of the world in which she finds herself nor the reality of any part of herself. Rather, in a speech that defies the attempt of both Chinese patriarchy and American racism to reduce and silence her, she expresses her intention to face that world as herself, rather than as some version of herself that will satisfy one or the other forms of power. She is willing to embrace her own weaknesses: "Even if I am stupid and talk funny and get sick, I won't let you turn me into a slave or a wife." And she is ready as well to embrace her own strengths, even if they challenge both Chinese and American stereotypes: "I'm smart. I can do all kinds of things. . . . I can make a living and take care of myself. . . . I can do ghost things even better than the ghosts can" (*WW,* 201).

Not only can she face the American world and make her way in it, but she also insists on doing so as a Chinese. Although she casts off ancient ties that will hobble her—"At college I'll have the people I like for friends. I don't care if their great-great-grandfather died of TB. I don't care if they were our enemies in China four thousand years ago" (*WW,* 201)—she still holds on to China when it strengthens her. The voice that defies China is the voice of a particularly Chinese form of heroism and passion, "pouring out . . . in the voice of the Chinese opera. I could hear the drums and the cymbals and the gongs and brass horns" (*WW,* 203).

With this the "sitter" is driven off, disappearing the way the Sitting Ghost disappeared in the face of Brave Orchid's defiant strength. But there is a difference. Brave Orchid's defiance wins her the homage of the other young women at medical school, who help chant her spirit back to the safety and comfort of home. For all the disruption of Brave Orchid's world, it is one that can be repeatedly restored through one's own unflinching determination. But Maxine inhabits a different environment, and her defiance has the opposite effect; by embracing ambivalence she has, in her mother's eyes, become a ghost herself, and ghosts are doomed to wander, seeking the home that is eternally lost. " 'Ho Chi Kuei,' " her mother shouts at her, labeling her as a type of ghost. " 'Get out, you Ho Chi Kuei. Get out' " (*WW,* 204).

An Ancient Figure of Synthesis

Kingston does not leave matters here, however. Maxine is not No Name Woman, banished for defiance, accepting of a fate which causes her "body and her complexity to disappear . . . a tribal person alone" (*WW,* 14). Rather, Maxine seeks, once again, to find "ancestral help," this time by rewriting the figure of Ts'ai Yen, a Chinese princess captured by barbarians who became China's first renowned woman poet. Through her reimagining of Ts'ai Yen's story, Kingston works one final transformation, creating a figure who faces, communicates, and even creates beauty out of the pain and loss that results from being of two opposing worlds.

The historical Ts'ai Yen is particularly suited for an examination of questions of exile, loss, and the confusion of contradictory cultures, her third-century experiences strangely paralleling those of the Chinese in

America. Captured by Huns, Ts'ai Yen was carried away to the north, where she became the concubine of a chief and bore two sons. Later she was ransomed, but although she escaped the Huns, her two sons were left behind.[2] In two of her poems that have been translated into English, "The Lamentation," and "From 18 Verses Sung to a Tatar Reed Whistle," the poet writes of her captivity against the background of a China in chaos.[3] Like the China that Kingston's parents have left behind, the China of Ts'ai Yen's time is portrayed as a country weakened both physically and spiritually, in which a "pitiless" heaven "sent down confusion and separation." Overpowered by the Huns, Ts'ai Yen writes, "our people lost their will and integrity" (Rexroth and Chung, 4). The barbarian captors are "nothing like us Chinese, / They pay no heed to righteousness or reason" (Liu and Lo, 37). They are "savage," with no reverence for their ancestors ("It is the custom here to kill the old and weak / And adore the young and vigorous" [Rexroth and Chung, 5]) and with no sense of home, eternally wandering. Ts'ai Yen declares: "How I hate to live this way." Her one desire is that "someday I can see again / The mulberry and catalpa trees of home" (Rexroth and Chung, 5).

Despite her loathing of the barbarian life and her longing for China, Ts'ai Yen loves her half-barbarian children. In "From 18 Verses Sung to a Tatar Reed Whistle," we see how she "reared and nurtured" them "unashamed / Sorry only that they grew up in a desert outpost." When the news comes that she has been ransomed, Ts'ai Yen is torn in two, divided between her love for her children and her yearning for her homeland. Upon leaving the barbarian land for China, she expresses her feelings of loss:

> Before I missed my homeland
> So much my heart was disordered.
> Now I think again and again, over and over,
> Of the sons I have lost. (Rexroth and Chung, 7)

Ts'ai Yen finally arrives in her beloved China, but there, she says: "I try to strangle my sobs / but my tears stream down my face" (Rexroth and Chung, 7). In the poem "The Lamentation" the author writes again of being ransomed and of being forced to leave her beloved children. When she returns to China she finds all of her family gone and her home "overgrown with thorns and brambles." So fearful is this scene of loss that she feels that her soul has left her body. Like those exiled from modern China, including Maxine's parents, who continue to dream of returning to China, Ts'ai Yen no longer has a home anyplace: "Rootless, despised and miserable, / I constantly fear to be abandoned again. / Human life lasts but a moment, / But grief is my lot till my days end" (Liu and Lo, 37).

Kingston creates the book's final transformation by likening Ts'ai Yen's barbarian captivity to the exile of Chinese women in America, women such as Maxine's mother Brave Orchid. In both situations China has been weakened and is unable to afford protection to its people; in both, a Chinese woman must live with the loss of home, among rootless barbarians who often seem not to grasp concepts that seem to be fundamental to humanity. For both figures, the yearning for home is complicated by the birth of "half-barbarian" children who will forever link their Chinese mother to the new land.

Rewriting the story of Ts'ai Yen, however, Kingston invites us to identify with both the banished princess and her abandoned children. Whereas Ts'ai Yen expresses only the grief of a mother at leaving her children, Kingston is concerned with the emotions of children such as herself who, as a result of their "half-barbarian" status, can never be certain that they will not, on some level, be abandoned by their Chinese mother. Ts'ai Yen's half-barbarian children resemble Maxine and other Chinese American children who are not viewed by their parents as fully human, having "been born among ghosts" and "taught by ghosts" and are themselves "ghostlike." The parents call the children "a kind of ghost" (WW, 184), and Maxine often feels herself to be inferior to "real" Chinese children. She sees that her mother's "enthusiasm" for her is "duller" than that felt for the slave girl Brave Orchid once bought, and also that she will never be treasured like the two babies Brave Orchid lost in China, "the older brother and sister who died while they were still cuddly" (WW, 82). Brave Orchid seems to see Maxine as a bad bargain when compared to "real" Chinese children, ruing the fact that children were given away for free in China; meanwhile, she tells her daughter, "Here I was in the United States paying two hundred dollars [in hospital fees] for you" (WW, 83). Maxine fears that she will be sold or married off if the family ever returns to China, and, as if tormented by the sense of her own possible abandonment, dreams recurrently of lost, "shrinking babies," (WW, 96), babies she must try to protect but who continually "slip between [her] fingers," babies whom she accidentally scalds in the bathtub, despite her care (WW, 87).

In Ts'ai Yen's poems there is only the grief of a woman ripped first from the world as she knows it, then from her children, left finally with neither. Kingston transforms that grief—along with the implied grief of the abandoned children—into something entirely new. In Kingston's revision of Ts'ai Yen, the poet manages to move beyond her sense of her captors as "barbarians" and "primitives," whose "only music" is the deadly sound of their whistling arrows (WW, 208). In the end, through the medium of art, she manages to grasp that the barbarians too feel human emotion; she knows the barbarians to be human when she hears the "yearning" beauty of their flute music. As she is able to see the barbarians as humans, she herself is transformed, as if this realization has given her a deeper understanding of her own humanity. And she sings in a voice that "matched the flutes," expressing her own emotions, her "sadness and anger" in a way that makes her comprehensible— human—to the barbarians (WW, 209). Not only does Ts'ai Yen manage to bridge the divide between herself and the barbarians, to transform each into humans in the eyes of the other, she also bridges the divide between herself and her half-barbarian children. Children and mother often cannot understand one another. Like Brave Orchid's children, Ts'ai Yen's children do not speak Chinese effectively; both sometimes mock the incomprehensibility of the Chinese mother. "Chinese people are very weird," one of Brave Orchid's children says. Ts'ai Yen's children "imitated her with senseless singsong words and laughed" (WW, 208). But that relationship is also changed by Kingston, as Ts'ai Yen's song speaks to her children as well, who no longer laugh, but "eventually sang along" as their mother leaves her tent to join the barbarians by their fire (WW, 209).

With this, Kingston works her final transformation of the book, changing grief, loss, and subjugation into a new, bold beauty, a heroism that surpasses that of Kingston's other heroines. No Name Woman showed a spirit of defiance through her suicide, but it was at the cost of becoming an eternal outcast. The Woman Warrior sought to return the world to order but was forced to concede that the project had become too vast. Brave Orchid, the shaman, faced down fear, but often at the expense of those who depended on her for protection. Now there is Maxine, a girl who has been forced to embrace the various parts of her world, and the various parts of herself. To provide Maxine with ancestral help, Kingston draws an ancient figure of synthesis, Ts'ai Yen, a woman who knows her sorrow and her loss, but who can still see the reality of the world in which she finds herself and the humanity of those who inhabit it, particularly her own children. The breach between mother and child has finally been closed, at least in Kingston's imagination. At last they can understand one another, and the song they sing together symbolizes the hope that all breaches, however wide and dangerous, can somehow be closed.

Chapter Six
Finding Fathers

In *The Woman Warrior* Kingston transforms women from despised, often destructive outsiders to bold heroines, fighters who save their people and restore order to a world in which male power has been shattered. The author recognizes, however, the dangers of such heroism. Some woman fighters, such as the ferocious Brave Orchid, may leave in their wake a trail of victims. Those around Brave Orchid are in danger of losing their voices, their identities, and even their sanity as they are required to follow her into endless warfare. After examining the need for, and the dangers of, heroism, Kingston finds an acceptable role model for herself not in the woman warrior but in the figure of the exiled Chinese poet, Ts'ai Yen. With this figure Kingston again portrays a woman lost from home in a broken world, but one who responds not by fighting but by accepting the reality of both old and new, of loss and change, and working these together into a beautiful, if inevitably sad, synthesis.

With *China Men* Kingston undertakes a similar act of transformation, but now it is not women but Chinese men who, as workers in America, are viewed as despised, potentially destructive outsiders. Now it is the men who require "ancestral help" and on whose behalf Kingston seeks out, appropriates, and rewrites images of Chinese heroism. As *The Woman Warrior* is driven by Kingston's study of the mother, Brave Orchid, *China Men* is driven primarily by the study of the father, Tom Hong. But whereas both are transformed into mythic Chinese heroes, the nature of heroism is different. Brave Orchid is a ghost-fighting shaman, struggling to restore order to a world gone mad. In *China Men* the heroes do not fight. Their heroism lies in their ability to keep their sensitive inner selves intact in the face of lonely, demeaning exile. Kingston's male heroes are men whose qualities have not been recognized in the confusion of a turbulent time, and who wander eternally, seeking, like the fourth-century B.C. poet Ch'ü Yüan, to transcend the "muddy, impure world."[1] Against a background of such mythical Chinese heroes, Kingston examines the lives of the exiled and self-exiled, the thrills, loneliness, grief, and potential for self-knowledge. In so doing she transforms the father, Tom Hong, from a bitter, angry man who only breaks his silence to shout misogynistic curses, into an exiled hero-scholar.

Kingston's main focus in *China Men* is Tom Hong, but he is not the only China man in need of attention. In her portrayal of the two grandfather figures, one a plantation worker in Hawaii, the other a laborer on the transcontinental American railroad, Kingston changes the image of the Chinese "coolie," the soulless work machine, into a different sort of hero through the appropriation of a different sort of myth. The grandfathers are not like Tom Hong; they are not misunderstood poets, forever wandering like Ch'ü Yuan. Rather, they are cast in the mold of American pioneers, the founding fathers, men who built America but who, at the same time, never forgot home.

Finally, as she did in the final chapter of *The Woman Warrior*, Kingston draws a figure—in *China Men* it is the brother in Vietnam—who is more than a heroic fighter or survivor. Fighting and surviving, Kingston seems to say, are necessary but not sufficient. To build a life in the world, one must be able to form the parts of oneself and one's experience into an integrated whole. Like the exiled princess Ts'ai Yen, the brother negotiates the moral minefields of what he views as an unjust war, and the divisive force of cultural duality, to find a way to be both Asian and American.

But *China Men* has a second aim beyond transforming the men of Kingston's family from oppressed victims into heroes, whose suffering and whose bravery can at last be understood. Kingston also is intent on studying the connection between oppressed men and the women they routinely subjugate as part of a particularly male-dominant cultural vision, a vision that has been carried from China to America. As Kingston does not allow her understanding of the oppression of women to blind her to the plight of the Chinese man in America, she does not let her understanding of the oppression of Chinese men in America cause her to gloss over the continued sexism of Chinese men. As King-Kok Cheung has written, Kingston's *China Men* points "not only to the mortification of Chinese men in the new world but also to the subjugation of women both in old China and America. . . . [T]he author objects as strenuously to the patriarchal practices of her ancestral culture as to the racist treatment of her forefathers in their adopted country" (Cheung 1990, 240).

Becoming the Other

Kingston signals her intention to explore the connection between the sexist oppression of women and the racist oppression of men in the first images of *China Men*, as she rewrites the story of a man captured by women found in the nineteenth-century Chinese novel *Flowers in the Mirror*, by Li Ju-chen. In the novel a merchant, Lin, who has traveled far from home, is captured by women who are the rulers of an upside down land. The women, who have taken on the domineering characteristics of men, force the merchant into becoming an object for their sexual use. It is this scenario with which Kingston begins *China Men*, changing the story so that it is Lin's brother-in-law, the disappointed scholar Tang Ao, who is captured. By focusing on sexual oppression and hinting at the connection between the man who is forcibly feminized and the men who came to the United States, Kingston suggests that the oppression of women by Chinese patriarchialism and the oppression of Chinese men in a racist America feel the same, indeed, are the same. She shows, as David Leiwei Li has written, that "female identity is as much an arbitrary cultural and historical construction as the identity of 'Chinamen' " (David Leiwei Li, 488).

In making this connection Kingston demonstrates to men the double standard that rules their lives and implicitly asks them to consider how they can at the same time lament their own oppression and continue to oppress others. But if it is necessary for Chinese men to grasp that their suffering and that of the women they oppress are the same, the opposite is also true. It may be as hard, Kingston suggests, for a woman to understand the pain of a man feminized by racism as it is for a man to understand the pain of a woman feminized by sexism. And although some have felt that Kingston forsook the feminist cause by turning her attention to men, she sees this effort as part of her growth as a person and a woman.

Kingston signals her intention to make both men and women imaginatively identify with the plight of the other in an early version of the "On Discovery" section of *China Men*, which was published in a 1977 edition of *Hawaii Review* under the title "On Understanding Men." In an editorial note the piece is defined as a vignette meant "to serve as a transition between *The Woman Warrior* and *China Men*, a work in progress."[2] In this version Kingston opens with lines that are dropped from the version found in *China Men*, but which give a sense of Kingston's intention with the Tang Ao story: "My mother tells both boys and girls a story first told by Li Ju-chen, who lived just after Jonathan Swift. Li taught that men must understand women and that women suffer" ("OUM," 43). At the end of the *Hawaii Review* piece is another sentence dropped for the final version of "On Discovery." "What tortures might [Li] have chosen for a woman who could understand men?" ("OUM," 44).

Kingston suggests that, to understand the pain of women, men must imaginatively *become* them. In the same way women must imaginatively become men to understand the constraints by which they are bound, to understand their pain and, in the case of men like Tom Hong, their anger. And the daughter must work hard to understand a father as angry and abusive as her own: "You were angry," the daughter writes to the father. "You scared us. Every day we listened to you swear, 'Dog vomit. Your mother's cunt. Your mother's smelly cunt.' You slammed the iron on the shirt while muttering, 'Stink pig. Mother's cunt'. . . . Worse than the swearing and the nightly screams were your silences when you punished us by not talking. You rendered us invisible, gone" (*CM*, 12, 14). In *China Men* it is this angry father that Kingston sets out to imaginatively become, finally knowing him as a man who has been nearly destroyed by his losses and his suffering. Through this knowledge, Kingston is able to transform him from the abusive father of her memory to an exiled and misunderstood poet.

Kingston begins by linking Tom Hong to Tang Ao, the disappointed, wandering scholar in *Flowers in the Mirror,* conflating the characters of Tang Ao and his brother-in-law Lin, who is captured and turned into a concubine. In the novel, which has been read as a "satire on social injustice in general and the suppression of women in particular,"[3] Tang Ao has passed the imperial examination and won high office, only to be demoted after being slandered to the usurper Empress Wu. Rather than accept this fate, Tang leaves the world of political intrigue and worldly vanity and embarks on a long voyage in search of immortality. He encounters many strange lands, among them such places as the Land of Courtesy and the Land of Dwarfs. He also calls at the Land of Women where women dominate men in a way that mirrors male-dominated Confucian China. There, Tang's brother-in-law, Lin, is captured and forcibly transformed into the "king's" concubine. The author does not spare the grisly details of how female "beauty" is achieved. Lin's feet are bound so tightly that "before two weeks were over, [they] had begun to assume a permanently arched form, and his toes began to rot." Soon "his feet lost much of their original shape. Blood and flesh were squeezed into a pulp and then little remained of his feet but dry bones and skin, shrunk, indeed, to a dainty size" (Li Ju-chen, 113). For a time Lin experiences what it is to be "no longer in command of his own destiny" (Li Ju-chen, 112), but he is finally rescued and resumes his travels. Meanwhile, Tang, the disappointed scholar, has come upon a "fairyland," where he is determined to stay, and he disappears from his traveling friends.

Feminized Fathers

Tang Ao and Lin are not the only characters in *Flowers in the Mirror* that particularly interest Kingston, for Li has also created a corps of 100 young women, led by Tang Ao's daughter Little Hill. As Kingston links Tom Hong to Tang Ao/Lin, the connection between Little Hill and Tom Hong's daughter, the narrator of *China Men,* is also apparent.

Little Hill and the other young women are actually immortal flower fairies who have been banished from heaven to live a time on earth. They are being punished because they offended heaven by obeying the usurper Empress Wu, who drunkenly commanded that all the flowers on earth be made to bloom on the same day. On earth the fairies transcend the roles usually assigned to women by becoming warriors and also scholars, as the empress—a figure who is given both positive and negative attributes—has begun allowing women to take the imperial examinations previously reserved for men. Like the swordswoman in *The Woman Warrior,* however, these brave young women do not allow their sense of enhanced opportunity to reduce their filial devotion, and Little Hill, upon learning of her father's disappearance, sets out to rescue him. The author makes clear that filial devotion is not reserved for males, having his character Little Hill write the poetic lines, "No matter I was not born a lad / I'll cross oceans to bring you back!" (Li Ju-chen, 133). As she searches for her father, she receives a letter telling her that she should return home to take the examinations and then they will meet. She passes the examination, then joins the other flower fairies in a fight to remove the usurper empress. As a result of the author's death, the novel comes to an abrupt end at this point (Scott, 106).

Although Kingston does not tell the story of Little Hill, a cursory look at *Flowers in the Mirror* allows us to better understand Kingston's use of the book and her aims in *China Men.* By conflating the figures of Tang Ao and the merchant Lin, Kingston can cast the father, Tom Hong, both as the disappointed, wandering scholar and as the man who

has been forcibly feminized in a strange land. Kingston casts herself in
the role of Little Hill, a daughter whose life is still ruled by filial devotion, even though she is a bold fighter and scholar. She is also a daughter
who does not hesitate to take over male tasks when the men are unable
to act.

Like Little Hill, Kingston does not give up on her father, even
though, as in the case of both Tang Ao and Tom Hong, he seems to have
given up on his daughter and on everyone, retreating into his own private world. Tang Ao, as a result of the perfidy at the imperial court,
which has dashed all of his hopes for advancement, retreats into a mystical fairyland; Tom Hong, as a result of a China in turmoil, the failure of
his own career as a scholar, and failures in the United States, retreats
into solitary anger, severing himself from his family, refusing to remember home, a man who "says with the few words and the silences: No stories. No past. No China" (CM, 14). Like Little Hill, Tom Hong's daughter sets out to find him and pull him back from his solitary retreat. She
does this through the act of writing China Men, saying to the father: "I'll
tell you what I suppose from your silences and a few words, and you can
tell me that I'm mistaken. You'll just have to speak up with the real stories if I've got you wrong" (CM, 15).

The central story Kingston tells is how her father has been, like Tang
Ao, captured, feminized, and stolen from himself. In "The Father from
China" section, she begins by showing Tom Hong as an infant, switched
with a baby girl by his father, who yearned for a daughter. The exchange
is soon discovered by the boy's mother, who rages at the father for being
"crazy" and an "idiot" for "trading a son for a slave," and at the girl's
family for trying to trade something worthless for something valuable.
The family concurs with her accusations that a girl is less valuable than a
boy and "hung their heads" (CM, 21). Kingston establishes the pattern
for what is to come, hinting that anyone, given the right circumstances,
can be feminized and thus devalued. At the same time Kingston suggests that, although the Chinese culture in general holds that girls are
useless, it is still possible that they be valued, that even a Chinese man
may "value girls" as her paternal grandfather clearly does, in his yearning for a daughter.

When Tom Hong decides to go to America with the other men of his
family, he starts down a road that will inevitably lead to a general loss of
identity. To get into the United States the men must purchase papers
from legal U.S. citizens, which purport to show that they are the offspring of these men. Those who have become citizens have often taken

the precaution of declaring the birth of a son every year, thus creating many slots for the entry of supposedly legal sons. To get through immigration the men must give details about the family they claim to be part of. Thus, each man must replace his own identity, must "memorize another' man's life, a consistent life, an American life" (*CM*, 46). Already, before he even gets to America, Kingston's father's identity begins to break apart; he will travel to the United States with "two sets of papers: bought ones and his own, which were legal and should get him into the Gold Mountain according to American law." He cannot necessarily expect to rely on his own papers, however, for they are "untried," whereas the "fake set" has worked for previous owners (*CM*, 46). The China men may try to hold onto their own identities, Kingston suggests, but they must always be ready to give them up and switch, if necessary, to an identity more acceptable to those in power.

Kingston makes her most unmistakable point about this loss of identity and the resulting feminization of the Chinese men in America, by having her father, in one version of the story of his immigration, arrive as a stowaway on a ship. He makes the trip in the cargo hold, curled up inside a wooden box which Kingston compares to the "palanquin" (*CM*, 49), or sedan chair, that is used to carry a bride to her husband's family. In an earlier passage Kingston has shown how the bride is hidden in layers of veils, her own identity symbolically blotted out and her ability to control, or even see, the path of her own destiny blocked. While guests compare the bride in her box to a queen, they simultaneously compare her to the victim of an abduction: " 'The men are kidnapping her' " (*CM*, 31). The palanquin was seen as a bridge to the woman's new life, a bridge that would be burned behind her: "She would go no more to her parents' house except as a visitor; the visit a woman makes to her parents is a metaphor for rarity" (*CM*, 32).

Similarly, Kingston's father makes the transition to his new home trapped in a box, unable to see where he is being taken. In the fear and confusion of his entrapment, his own identity is lost, and he finds himself taking on another identity to suit his new home. In the box he begins to "lose his bearing"; he "felt caught," imagining many fearful fates. He imagines the voices of his family, but the voices do not speak of home. Instead of reminding him of who he is, they separate him even more from his past, spinning fantasies of the new land, the abundance of food, the easy wealth—"You can get rich picking over what [the Americans] drop"—and the wonders of this strange, new world: "Skyscrapers tall as mountains. . . . They'll invent robots to do all the work, even answer the door" (*CM,* 50). When he finally arrives in the United States, it seems that his captivity in the box has worked in the same way as does a bride's captivity in her palanquin. Carried blindly to a new environment, the prisoners both lose sight of the way home and of who they used to be. Both arrive with no identities, ripe for molding by the new environment. As the new bride must take her husband's family as her own, even though she will always be an outsider there, the emigrant father must take America as his own—"Gold Mountain, his own country"—even though he will always be seen as an alien (*CM,* 52). In this he, like the bride, the subjugated woman, is feminized, as both are changed into objects that exist to absorb the fantasies and serve the desires of others.

A Fantasy of Freedom

When a little later we see the father and his friends in New York, all of the men seem to have been purged of any connection to their previous identities; they are "free: no manners, no traditions, no wives" (*CM,* 61). At least they are free of their pasts, but they are possessed now by the fantasy of America and seem to have become blank screens on which the novel excitements are projected, as they visit the Statue of Liberty, go to movies, window-shop Fifth Avenue. Like women, whose lives are controlled by others and who must create an appearance that is pleasing to those in power, the China men are preoccupied with their own adornment, spending large sums on suits, hats, and silk socks so that they will look as much like prosperous Americans as possible. As if secretly aware of the extent to which they have been stolen from themselves, and constantly needing verification that they still, on some level, exist, they constantly seek out their own reflections, hoping to see reflected back to them the new American appearance they have cultivated so assiduously. They look for themselves "in windows and hubcaps. They looked all the same Americans" (*CM,* 64). So thoroughly do the men seem to exchange their previous identity for one supplied by the fantasy of America, they begin to see themselves as fantasy figures. At the dime-a-dance parlors, where Ed basks in the presence of blonde women, he acts out gestures he's seen in American movies: " 'What's your name, sweet heart?' he said like in the movies. . . . He saw himself and her in the mirrors, and they looked like the movies" (*CM,* 65). The men do not, of course, attempt to integrate their previous existence into this scene from the movies: "Not one of the four of them told any blonde that they were married and were fathers" (*CM*, 66).

Through her juxtaposition of "The Father from China" with the tale "The Ghostmate," Kingston underlines the implication that Ed and his friends, for all their purported freedom, have actually been stolen from themselves. In "The Ghostmate" we are shown a man who appears to be freed from the sameness and drudgery of home, from his unglamorous wife and family responsibilities; indeed, he seems to have found paradise when a beautiful woman invites him into her luxurious home, pampering him endlessly and giving him everything he could desire. Although the experience is delicious, the man, we come to see, is actually being emptied of experience and character, reduced to a plaything, existing at the pleasure of another: "[H]e feeds [upon the fancy foods] like a zoo animal, a pet" (*CM*, 77). He does not exactly forget his old life, "but remembers it like a bedtime story heard as a child." Even his family is no longer real: "Now whenever he conjures up thoughts about his family, he sees their black and white portraits" (*CM*, 79). For him, as for the China men in New York, the emotion and complexity of family life has been flattened into a photograph.

Both Ed and the young man in "The Ghostmate" are, despite the thrill of their new lives, in reality dying inside. When the young man finally breaks away from the beautiful woman and wanders in a daze back to his home, he finds that he is wasted and disheveled: "Look at you," his friends cry. "You're so thin. Have you been ill? Why, I can feel your bones. What black bags under your eyes, and why do you let your hair hang like this?" (*CM*, 81). And he realizes that the beautiful woman was only a deadly illusion, bent upon stealing him from himself. Similarly, Ed's glamorous life in New York proves to be an illusion. He is not really a Fifth Avenue swell but a laundry man who slaves late into the night and then falls down exhausted on his ironing tables. He will not get to go home with the blondes he pays to dance with. Also illusory is the friendship he forms with Woodrow, Roosevelt, and Worldster, the other China men who seem to make up a new family to substitute for the constraining, traditional structure of parents, wives, and children. Although the friends seem devoted to one another, the other three conspire to swindle Ed out of his share of the laundry.

As the young man in "The Ghostmate" is pulled back to reality by people from home, Ed is reconnected with his past by his wife whom he sends for. While he has been imagining himself as Fred Astaire, she, like the hardworking wife of "The Ghostmate," continues to struggle with the problems he has left behind, enduring the deaths of their two children and laboring to build roads to pay off the family labor tax; she escapes the region just ahead of the invading Japanese. (It is to Ed's credit that he sends for her; the other men, hearing that he has done so, ask, "Why did you want to do that?" [CM, 68].)

Although her husband protests, the wife unpacks jars of seeds, which she plants in cans on the fire escape, bringing life from the old world into the new, perpetuating the connection between past and present. And she unfurls the canopy from their marriage bed—"the only thing we have left from China"—with its Chinese symbols, a red phoenix and a red dragon, and its English greeting, "Good Morning," which, as a bride, she copied from a needlework book. Even in its beginning, Kingston indicates, their marriage has been a union of Chinese past and American present. And it is the wife's job to reconnect Ed to his past. Although Ed and his friends have dropped the Chinese holidays, Ed's wife brings them back. And while Ed is still bedazzled by the wonders of America, his wife is not and continually pulls him back to his Chinese identity: "When do you think we'll go back to China?" she asks, as Ed shows her the sights of New York. Asked to admire an American aquarium, she is not impressed, commenting, "There are bigger fish in China" (CM, 71).

Kingston's portrait of Ed in New York offers one vision of how the Chinese men are stolen from themselves, turned into objects, like young brides being carried to their husband's families. Another view of how the Chinese men were taken from themselves is presented by her portrait of the "legal father," an alternative version of how her father may have reached the United States. In this version her father does not stow away in a cargo box but finds himself in what amounts to a box all the same. As he attempts to enter the country legally, he is detained, along with other Chinese immigrants, at an immigration station off the California coast. Here, he, like the others lost in the San Francisco fog, is in danger of being lost to himself. Part of the men's loss is the result of the failure of the Chinese male-dominant power structure. They lament that their emperor, at the top of China's chain of male dominance, is "too weak to help them" escape their imprisonment by the Americans. The loss of male power is physically demonstrated to the men; they must live on a floor that is below the women's prison, so that the men are "trodden over by women" (CM, 55). For men who have avoided the bad luck and pollution of even walking under women's pants on a clotheslines, this first American living arrangement seems to be a humiliation the American "demons" have planned (*CM*, 55). Trapped, humiliated, and lost in the fog, the men, who had come to "do mighty American deeds," are instead "corralled," locked into another box, as one of the poet-immigrants writes, " '[T]his wooden house my coffin' "(*CM*, 56).

As with the father who entered the country as an illegal stowaway, the "legal father" does not use his name but plans to find a new American name. And as the "illegal father's" past seems to be obliterated during his time in the cargo box, the legal father also has his past wiped out as part of the passage into America, this time by immigration officials who invalidate his ancestors: " 'Your grandfather's papers are illegal,' " he is told. " 'And your father is also an illegal alien.' One by one the demons outlawed his relatives and ancestors. . . . and put an X across the paper that had been in the family for seventy-five years" (*CM*, 59).

In painting these two portraits Kingston demonstrates how the loss of self attendant upon humiliation and subjugation is a function of power arrangements, rather than of something inherently inferior in the victim. In doing so she continues to suggest the similarity between women subjugated by men, and men subjugated by superior political and economic power.

Still, the daughter, like the wife, seeks to pull the father back to the "real" world, the proper world of the Chinese kinship system. Kingston suggests that, because the father has been subjugated by racial and cultural discrimination in a way similar to the subjugation that women have always experienced, his wife and his daughter understand his suffering and find a way to pull him back into a loving kinship relationship. To do this Kingston must provide an explanation for her father's anger, abusiveness, and silence to replace the one imagined by Kingston and her brothers and sisters, which was that he was full of hate, both for them and for their shared Chinese legacy: "We invented the terrible things you were thinking. . . . That you hate daughters. That you hate China" (*CM*, 14). Like Little Hill, Kingston has set out to find her father, discovering imaginatively a man who has been captured, degraded, and stolen from himself, driven to rage and to silence. Not only must she find her father, however, but she must also save him, as Little Hill attempts to save Tang Ao, bringing him back to life in the world.

A Poet in Exile

In the "American Father" section of *China Men*, Kingston saves her father by identifying him with another figure from Chinese story,

fourth-century B.C. poet Ch'ü Yuan, author of the elegy *Li Sao,* which
Kingston gives variously as *Lament on Encountering Sorrow, Sorrow after
Departure,* or *Sorrow in Estrangement.* Examining Kingston's portrait of
Ch'ü Yuan alongside her figure of Tang Ao, we can better understand
the portrait she attempts to paint of Tom Hong. Perhaps Kingston
seizes upon Ch'ü Yuan's *Li Sao* as a vehicle by which to recover the
image of her father because it is a work of which the father approves
wholeheartedly and which he takes to be quintessentially Chinese: " 'All
Chinese know this story,' says my father; if you are an authentic Chinese,
you know the language and the stories without being taught, born talking them' " (*CM,* 256). This is the defining Chinese story, the father
seems to say, and so Kingston uses the story to redefine the father, give
him back his Chinese identity, and place him in the United States.

Like Tang Ao of *Flowers in the Mirror*—and like Tom Hong—Ch'ü
Yuan has been ill-served by his monarch and his fine qualities have been
trampled in the turmoil of a confused age. And like Tang Ao and Tom
Hong, Ch'ü Yuan seeks to escape the "muddy impure world, so undis-
criminating" (Birch, 47), retreating into solitary reveries.

As Tom Hong experienced the collapse of imperial China and Tang
Ao saw a usurper take over the throne, Ch'ü Yuan lived in the turbulent
Warring States period, which began in the fifth century B.C., and during
which China was split into a number of hostile factions. A member of
the royal house, he was a favorite advisor to the king, credited with
bringing about important reforms, including diplomatic initiatives that
strengthened the position of the state of Ch'ü[4] in relation to its enemies.
But his success drew the envy of courtiers, who slandered him to the
king, and Ch'ü Yuan was demoted and banished. The diplomatic ties he
had forged came undone, leaving the kingdom vulnerable to attack.[5] In
exile the grief-stricken Ch'ü Yuan lamented both his own losses and the
corruption of the age.

In Kingston's version of *Li Sao* the poet grieves over his own banish-
ment, his eternal homelessness: "No home anywhere. He saw the entire
world, but not his homeland. . . . He was an orphan who traveled everywhere because one place was denied him" (*CM,* 257). Kingston's portrait also shows a man whose fine qualities have been ignored: " 'The
crowd is drunk,' " Ch'ü Yuan says. " 'I alone sober, I alone am clean, so I
am banished. The world has gone bad' " (*CM,* 259). Kingston's version
resonates against the background of the poem itself, which, as given in
Cyril Birch's edition, contains these elements but which also expresses a
more intense sense of love for country, as represented by the monarch. "I

do not care, on my own account, about this divorcement," the poet Ch'ü Yuan writes of his exile. "But it grieves me to find the Fair One [his king] so inconstant" (Birch, 52). Kingston seldom speaks directly of the collapse of Imperial China, but her use of *Li Sao* suggests that this catastrophe is always echoing in her father's life.

Ch'ü Yuan is also shown struggling to maintain his own inner purity, in an impure world: "If only my mind can be truly beautiful / It matters nothing that I often faint for famine"; and "I will no longer care that no one understands me, / As long as I can keep the sweet fragrance of my mind" (Birch, 53). Even this desire to protect the mind at least from the tribulations of the world is misunderstood and deposed by lesser beings: "Why be so lofty, with your passion for purity?" the poet is asked (Birch, 55).

In the end, Ch'ü Yuan drowns himself because "there are no true men in the state: no one to understand me" (Birch, 62). But, like Tang Ao and Tom Hong, Ch'ü Yuan turns out to be less misunderstood and more beloved than he realizes, for the story is told that those who loved Ch'ü Yuan came to reclaim, if not his body, then his spirit. When news of the poet's suicide reached the people who understood his virtue, they are said to have sent out boats to search for his body. This storied event is still commemorated among some Chinese communities in the annual Dragon Boat Festival (Scott, 31). In Kingston's version the people seek to entice the poet back to life by reminding him of earthly pleasures such as foods, songs, and chess games. " 'Return, O Soul. Return,' " they call (*CM*, 260). Not finding him, they prepared rice cakes, racing in their boats to be the first to sacrifice the cakes to the dead man.

While Kingston has shown her father's humiliation and his feminization, casting him as Tang Ao, captured and feminized, she also casts him as the banished poet Ch'ü Yuan, an especially sensitive man, who nourishes a rich, pure inner life, despite his hardships and the coarse brutality of his world. She first makes the connection between Tom Hong and the poet by showing her father as one who also displays from birth an unusual sensitivity. Ch'ü Yuan was marked "from birth [with] inward beauty" (Birch, 51); the father as an infant is seen as destined for finer things than his brawny brothers: " 'Your little brother is different from any of you,' " Kingston's grandmother tells her other sons. " 'Your generation has no boy like this one. Come. Look. . . . Look at the length of his hands and fingers. . . . This kind of hand was made for holding pens. This is the boy we'll prepare for the Imperial Examinations.' The other boys were built like horses and oxen, made for farmwork" (*CM*, 16). The

boy's mother dresses him as a little scholar; he is given lessons, and soon
he shows signs of prodigy, " 'playing with big words' " like the famous
poet Tu Fu (CM, 23).[6]

Like Ch'ü Yuan, Bibi, as Kingston's father was known as an infant, is
the object of jealous anger from those who are coarser and less talented.
In Bibi's case his older brothers resent his scholarly activity and the
attention it commands. They catch Bibi outdoors "scratching the
ground with a stick" and say to one another, " 'Even outdoors he's writing. Let's torture him.' " They dance around him singing their disdain,
" 'Poetry addict, poetry addict . . . won't work for rice, shoulders a hoe
but forgets to till. Poetry addict won't comb his hair, defends his home
with a rusty sword' " (CM, 24).

As Bibi goes off to take the Imperial Examination—the last ever
given—Kingston compares him to the great poet Tu Fu, both mentally
flying toward an expanding intellectual world. As Bibi stays up all night
studying for his exam, Kingston again links him to famed scholars and
poets by borrowing stories associated with real historical figures and
attributing them to the father. Like the ancient scholar Ju Yin, he uses
fireflies to illuminate his reading. Like another ancient scholar, Sun Jing,
he ties his pigtail to a high beam so that he will be jerked awake if he
dozes off and can continue studying. Like Su Jin, he jabs an awl into his
thigh so that the pain will keep him alert for his studies.[7]

The father does not win top honors in the examination, but this too
links him to the great poet Tu Fu, who, as Kingston observes, failed the
imperial exam numerous times, even failing "a special test arranged in
his honor" (CM, 28). Like Tu Fu, Kingston implies, her father is a creative thinker, not a career-minded crammer. He does well enough, however, to get a job as a village teacher. Here, the connection to Ch'ü Yuan,
whose fine qualities were ignored by an insensitive public, is most pronounced. The father tries to take his students beyond rote memoriza-
tion, to teach them an appreciation of the poetry they are reciting.
Rather than "marvel[ling] that they had a teacher who knew the mean-
ings of the texts and not just rote" and rising to the challenge he presents, the students retreat into boredom and blame. The teacher must
be inept, the boys reason, because they would have to think more than
is their habit to understand what he is saying. Like Ch'ü Yuan, whose
life at court is destroyed by crude inferiors, the father's life is ruined by
the dull students who "ruined his eating; they ruined his sleep. They
spoiled the songs of birds. And they were taking his books and calligra-
phy from him too—no time now for his own reading, no time to prac-

tice his own writing. Teaching was destroying his literacy" (*CM*, 39). Also like Ch'ü Yuan, he is a victim of a world "blinded with its own folly / How can you show men the virtue inside you?" (Birch, 59).

Finally, the father is driven out, "made susceptible" by his suffering in the classroom to the stories about magical Gold Mountain. As both Ch'ü Yuan and Tang Ao, misunderstood and maligned, leave the world to wander in exotic fairylands, the father leaves for the America that is described by returning travelers, a place of unbelievable wealth, the streets paved with gold, the "very dirt atwinkle with gold dust" (*CM*, 41).

In the United States the father continues to be identified as a scholar and a poet, the one who "heartens" the other men by reading from Li Po, whose poems he carries with him. The father anonymously writes a much-admired poem on the wall of the Angel Island internment cell, and he applauds and encourages the incipient poetic efforts of the illiterate men. In New York the father, now called Ed, keeps up his spirits at the ironing tables by singing the old poets. It is suggested later, however, that Ed may have been punished for his special sensitivity to literature once again: "You were always reading when we were working," one of his friends tells him, apparently to explain why Ed has been swindled out of his share of the laundry business (*CM*, 73).

By juxtaposing the figures of Ch'ü Yuan and Tang Ao with that of the father, Kingston suggests that it is not necessarily the greedy or even the ambitious who came to America, but that in some cases it is the too-sensitive, and the heart-broken, driven out of real life, forced to wander eternally in a fairyland that is, at times, fabulous and exotic, but which will never be home. With this portrait Kingston erases the image of the man filled with hatred, transforming him into one who, like Ch'ü Yuan after years of wandering, is still overcome with his loss and who has retreated into some pure, inner part of himself, the only place he can protect from the depredations of a hostile world. No longer are her father's long, angry silences hate filled. Now they can be seen as the lonely refuge of an exiled poet.

Kingston also transforms the depression that overcomes Tom Hong into the suffering of a hero, even though the father's paralysis is seen in his own home as anything but heroic. The mother, here referred to as MaMa, operates very differently from her husband. Herself a tireless fighter, as shown through the portrait of Brave Orchid in *The Woman Warrior*, she believes that her husband's weakness has caused the loss of everything from the laundry in New York to the gambling job in Stockton to his land in China. To the author's younger self, meanwhile, the father seems merely absent, apparently having "lost all his feelings," experiencing neither love nor pain. But the adult author, reading against the background of Ch'ü Yuan and Tang Ao, can see that her sensitive, heart-broken father has simply "run down and stop[ped]" (*CM,* 248), that, like Ch'ü Yuan, whose grief drove him to suicide, he has finally given up his lonely struggle.

By working this change upon her father, Kingston succeeds where Little Hill fails. Apparently as a result of the sudden death of its author, *Flowers in the Mirror* ends abruptly with Tang Ao still lost. But Kingston finds her father where he has hidden, discovering the sensitive man behind the anger and depression. She contributes further to this portrait by seeking him out in his secret places, which function as metaphors for the father's inner life. She finds him in the cellar under the house, where the supposedly bottomless well is "a hole full of shining, bulging, black water, alive, alive, like an eye, deep and alive" (*CM,* 238), managing to glimpse the well although her father tries to keep her away from it. The well, like the father, is dangerous and mysterious, but full of secret, brilliant life. And through a long and frightening passage, it finally connects America and China. The father is also reflected in the attic, a place of hot, "too thick" air that is still extravagantly spacious. Like the father's inner life, the thick air of the attic is always there, floating silently above the crowded hubbub of family life. But the best metaphor for the secret life of the father is found in the gambling house he ran, another "secret place." No one looking at the shabby, lifeless outside of the building would understand the rich life within; it is quiet and orderly, and although it is a gambling house, it is also a house of poetry as the men gamble on word games where "you had to be a poet to win, finding lucky ways words go together" (*CM,* 241). Here the father seems to be in his element, presiding serenely over a world in which men come together in search of poetry and fortune, and where the two are inextricably linked. In the gambling house Kingston even discovers her father's concern for her, a concern that is not usually evident. She learns that the father has named his first child after "a blonde gambler who won." He has given her a "lucky American name" (*CM,* 243).

In the "American Father" section Kingston shows Tom Hong literally pulled up out of his depression, brought back to life, by his increasingly "wild" children. They "goad" and "irk" and "*gik*" him until "the gravity suddenly let go of him" and he is up out of his chair, chasing them, beating one of the sisters—they are unclear which—with a coat hanger. After this he does not return to his chair but goes out and opens a new laundry, starting life anew.

Revived, he makes for himself one more secret place, allowing his daughter a last metaphor for the father's inner life. This is the basement under his new laundry, a vast, dark place, a world unto itself, a dark mirror of life above ground. It is an unchanging world of "sunless, rainless city soil," and in its secret, mysterious, and labyrinthine vastness—"we never found the ends of some tunnels"—the basement seems to mock the smug complacent life above ground of those who do not understand the complex depths that hide beneath deceptively simple surfaces: "The people who lived and worked in the four stories above us didn't know how incomplete civilization is, the street only a crust" (CM, 254). The real world, Kingston suggests, is underground. And this is where the daylight world is explained: " 'Now we knew the secret of cities,' " Tom Hong's children tell each other. If the basement is an alternative world, one that is deeper and more complex than the sunny, surface life, it is also a place to shelter from the potential horrors of the world and to carry out subversive retaliation. For example, the father has stocked distilled water against the threat of air raids, as his children recognize: "Here was where we would hide when war came and we went underground for gorilla [sic] warfare" (CM, 255).

This space mirrors Tom Hong, who in his dark, complex, and ultimately unknowable privacy is more intensely alive, Kingston suggests, than those who go easily and sunnily along on the surface. Although it may appear that Tom Hong is only hiding in his silence, as in his basement, he is actually securing and protecting a place from which to carry on ceaseless clandestine warfare. In showing the father's secret underground world, Kingston echoes the scene with which Ralph Ellison begins The Invisible Man, in which the narrator finally becomes "aware of [his] invisibility" to those above ground, who see only "my surroundings, themselves, or figments of their imagination—indeed, everything and anything except me."[8] Invisible in the world of light above ground, he builds his own world below ground, realizing, "I . . . did not become alive until I discovered my invisibility" (Ellison, 7). Like the Chinese heroes who were maligned and misunderstood, and like African Americans who have been the object of racial stereotyping, the father has been driven underground, mentally and physically, but survives there, his sense of himself intact, if invisible, to the "dusty world."

Kingston links the father to yet another poet, Kao Chi,[9] who was "executed for his politics" in 1374 and who, she notes, was "famous for poems to his wife and daughter" (*CM*, 255). Once again Tom Hong is cast as a hero exile, now with the added quality of the ability to love his female relatives. The father is not shown writing poems for his daughter, but he is capable of giving her a gift of feeling, presenting her with a picture from the newspaper showing redwoods in Yosemite, telling her, "This is beautiful." Also like Kao Chi, Tom Hong gardens. Although he has seemed to live only in a hellish present, cut off from both past and future, Kingston links him to the great poet exiles of Chinese tradition, transforming him into a man with both a past and a future. His past is China; his future is his family and the seeds of love that he has, despite all appearances, planted. This then is our last image of Tom Hong, as a gardener, a man planting "from seed pits . . . peaches, apricots, plums of many varieties—trees that take years to fruit" (*CM*, 255).

The Grandfathers: Room for Paradox

Because Ed Hong seemed to have lost China, Kingston takes upon herself the task of finding the China in him, linking him to the heartbroken, exiled poets of Chinese history and literature. But as she looks at her two immigrant grandfathers, Kingston's project is different. Unlike Ed, the grandfathers appear never to have been in danger of losing China; both came to America, but both are shown returning home after sojourns in this country. Ed Hong finally realizes that, for better or worse, he is in the United States to stay, owning his own house and business and raising a family there; the grandfathers have no such ties. As Ed is in danger of losing China, the grandfathers are in danger of losing America. Ah Goong, the grandfather of the Sierra Nevada, along with the other Chinese men who helped build the transcontinental railroad, stand the chance of being driven out after their labor is no longer needed, and as the continued presence of the China men threatens Caucasian workers. Bak Goong, the great-grandfather of the Sandalwood Mountains, on the other hand, is not physically driven out, but he could be denied the chance to live a real life in America by overseers who cast the China men as soulless work machines and treat them as slaves.

If the grandfathers are in danger of losing America, Kingston shows, introducing a theme she will expand in *Tripmaster Monkey*, the United States is in danger of losing the grandfathers by excluding them from American history, not realizing their role in building the country, not grasping or appreciating their contribution. So full and rich are these men's inner lives, Kingston declares, that it will be America's loss. And so Kingston has set out to weave her grandfathers into the fabric of American myth, seeing her book as a continuation of William Carlos Williams's work of alternative American mythology, *In the American Grain*. Rather than "inscrutable" coolies, work machines with no discernible subjectivity, she shows the grandfathers as men of passion and pride. Though she fully acknowledges the injustice and mistreatment to which the Chinese men were subjected—the section "The Laws" details the institutionalized oppression of the Chinese in the United States—Kingston sees these figures not as victims but as heroes who overcame their hardships to build a country, as founding American fathers.

With Bak Goong, the great-grandfather who went to Hawaii, Kingston creates a figure of whom she can approve wholeheartedly. In his determination to become big enough to encompass all of his experiences, all of his worlds, and in his insistence on finding and keeping his own voice, he resembles no one as much as the autobiographical narrator of *The Woman Warrior*. Bak Goong can also be seen as a direct forbear of Wittman Ah Sing, the protagonist of *Tripmaster Monkey*, who grasps the unity of all experience, and who, also, is "one of those who talks himself through fear" (*TM*, 97).

In her portrait of Bak Goong, Kingston again suggests the chaotic background against which all of her Chinese characters are painted. The great-grandfather is shown to be fleeing upheaval of every kind, from the fanatics of the Taiping Rebellion to patrolling foreign invaders, "British demons with big noses and guns" (*CM*, 92). As he traveled through China on the way to the ship that would take him to the United States, he knew that he "was walking on dangerous and sick land" (*CM*, 92). Unlike Tom Hong, however, who seems to leave China, at least in part, as a result of his personal disappointments, Bak Goong does not take with him a sense of personal injury. Rather, recognizing "a century sized upheaval," he sensibly "turned his back and walked away" (*CM*, 93). But it is not only disaster that prompts Bak Goong's departure; he is also, Kingston claims, propelled by a sense of adventure that particularly infects the Cantonese: "Hong Kong off the coast tugged like a moon at the Cantonese; curiosity had a land mass to fasten upon, and beyond Hong Kong, Taiwan, step by step a leading out. Cantonese travel, and they gamble. . . . So the ocean and hunger and some other urge made the Cantonese people explorers and Americans" (*CM*, 91).

As was the "illegal" Ed Hong, Bak Goong is also shown locked up in the bowels of a ship, cramped and miserable as he is transported to his new life. Unlike Ed, however, Bak Goong does not become disoriented, does not "lose his bearings" or become separated from his past by exotic fantasies. On the contrary, the extremity of this experience—along with the opium he samples—enlarges his vision and propels him into an understanding of the connectedness of all life, both his prosaic past and his exotic future: "Though he was leaving his good wife and his village, they were connected to him by a gold net or light" (*CM*, 95). Here in particular the great-grandfather resembles the swordswoman of *The Woman Warrior* during her lonely time of testing, as she manages to make her mind large "as the universe is large" so that "there is room for paradoxes" (*WW*, 29). When Bak Goong arrives in Hawaii and is overcome by its exotic beauty, he does not, like Ed and his friends in New York or like the young man in "The Ghostmate," become so mesmerized by this fairyland that he forgets home and thus, as Kingston sees it, begins to die inside. Rather, eating the exotic new fruits, he thinks of his wife, wishing he could share the thrilling new experiences with her.

As Bak Goong does not forget wife and home, he and his companions do not, in direct contrast to Ed and his friends in New York, lose civilized ways, do not take their new situation as an invitation to "gulp" and "jab" at the table. Although the Chinese men in Hawaii are strangers to one another, they "ate like a family," keeping the idea of family alive (*CM*, 99). Whereas Ed and his friends seem happy to forget about Chinese tradition, ignoring the holidays, Bak Goong and the others carry these traditions to the new land. If anything, Kingston suggests, the traditions are improved upon by the men in Hawaii: For a New Year's festival Bak Goong helps build a dragon, one that "was more splendid than any village dragon he had left behind. None of the men had seen a longer dragon in China. 'This is the longest dragon in the world,' they said" (*CM*, 108). The men in Hawaii do not allow themselves to become objects manipulated by the forces of the new world; rather, they are subjects, founders. It is they who define America; America does not define them. Bak Goong declares, "We can make up customs because we're the founding ancestors of this place" (*CM*, 118). The customs may change, but they will live; indeed, Kingston implies, they will be revitalized by the immigrant experience.

Chinese Warriors, American Pioneers

As he breathes in the perfumed island breezes, Bak Goong recognizes the danger of being overcome by this unearthly beauty and becoming lost to himself; he looks back to China for steadying influences. He resolves to approach the new land not as an impressionable new bride, a blank slate, upon which anything can be inscribed, but as the warrior of Chinese legend: "If he did not walk heavy seated and heavy thighed like a warrior, he would float away, snuggle into the wind, and let it slide him down the ocean, let it make a kite, a frigate bird, a butterfly of him" (*CM*, 97). To prevent this danger he identifies with the great figures of Chinese history: "He sang like the heroes in stories about wanderers and exiles, poets and monks and monkeys, and princes and kings out for walks" (*CM*, 98). His ability to see himself as a warrior, even as others see him as a slave, is a sharp contrast to the self-image of the Chinese men who, along with Kingston's father, are detained on Angel Island. These men cannot see themselves as heroes, having come to "a part of the world not made for honor, where 'a hero cannot use his bravery' " (*CM*, 55).

Although the Sandalwood Mountains are beautiful, they are untamed, and it is the job of the China men to clear vast, tangled forests (*CM*, 98). The work is hard and the conditions degrading, sometimes literally killing, but the men are not victims, helpless sufferers. Not only does Kingston portray the men as mythical Chinese warriors, she also casts them as American frontiersmen, describing their work in the language of American pioneering mythology, as the men "hack a farm out of the wilderness" (*CM*, 98) so that they will be "the first human beings to dig and see the meat and bones of the red earth" (*CM*, 103). If the great-grandfather is an American pioneer, he is also linked to another stock figure of Western mythology, the brave knight on a romantic, heroic quest. Like the prince in "Sleeping Beauty," Bak Goong must fight his way through a "strange forest" of thorns and branches (*CM*, 98), until "one day, like a knight rescuing a princess," he breaks through (*CM*, 103). At the same time that Kingston paints the great-grandfather as a cross between Paul Bunyan and a knight in armor, she also takes care to maintain a down-to-earth Chinese identity: seeding the cleared ground, Bak Goong is shown wanting "to sing like a farmer in an opera" (*CM*, 103).

If Bak Goong resembles the narrator of *The Woman Warrior* in his determination to make his mind large enough "for paradoxes," he also resembles her in his sense that his very life depends on his ability to find his voice and express himself. Kingston seems here to meditate anew on the role of speech, particularly for those struggling to hold disparate worlds together.

Like Maxine, the young protagonist of *The Woman Warrior,* Bak Goong is inhibited from speaking. Both are silenced through the dictates of white power; Maxine loses her voice when confronted with the need to speak English in school; Bak Goong is silenced by field overseers who do not want the Chinese men to talk while they work. As both school girl and laborer are denied their voices, they are also in danger of being rendered invisible to the world and even to themselves. Furthermore, in being denied voice, they are being denied the means of working the difficult but necessary transition between the old world and the new, of bringing those two worlds together. Bak Goong and the other China men need to talk to help one another cope with the difficulties of the new life and to give one another advice. They need to tell stories to make one another laugh, to transport the wit and humor of the old world to the new, and to make the work go easier. And they need to talk simply to come to terms with their new experiences and sensations; for Bak Goong, talking is a way of expressing and understanding the self, integrating the old self with the new one. He wants to talk about the awesomeness of his task in clearing the land, how he "sawed through trunks and the interlocked branches held the trees upright." He needs to talk to help himself understand how to keep going: "Actually, I like being bored. Nothing bad is happening, no useless excitement." And he wants to talk about the sheer wonder of his adventures, for "How was he to marvel adequately, voiceless." He must marvel, and he is impelled to use his voice, constantly, to hold his worlds together: "One day—he could not help it—he sang about the black mountains reddening and how mighty was the sun that shone on him in this enchanted forest and on his family in China" (*CM,* 100).

For Bak Goong, as for Maxine, enforced silence is linked to both physical and mental illness. Bak Goong is forbidden to talk in the fields but still manages some expression, "scolding" his white masters in phrases "disguised as coughs." Although his speech is constricted, even this effort keeps him from sinking into despair; though he feels hopelessness, it is "dispelled upon speaking it. The suicides who walked into the ocean or jumped off the mountains were not his kindred" (*CM,* 104). Still, his speech inhibited, Bak Goong is felled by illness. Similarly, in *The Woman Warrior,* Maxine falls ill after confronting the silent girl, and the imperative to silence that is still within herself. In his fevered dreams Bak Goong feels that his "tongue was heavy and his throat blocked. He awoke, certain that he had to cure himself by talking whenever he pleased." The illness, he tells the others, "is a congestion from not talking. What we have to do is talk and talk" (CM, 115).

Following his own advice, he tells the men an "apt story," which Kingston implies is a Chinese myth, the men having "heard it already in the long ago place where there had been mothers and children" (CM, 116), but which also bears a distinct resemblance to the story of King Midas of Greek mythology. In both stories a man is commanded to keep silent about a royal person's animal ears; the silence becomes unbearable, and the man digs a hole shouting into it, then covering the hole to bury the secret. The earth itself breaks the silence, as the secret blows in the wind for everyone to hear. Silence and secrecy are unnatural, Kingston seems to say, in East and West alike. Bak Goong and the others, inspired by this story, dig their own hole. In defiance of their overseers' orders, they shout into the hole everything they are thinking and feeling, from "I've become an opium addict" to "I want home" (CM, 117). The men realize that they are not talking just to themselves or each other, but that they are "planting" their words so that they will grow and spread; the thoughts and feelings of the China men will become a part of the American landscape.

With this, Kingston transforms the men from victims to "founding ancestors." Not only do the men find their voices, but their stories become strong, survivor stories. For those whom society would silence, the author implies, speech becomes so important that their words are infused with special power; their stories endure and spread. Furthermore, in speaking up, the men have demonstrated their own, determined humanity and have won the grudging respect of the overseers, who no longer punish them for singing and talking at work and who no longer dare to "accompan[y] the knife-wielding China Men into deep cane" (CM, 118). Most important, speech, which constantly works to establish the connection between the self and its experiences, allows the great-grandfathers to keep the connection between the old and the new, to do what the father, in his silence, has so much difficulty in doing, to make "their lives of a piece" (CM, 118).

Building Gold Mountain

Kingston envisions another founding father in reimagining her paternal grandfather, imbuing him with the mystery of the railroad, which dominated her childhood landscape. A man marginalized not only by American racism but also by his own family, who hid and ignored him after he was bayoneted in the head by a Japanese soldier, he is rehabilitated by his granddaughter, who understands his heroism in terms of the railroad he built and "left for his message" (CM, 126).

The message left by Ah Goong is, like that of Bak Goong, the story of men who struggle against loss and uprootedness, but who find a way to connect their two worlds and to know themselves, finally, as the builders of America. As we understand Bak Goong by seeing him hack through an enchanted forest, freeing the land as if it were a sleeping princess, we understand Ah Goong first by seeing him fell a redwood. Kingston shows the huge tree suffering as it falls, "screeching like a green animal." The tree does not succumb immediately, but "pushed at the ground with its arms." It "lay like a long red torso; sap ran from its cuts like crying blind eyes" until "at last it stopped fighting" (CM, 128). Although the tree is in America, its roots, "like claws, a sun with claws," comes from deep in the earth, perhaps from China on the other side of the globe. The roots suggest the imperial Chinese dragon, hinting of the fall not only of China but of Ah Goong, himself driven out of China by the troubles there and by a wife who "forced" him to leave to make money (CM, 127). To go on with his life, Ah Goong must, like the great uprooted tree, join his strength with that of a young, driving country.

Like Bak Goong in Hawaii, Ah Goong is astonished by the exotic beauty of the new land, but, farther from home and in a less inviting climate, he feels, in the icy nights of diamond-like brilliance, his heart "breaking of loneliness at so much blue-black space between star and star" (CM, 129). But Ah Goong does not lose himself and his past in that cold, empty space; rather, he finds in the space the very stars and moon that he saw in China. He clings to this discovery, even though other China men disagree: "Nah. Those are American stars" (CM, 129). Not only does Ah Goong find the stars of China in the sky above, but he finds the two stars that will help him come to terms with his own loneliness, those representing Spinning Girl and Cowboy, two lovers who, in a traditional story, are separated all but one night a year. He also notices in his new country familiar birds—magpies—which are said to form a bridge upon which Spinning Girl and Cowboy meet. With these he had "found two familiars in the wilderness: magpies and stars" (CM, 130). Unlike Ed and his friends, who seem to have lost the holidays along with their families and home lives, Ah Goong observes the holiday associated with this meeting of the stars. Also unlike the Chinese men in

New York, he seems to recognize the role women play in maintaining tradition, and to honor that role by replicating it in the women's absence: Even though there were "no women to light candles, burn incense, cook special food, Grandfather watched for the convergence and bowed" (CM, 130).

Ah Goong encounters the cold, high emptiness of America again as he is lowered into space, swinging in a basket to plant gunpowder charges in the mountain face. Like the "blue-black" spaces between stars, the empty sky into which the basket men "swung and twirled" symbolizes the new world as it appears to the China men. Cut loose from everything that holds them in place, even gravity, the men could easily cut the last ties that bind them to life: "[H]e could just cut the ropes, or, easier, tilt the basket, dip, and never have to worry again" (CM, 131). Even those who want to live could go flying out into cold space, like the two men Ah Goong sees blown up, one screaming, one silent, both losing their lives as they plummet through empty space.

But faced with this terror of limitless space, Ah Goong is not, like Ed Hong, tempted to cut himself loose. Nor is he paralyzed by fear that he will be blown out into the sky. Rather, he sees in the empty sky an opportunity to take possession of the new place, first urinating into it, making himself part of it: "I'm a waterfall." Then, moved by the beauty that he experiences along with the terror as his basket swings in the sky, he ejaculates into the space, mates with the unknown newness of this country, establishes himself as one of the fathers of the new world that the railroad workers are helping to build: " 'I'm fucking the world,' he said. The world's vagina was big, big as the sky, big as a valley" (CM, 133).

As Ah Goong does not lose himself in the emptiness of the sky, he also does not lose himself when he is required to tunnel through seemingly impenetrable granite. Here, too, Kingston replaces potentially paralyzing fear with the opportunity for bold, heroic action, as Ah Goong "bite[s] like a rat through that mountain." And as he uses the stars to connect him to home and family, so he transforms the sound of the men's steady hammering into the sounds of home: "holidays and harvests; falling asleep, he heard the women chopping mincemeat and the millstones striking" (CM, 134). But Ah Goong does not simply remember home; he is not simply biding his time, captive in an alien land, until he can return. Rather, he has brought China with him, marrying it to the new land, making America his. When other men express their fear of dying and being buried in the American mountains, "nowhere," Ah Goong protests: " 'But this is somewhere,' Ah Goong promised. 'This is Gold Mountain. We're marking the land now . . . your family will know where we leave you' " (CM, 138).

Finally, Ah Goong and the China men take possession of Gold Mountain by going on strike to protest the extension of the work day to 10 hours, asserting their rights in a land theoretically founded on concepts of equality. As Kingston paints the men, they are entirely unwilling to view themselves as wage slaves; rather, they see themselves as pioneers, and builders: "No China Men, no railroad. They were indispensable labor. Throughout these mountains were brothers and uncles with a common idea, free men, not coolies, calling for fair working conditions" (CM, 140). To underline Kingston's sense that these men have brought China to American soil, that they have indeed revived a failing China in the new land, the strike notices are wrapped in traditional foods that the men pass around to celebrate the summer solstice festival. In this the railroad workers are portrayed both as American heroes, fighting for their rights, and mythical Chinese warriors, like those who circulated "the time and place for the revolution against Kublai Khan by a message hidden inside autumn mooncakes" (CM, 140).

The men are strengthened by remembering this story, as the grandfather will be strengthened later by watching a theater production of scenes from Romance of Three Kingdoms, with its hero, the warrior Guan Goong, who is also the god of war and literature.[10] Guan Goong is a mighty warrior, but he is also a man of sensitivity, known for the pact of friendship and loyalty he makes with two comrades in a peach garden. Seeing the play, Ah Goong is "refreshed and inspired," knowing that he has been accompanied to America by "Grandfather Guan, our own ancestor of writers and fighters, of actors and gamblers, and avenging executioners who mete out justice. Our own kin. Not a distant ancestor but Grandfather" (CM, 150).

Although the strike ends in compromise, it can be seen as representing a victory for the right of the Chinese men to have a say in their own work. When the railroad is finished, Ah Goong hears the speeches proclaiming that "only Americans" could have accomplished such a feat; he does not pause to wonder if the white speaker includes him in this category. Rather, he is certain that "he was an American for having built the railroad." And although in Kingston's version it is a white man in a top hat who drives in the golden spike, uniting the two halves of the transcontinental railroad, that spike does not really complete the great project. Rather, it is a steel spike, held and hammered in by the Chinese men, which actually holds the country together" (*CM*, 145).

The railroad built, Ah Goong is driven out, along with the other Chinese men who now threaten white workers. The grandfather seems to disappear after this, and family legend has it that he turned into a bum, a "fleaman," who, rather than sending money home, had to be brought back to China at great cost to the family. But Kingston counters both American and Chinese family stereotypes. As the Americans do not realize that he is one of the heroic pioneers, so the family did not realize that his American experiences had value beyond funds sent back to China, "did not understand his accomplishments as an American ancestor, a holding homing ancestor of this place" (*CM*, 151).

A Real American

With the final section of *China Men*, "The Brother in Vietnam," Kingston introduces the theme of war, a subject that, she shows here, dominated her life and imagination as a child and which will increasingly concern her in *Tripmaster Monkey* and in works now in progress. Here, Kingston examines the relationship between war and Chinese men, particularly her youngest brother who, although opposing the Vietnam War, enlists in the navy and is sent to Asia. Being an American serviceman sent to an Asian land war forces the second-generation brother to come to terms with his Asianness and his Americanness, and to synthesize the two into a unified whole.

Although war is often seen as a unifying force, solidifying the individual's sense of national identity, Kingston shows that there is no easy sense of identity for Chinese Americans. Identity becomes a particularly vexed question for them when confronted with the Vietnam War. Seen as the "other" by both Americans and Asians, Chinese Americans can have no clear sense of the enemy to be fought and the community to be defended. Furthermore, for Chinese Americans, who had seen invasion, revolution, and factional warfare rip apart their homeland and for whom World War II began in 1937 with the Japanese assault on China, not with Pearl Harbor in 1941, war had been a continual horror in a way not experienced by most Americans. Indeed, Kingston contends, it was largely to escape war that the Chinese came to America: "Freedom from the draft was the reason for leaving China in the first place. The Gold Mountain does not make war, is not invaded, and has no draft.

The government does not capture men and boys and send them to war" (*CM*, 269).

But although the Vietnam War has the feel of a recurring nightmare, the brother does not become lost to this horror. Rather, Kingston shows a character who has managed to form a coherent, if hard-won identity that is both Chinese and American, both pacifist and patriotic.

War, Kingston has shown, was a dominant motif of her childhood. Her sense as a young girl was that "there had always been war, whether or not I knew about it" (*CM*, 264). As World War II rages, movies and magazines are filled with images of destruction. The adults hold parades to raise money for Chinese war refugees, and "all the talk was about war and death" (*CM*, 268). Pleas for peace use up all the girl's wishes on stars, as well as all of her childhood magic, all "the magic rings, bracelets, wands, the fairies with dandelion skirts, the fish I let go" (*CM*, 267).War was always there, a maelstrom into which all tranquillity and happy hopes could apparently be drawn at any time. Against this background war loses any shred of nobility or glory; it is simple obliteration, and Kingston quotes an adult saying, "To go to war is to mingle with the desert sands" (*CM*, 268).

But World War II has an effect on the Chinese American child that goes beyond the well-known horrors of conflict. War, particularly war in Asia, contributes substantially to the identity confusions that already plague Asian Americans, who are imbued with no easy national or racial sense of "us" and "them." As a girl, for example, Kingston knew that the Japanese were the enemy. Cartoons in Chinese magazines showed Japanese soldiers torturing both Chinese women and American soldiers. But although the Japanese are the enemy of both the Chinese and the American parts of herself, the girl at the same time identifies with the Japanese American children whose lives have been shattered by war. As the AJA (Americans of Japanese Ancestry) children came home from school to find their parents taken to a concentration camp, Kingston's girl feels that any day she could come home from school "to find a bomb crater or a house that would be empty" (*CM*, 275). There is the underlying sense that, even though the Japanese are at war with both China and America, it is the AJA children's Asianness that makes them vulnerable, not the political configurations of World War II.

Once the United States entered World War II, American propaganda began to claim the Chinese for the Allied cause. But this same propaganda underlined the ongoing sense that the Chinese were alien others. Kingston's girl studies the character Chop Chop, who is featured in the comic book *Blackhawk,* about a squadron of World War II allied pilots. Chop Chop, the only Chinese on the team, is embraced and praised, but always in terms of the most egregious racial stereotyping: "Very clever these Chinese," the American squadron leader says, "I always said little Chop Chop is the smartest of the Blackhawks." Besides being "clever" Chop Chop wore "slippers instead of boots, pajamas with his undershirt showing at the tails, white socks, an apron; he carried a cleaver and wore a pigtail, although the Chinese had stopped wearing these in 1911. He had buck teeth and slanted lines for eyes and his skin was a muddy orange." He was "fat and half as tall as the other Blackhawks, who were drawn like regular human beings. . . . It was unclear whether he was a boy or a little man" (*CM,* 274). Hungry both for peace and for positive images of the Chinese, the girl is pleased by the "compliments" to Chop Chop's intelligence, the racism of the portrait registering only subconsciously.

After the defeat of Japan, the next enemy in the young girl's life is the Communists, who again complicate the simple equation available to Caucasian Americans of "us" and "them." The Communists in China are a double threat, simultaneously persecuting Hong family members in China and appearing to threaten the West Coast with nuclear annihilation. Despite the atrocities committed by the Japanese, the Chinese Communists seem even worse. "I wish the Japanese had won," the mother says (*CM,* 276). Now it is not just the Japanese who are monsters but the Communists as well. They seem not even to be fully human, but to be "monkeys trying to be human beings; they were pretending to explain and reason, putting on serious faces" (*CM,* 276). The identification of the Chinese Communists as evil monsters, however, has unsettling implications for the Chinese in the United States, who are still the victims of racist stereotypes. As portrayed in the *Blackhawk* comic book, the Chinese are not quite fully human, no matter what their allegiance. Confusing questions arise for Kingston's young protagonist: Are the racist assumptions that the Chinese are less than human justified in the case of the Communists? Are there human and inhuman Chinese? Can Americans—who are notorious for their inability to tell the Chinese apart—tell the difference?

During the Korean War the young Kingston and other school children were issued dog tags, presumably so that their bodies could be identified in case of nuclear attack. The function of the dog tags is to specify identity, but in this case they serve to underscore that there is no clear identity available to the Chinese American children who cannot fit themselves into the available categories. Indeed, the form the children must complete to get their dog tags engraved raises more problems of identity; it seem as though the Chinese American children may not actually exist, at least in American terms. The first problem is the category of religion, which the mother says is "Chinese." The girl, however, knows this is not what is meant by religion. Nor are Chinese American children able to fit into the categories given for race, which are designated as either black or white. As a result the children are given an "O" in each category for "Other." Since the girl's blood type is "O," her dog tag appears to give her identity as a string of zeroes. The zeroes suggest not only that the Chinese American, and other Asian children, cannot be placed in American life, but also hint again of the connection between the Asian American children and the evil Japanese of World War II; for a child of the World War II era, the zero is unavoidably linked to the infamous Japanese fighter plane. Again, the distinction between the "good" Asians and the "bad" ones is blurred. In being issued dog tags, the Chinese children seem to be accepted into the fold of Americans to be identified and protected. But in this very act of identity and acceptance, the children are shown that they have no clear place and that, in their Asianness, they are linked with those whom they have been taught to view as America's worst enemy.

With the war in Vietnam all of these contradictions seem to be concentrated in the person of Kingston's younger brother, who, it seems certain, will be drafted to fight the Chinese-backed North Vietnamese. Although he is an American, he is still an Asian, and he senses he will be particularly hated by the Vietnamese, as his participation in the war will be taken as an act of betrayal: "The Japanese and Chinese Americans warned one another what would happen if they got captured: the Vietnamese would flay Asian Americans alive" (*CM*, 277). Once again, Asian Americans can find no place in the system that the United States has set up to identify people, in this case draft-age men. A pacifist, who opposes the war, he cannot even try to get classified as a conscientious objector because that status is based on identifiable religious beliefs, and Kingston's brother "does not have [a religion]" (*CM*, 277).

Not only does the brother lack an identifiable—that is Western—religious affiliation, but his political views are not necessarily seen as those of a real American. Rather, due to his Asianness the brother's antiwar views are seen as stemming from suspect special interest. When the brother asks the disadvantaged students he teaches to envision a society where there is more attention paid to human welfare than warfare, the students reply: " 'You think like that because you're a Communist. That's a Communist question.' Any criticism he had of America they dismissed as his being gookish" (*CM*, 279). The heightened sense of enmity with Communist China keeps alive the racist notion that the Chinese might be subhuman monsters, eternal opponents of the "real" people of the world. When the secretary of defense declares the Chinese to be "the enemy of the world," the brother stops reading newspapers.

Although the brother abhors the war, and although his own identity as a full American is constantly undercut by the perception that he will always be an Asian Other, he refuses to escape the war by fleeing to Canada. As Kingston indicates, there has been a change from the generation of Tom Hong to that of the American-born brother. Whereas Kingston reads Tom Hong as one of the wandering exiles of Chinese mythology, this role does not fit the brother. He is no Ch'ü Yuan whose high-minded opposition to war in ancient China resulted in a life of lonely exile. Rather, the brother struggles to find a way to survive the war without abandoning his honor or his life which, for better or worse, is an American life. As he is not Ch'ü Yuan, ready to sacrifice himself on the altar of his own purity, neither is he a China man of his grandfather's generation, an alien, expendable, easily shunted aside. Although some may see him as the Other, and although he accepts his own complex identity, he still views himself as fully American and entitled to live his life in the country of his birth: "He did not want to live the rest of his life a fugitive and an exile. The United States was the only country he had ever lived in. He would not be driven out" (*CM*, 283).

Making his own painful compromise with a war he abhors, he enlists in the military, to "be a Pacifist in the Navy. . . . He would not shoot a human being; he would not press the last button that dropped the bomb" (*CM*, 285). Even as an enlistee in the service of his country, he is still Other, who cannot be seen as a full American. Although "nobody called him chink or gook or slope or Commie," his commander does keep asking him where he is from, which the brother interprets as saying, " 'Remember you're not from Vietnam. Remember which side you're on. You're no gook from Vietnam" (*CM*, 286). If the commander identifies him as fundamentally "Oriental," so does Bill, a hippie pacifist and sinophile who had "a thing for the Orient." And when the brother teaches English classes to nearly illiterate recruits, his students are impressed by how well he has mastered their language: "You speak English pretty good" (*CM*, 290).

As the brother's ship nears Asia, all the paradoxes he must face as both Asian and American begin to surface in dreams that reflect the confusion as to who, exactly, is the enemy, and the way in which the Asian enemy and the Asian self seem to melt together. The brother dreams he is fighting ferociously against an enemy who has captured and victimized a city, torturing its people. The brother fights ferociously, "hacks into the enemy. . . . When he stops, he finds that he has cut up the victims too, who are his own relatives. The faces of the strung-up people are also those of his own family, Chinese faces, Chinese eyes, noses, and cheekbones" (CM, 291).

When the brother reaches Taiwan, he has to worry about being Other in a different way. As he is not seen as a real American because he is Asian, neither can he be seen as a proper Chinese because he is American. Now he must fear that the old Chinese houseboy will "scorn him for speaking the wrong kind of Chinese, scold and mock, turn him into a child, a bad Chinese who couldn't speak right, and that he will be blamed for everything from being in the navy to the colonization of Asia" (CM, 295). He can blend into the Taiwanese crowds when he wears civilian clothes, but he cannot always understand what people are saying and feels more at home on the military base. In Hong Kong, where he hears Cantonese that is close to what his family speaks at home, he tries to find the address of relatives. Again he worries that he will be mocked for not knowing the proper customs, or that they will be so destitute that he will have to spend the rest of his life trying to help them. In the end, he does not find the family; the street numbers he has been given seem not to exist. In neither Taiwan nor Hong Kong does he find "home." Finally, Kingston seems to suggest, there is no one place where Asian Americans are fully at home, neither in America nor in Asia.

But at the same moment that the Vietnam War underlines the way in which the brother is not perceived by Americans as fully American or by Asians as fully Asian, it also, surprisingly, provides the brother with an American identity in legal terms, an identity denied the early China men, whose citizenship was always in jeopardy, and for whom deportation eternally loomed, even after decades in the United States. When he receives a high-level security clearance, the brother sees that "the government was certifying that the family was really American, not precariously American but super-American, extraordinarily secure—Q Clearance American" (CM, 299). This must mean, the brother decides, that his family in the United States has been finally validated. This has occurred despite all the fears of deportation, despite the desperate methods the family took to reach America, despite the fact that they were related to the "enemies of the World":

> The Navy or the FBI had checked his mother and father and not deported them. . . . And the government had forgiven whoever it was who had almost got caught stowing away. . . . The Communist grandmother, aunts, and cousins, potential hostages, were not hurting his trustworthiness as an American . . . and it was all right that his mother was an alien. The government had not found him un-American with divided loyalties and treasonous inclinations. Though he was conveniently close to China, the U.S. government which could make up new laws, change the law on him, did not dump him there. (299)

The brother returns from war not in triumph but as one who has survived and come home and honor intact. It is by insisting that the United States *is* home, by refusing to be driven out, that the brother has finally won legal recognition for himself and his family.

It has been Kingston's task in *China Men* to find a new identity for the men of her father's and grandfather's generation, rereading them as mythical Chinese and American heroes. Kingston has shown that the men's primary task has been to manage their sense of homelessness and alienation in America, a condition that is, despite all efforts, permanent. But with the portrait of the brother, as with the portrait of Ts'ai Yen that closes *The Woman Warrior,* Kingston creates a figure who has found a way to unite both Asian and American within one body and one psyche, who, despite the ongoing imputation of duality by the cultures around him, is one and at home.

Chapter Seven
Tripmaster Monkey and the Scrutable Self

From her earliest work, Kingston has taken it as her mission to intervene in the process by which the identity of the powerless is invented by the stories of the powerful. If identity is an invention she suggests, identity can be changed, as stories that define identity can be complicated, altered, even reversed. In *The Woman Warrior* Kingston is concerned primarily with the identity of Chinese and Chinese American women and is intent upon transforming the identity that had been imposed on them as potentially destructive outsiders—"maggots in the rice," never fully members of the all-important, male-dominant kinship system—to that of heroines who save their families and the world, who clean it up and hold it together. Then, in *China Men* Kingston turns her attention to the identity of immigrant Chinese men. Now it is the men who, in a racist and xenophobic America, have been portrayed as a weak but potentially destructive Other, men whose menial labor is necessary to help build a new country, but who are not seen as entitled to the rights and privileges of American life. Kingston retells the men's stories, casting her father and grandfathers both as mythical Chinese heroes and as American founding fathers.

At the end of both *The Woman Warrior* and *China Men* Kingston also creates figures who manage to unite Chinese and American within themselves. In *The Woman Warrior* she alters the traditional story of Ts'ai Yen to create a figure who synthesizes two cultures, translates between them, and is able to love across cultural boundaries. With the figure of the brother in Vietnam, which concludes *China Men*, Kingston finds a character who is utterly clear about being both American and Chinese and who lives with the sometimes uneasy union of various parts of himself, refusing to be torn in two.

With *Tripmaster Monkey*, published in 1987, Kingston turns her attention to a young American-born Chinese man, Wittman Ah Sing, who must, like the brother in Vietnam, construct an identity by integrating his own dual inheritance, all the while negotiating a minefield of cultural stereotypes. But Wittman is given another task. It is Kingston's project not only to transform the identities of Chinese Americans, but to transform the identity of America itself, to integrate Chinese mythology, the Chinese experience, and Wittman's own personal experience into the imagination of his audience. Wittman seeks to do this through theater in much the same way that African Americans have used music to infiltrate and alter the American consciousness, filling it with an improvisatory idiom of emotion, complicating identities prescribed by the dominant culture.[1]

Wittman Ah Sing, living in the postbeatnik, early–Vietnam era, sees an America that is in trouble, that is increasingly held hostage by powerful corporate and military interests. Americans are being taught, he believes, to accept an identity that makes them servants of these powers, valuable only for their willingness to consume and to support wars of imperialism. Ultimately, Kingston's protagonist suggests, Americans' identification with corporate and military interests could result in their own annihilation in the form of nuclear destruction. Even children's comic books, with their scenes of gore, are "brainwashing us for atomic warfare. . . . They are getting us inured so we could entertain the possibility of more nuclear fallout. . . They tried to make us despair of ridding ourselves of evil" (*TM,* 98). As mainstream Americans are increasingly trained to identify themselves in terms of their relationship to corporate and military culture, Kingston suggests, their authentic selves have been rendered invisible, both to themselves and others. Echoing Ralph Ellison in *Invisible Man,* Kingston suggests that white middle-class Americans are also defined by the stories told by the powerful, albeit to a lesser extent than those who have been marginalized in the traditional terms of class and race. As the "invisible" narrator, who has been forced to go underground to know himself, says to his white readers, "Who knows but that, on the lower frequencies, I speak for you" (Ellison, 581).

Constructing Identity in a Postmodern America

As Wittman works to construct his own identity, he suggests that the dehumanizing forces of racism are on some level the same as the isolating soul-death of consumerism and the dehumanizing energies of militarism. Wittman will combat these forces that seek to empty out the individual, filling him back up with an identity that reflects the needs of those in power. He will do this by filling the American imagination with the stories of community, heroism, and loyalty found in Chinese myth and in the struggle of the Chinese experience. As blues and jazz bespeak emotions shared to some extent by black and white Americans, so, Kingston suggests, the Chinese American experience speaks to a struggle that is actually shared with mainstream Americans, the attempt to know oneself in ways not specified by the narratives of those in power. Because the Chinese have a long tradition of evading corrupt officials in China and immigration officials in the United States, Kingston concludes that they are perfectly suited for the job of subverting the narratives of power: "outsmarting the government is our heritage" (*TM*, 249).

Although it may seem far-fetched to suggest that an imaginative engagement with Chinese story will, as Wittman says to his Caucasian wife, Tana, "turn you into a Chinese" (*TM*, 172), it can be argued that this is precisely what has made Maxine Hong Kingston Chinese. As a young person she has never been to China, does not speak acceptable Chinese, is viewed as a barbarian by immigrant relatives, and is mystified by much of Chinese tradition; but she is Chinese, it appears, because her imagination has been formed by Chinese myth, the repository of Chinese feeling and experience that has come to her through her parents' stories and songs. It is to these mythological works and figures that she turns as she attempts to understand through her writing "what is Chinese, and what is the movies," that is, Western cultural stereotype (*WW*, 6).

If Kingston's Chinese identity is formed by myth and story, it is an identity that is, like these stories, improvisatory and performative, constantly remaking itself, as do the tales told by Kingston's immigrant parents. Despite the critics who disapprove of Kingston for the liberties she takes with Chinese stories, Kingston grants herself and others permission to engage these stories in whatever ways they choose, telling the stories so that they make sense in their present environment. Having heard the stories all of her life, Kingston says, she believes they are hers to use as she sees fit: "They're mine. They are part of the psyche I inherited" (Simmons).

While Kingston has been criticized for failing to adhere to canonical versions of Chinese stories, it may be noted that many of the stories Kingston uses in *Tripmaster Monkey* evolved from constantly shifting oral accounts. *The Romance of Three Kingdoms* is, according to James J. Y. Liu, "based mainly on written historical records but also partly on oral recitals. . . . Although intended as popularization of history, the book may be considered a literary work of art because the incidents and characters owe much of their lively presentation to the imagination of the author (or authors). *The Water Margin* or *Tale of the Marshes,* as it is also translated, is also based on historical events which give rise to legends told orally, and eventually these stories were joined into one long narrative" (Liu, 70). *Journey to the West* is based on the historic journey of a Buddhist monk to India to bring back Buddhist scriptures, but this event too has been widely interpreted, giving "rise to legends, which formed the basis of various oral tales, dramatic works and simple written accounts" (Liu, 73). Only eventually, Liu notes, were the stories linked together in novel form.

As Kingston does not feel the need to keep these stories within the boundaries of an official canon, neither are they kept within national or cultural boundaries. Rather, Kingston has consistently shown the determination to retell Chinese stories in a studiedly American context, to create a synthesis that defies racial, cultural, or national boundaries. Only in this way can a Chinese American self be imagined that will be at home in American culture; only by integrating Chinese stories into its imagination can an American culture be imagined that will fully be home to a Chinese American. As A. Noelle Williams has noted, Kingston asserts that it is not only possible but necessary to tell Chinese stories in an American context as "various identities need to coexist peacefully within the same individual for any of the unities the individual forms with various communities to be affirming rather than stifling."[2]

Monkey Spirit

It is Kingston's task to intervene in the process by which the identities of the powerless are invented by the powerful and to subvert the "mono-logic identities" that trap one in either-or power equations. Her agent in this is Wittman Ah Sing, who is imbued with the 1960s spirit of challenge to corporate and military authority, and whom Kingston models in part on the beatnik poets, such as Allen Ginsberg, who insisted on building a counterculture community among those who oppose the conformity of American life, and on "howling" out the alienated self. Wittman is also modeled on one of the most beloved anti-authority figures of Chinese literature, the trickster Monkey. Hero of the Chinese classic *Journey to the West,* Monkey is well suited to challenge forces of authority. A master of 72 transformations, Monkey cannot be trapped in any power equation.

As Wittman must battle his way to a true identity, Monkey must fight his way to enlightenment. In *Journey to the West* Monkey is chosen to accompany a Chinese monk on the perilous journey to India, where he will be given sacred Buddhist scriptures to bring back to China. The ostensible protagonist of the *Journey to the West* is Tripitaka, a character based on a historical figure who traveled to India in the seventh century to bring Buddhist texts back to China; the real hero, C. T. Hsia observes, is Tripitaka's protector, Monkey, "who suggests such Western figures as Prometheus, Faust, and Milton's Satan in his defiance of established authority and quest for knowledge and power" (Hsia, 133). But Monkey differs from these Western rebels in his sense of humor and "his ability to view himself in humorous light. . . . He is never too solemn even when fighting a whole battalion of heavenly troops. Without his sense of humor, Monkey would have become a tragic hero. . . . With his sense of humor, he can turn from rebel to Buddha's obedient servant without forfeiting our sympathy. . . . [T]o the end he retains the comic image of a mischievous monkey whose very zeal and mockery become an expression of gay detachment" (Hsia, 135).

As Wittman will be, Monkey is constantly faced with obstacles that must be overcome. Some, like the Demon King Havoc, are external. Some obstacles, like the Flaming Mountain, have actually been created by monkey himself, as a result of his inability to control himself. And although Monkey is the hero of *Journey to the West,* he still gets into trouble from which even his magic cannot extricate him. When this occurs it is a female who saves him, as he is rescued and set back on the proper path by Kuan Yin, the goddess of mercy, who, as she tells Monkey, "is trying to keep you on the straight and narrow for your own good" (Wu, 125). It is, Kingston has acknowledged, Kuan Yin who narrates *Tripmaster Monkey* and who keeps Wittman on track (Simmons). Sometimes she chides the wayward Wittman, who, like Monkey, must try to overcome his own rages and weaknesses to enlighten himself and his community. Sometimes she appears as a comforting mother, as in the book's last lines: "Dear American monkey, don't be afraid. Here, let us tweak your ear, and kiss your other ear" (*TM,* 340).

While Monkey is most accessible to English readers through translations of the novel, he has been highly visible to generations of Chinese as the central character of traditional stage performances. Dorothea Hayward Scott's description of Monkey as seen in traditional stage performances gives a sense of the character Kingston seeks to create with Wittman Ah Sing:

Monkey's stage costume was yellow and black and on his head he wore a
tam-o'-shanter-type hat with a pom-pom in the middle or a yellow and
black skullcap. He wore realistic painted-face makeup and his elaborate
facial contortions and grimaces were monkeylike. His was the supreme
athletic role and performance especially loved by children. He would leap
about the stage, jumping high over the heads of his opponents, turn
dozens of cartwheels with such rapidity that he could scarcely be seen,
turn backwards and forwards somersaults in the air, and perform mira-
cles of dexterity with his magic wand, symbolized by a slender silver-
colored metal stave, some four feet long. This he would twist and turn
over his head and behind his back, with such lightning speed that it
would become almost invisible; then it would be thrown in the air and
finally caught with a magnificent flourish. (Scott, 94)

Performing the Self

For Wittman, who takes on the flawed but finally triumphant role of
Monkey, the stranglehold of military and corporate power on American
life and the entrapments of racial stereotype present not a death sentence but an opportunity to pursue his own enlightenment and that of
his community, and to have as much fun as possible in the process. For
Wittman, as for Monkey, it is in encounters with those who would
destroy him that he most profoundly performs himself. His suffering,
then, is his opportunity, and he vows, "I will make of my scaffold a
stage" (*TM*, 30).

Wittman will gather on the same stage figures from all the great Chinese classics, will act out an array of character and story that will prove
dizzying to those who seek to reduce Chinese Americans to a set of
stereotypes. In addition to showing that the Chinese and the Chinese
American experience richly transcends any one model, he also offers,
through images of Chinese community and fidelity, a more soulful way
to live, combating the versions offered by the department store, the
employment office, and the movies.

Kingston knows and accepts the fact that the performance of Chinese
myth and experience will provide unfamiliar and difficult material for
some American readers. Reviewer Anne Tyler no doubt speaks for some
of these when she describes *Tripmaster Monkey* as "exhausting. . . . The
myths and sagas are particularly tiring. Wittman loves to tell lengthy
stories that possess the grandiosity and the meandering formlessness
common to folk legends. . . . After a while the merest mention of Liu Pei
or Sun Wu Kong, the Monkey King, is enough to make our eyes glaze

over" (Tyler, 46). But as Wittman imagines the play he will put on, bringing all the heroes of Chinese mythology onto the same stage, he declares his unwillingness to simplify for the benefit of American audiences. Increasingly, Kingston has said, she sees her mission as one of "educating a very ignorant America" (Simmons), and Wittman expresses a similar sentiment. In one of Wittman's speeches, Kingston seems to refer to the reception of *The Woman Warrior,* which, she believes was taken as a piece of beautiful Chinese exotica by many white reviewers. At the same time the book was criticized by some Chinese reviewers who saw it as delivering negative stereotypes of the Chinese for the gratification of mainstream America. Kingston has defended herself against both claims, and she seems to signal here an intention to forestall any such attack on the present book. The complexity of *Tripmaster Monkey* prevents readers from gliding through the book, mindlessly projecting onto it their own stereotypes of the Chinese. Wittman declares, "We keep the men's Chinese names, we keep the women's names untranslated too, no more Pearl Buck Peony Plum Blossom haolefied missionary names. No more accessible girls and unspeakable men. The women: Hoong Ngoak, Fa Moke Lan, Ku San the Intelligent, Mrs. Shen the Earth Star. Let the gringo Anglos do some hard hearing for a change" (*TM,* 138).

While Wittman's play and Kingston's book challenge audiences to break through easy assumptions, to expand their cultural horizons, Kingston also sees her stories as a gift given to cement a union. Significantly, Wittman's wedding gift to the Caucasian Tana is story: "That's it, my present to you," Wittman says. "Got no money. Got no home. Got story" (*TM,* 175).

Wittman, who begins the book lost in the literal fog of San Francisco and the figurative fog of Vietnam-era corporate America, turns to the stage and to the performance of Chinese mythical stories out of utter necessity, after he has explored and rejected the more readily available ways in which he might fashion an identity and find a community within which he can be known. His job in the toy section of a department store demonstrates the increasing soullessness of American culture, as mindless, violent toys are pushed on children and their parents, and as corporate management trainees are groomed for a life of vapid competition. Nor does Wittman's avocation as a beatnik poet provide the identity he needs, as the era of the beatniks has waned by 1963. And even among the beatniks, Wittman notes, a Chinese American is still subjected to stereotype; even "King Kerouac, King of the Beats" writes of the "twinkling little Chinese" he sees as he travels across America.

Wittman responds, "A man does not twinkle. A man with balls is not little" (*TM*, 69).

With the figure of the "Yale Younger Poet," whom Wittman finds hiding out in the bowels of the department store, Kingston seems to pause to consider whether literary stardom might relieve one of the need to construct an identity. The prize-winning poet, becalmed in the stockroom, seeks to replace "doing" with "being," as if one can simply pick up the winning marbles and go happily home. But this is not an option that Wittman, who has not yet given up on action in the world, is ready to take.

Fired from the corporate job he cannot help undermining with his mockery, Wittman tries to find his identity in the movies. At first he does, identifying with the members of the Puerto Rican gang members in *West Side Story:* "Oh, yes, that's me, that's me, a-crouching, and a-leaping, fight-dancing through the city, fingers snapping, tricking feet attacking and backing up and attacking, the gang altogether turning and pouncing—monkey Kungfu. 'You got brothers around. . . . You're never disconnected. . . . You're well protected' " (*TM*, 70). He cries when Maria sings, "There's a place for us." Then he realizes that all of the actors playing the roles are white because Hollywood doesn't cast nonwhites, no matter what the role. The gang members aren't really him but "two white-boy gangs." But "white boys don't need a gang because they own the country. They go about the country individually and confidently, and not on the lookout for who to ally with" (*TM*, 71). He finally sees the Hollywood vision of ethnic solidarity as a sham, a mask on the face of a power structure that has no intention of granting nonwhites a place in American life.

Trippers

As Wittman does not find acceptable identity or community in corporate America, in beatnik or artistic exile, or in Hollywood images, neither does he find these at the party of friends he knows from his days at the University of California at Berkeley. Here Kingston explores the possibilities provided by 1960s Berkeley counterculture, the drug trips, the social causes, the games that defy the conformity and compromises of adulthood. At first the party seems promising as Wittman admires the spirit of spontaneous, audacious, defiant play that is the party's motif. And he approves of the drug trips that allow one to envision the unity and the empathetic connection of all life: "All of them were calm, breathing in unison; they must be on that trip where the margins between human beings, and between human beings and other creatures, disappear, so that if one hurts, we all hurt, so that to stop war, all we have to do is drop lysergic acid into the water supply" (*TM*, 88).

At the same time, however, Wittman recognizes the fear and chaos that lurk just below the party's surface, and the surface of life in the 1960s. The drug trippers envision unity, but they also envision nuclear holocaust: "The monkey brains had attuned themselves in to an open channel to a possible future. If . . . bombs were to fall, light would flash through time, backwards and forwards and sideways. Images would fly with the speed of light-years onto this screen and onto receptive minds. Future bombs are dropping into the present, an outermost arrondissement of the Bomb" (*TM*, 96). And it is here, as drugs induce a focus on the possibilities of both human unity and nuclear annihilation, that the concepts of both *tripmaster* and *monkey* seem to be born. For the party is, in microcosm, the world of Wittman and his Berkeley friends: open, audacious, intellectual, with the potential for unity and fun, and at the same time unpredictable and chaotic, in danger of plunging headlong into paralyzing paranoia, fearful of the same military-industrial forces they seek to elude through their alternative consciousness.

The drug trippers at the party need a guide and choose a young man named Charley, who is notable for "his articulateness in the midst of revels" (*TM*, 102). In the same way Wittman, who can "talk himself through fear" (*TM*, 97), will be assigned the task of tripmaster for those in search of a new form of community and identity. In describing Charley's performance as guide, Kingston describes what both she and Wittman must accomplish, and what attitude they must take. They must emulate Charley, who "was beautifully keeping his charges from wigging out. He got them to be inhabiting the same movie. Here we are, miraculously on earth at the same moment, walking in and out of one another's life stories, no problems of double exposure, no difficulties crossing the frame. Life is ultimately fun and doesn't repeat and doesn't end" (*TM*, 103). This is Kingston's task and Wittman's, to speak to the open-minded, helping them control fear, and at the same time reinforcing the unity of all people and the joyous potential of life.

With this, Wittman has found his mission, to get everyone to "inhabit the same movie" and to "walk in and out of one another's life stories" with ease. He will seek to accomplish this mission through the theater, which is, Kingston's narrator says, nothing less than "the life of the human soul receiving its birth through art" (*TM*, 276). By getting everyone he knows to perform the mythical Chinese stories of heroism and community, Wittman hopes to inspire Americans with the bold tales that have inspired the Chinese. To "get everyone in the same movie," Wittman draws on 1960s notions of improvisational theater: "Audience participation—they eat and they're sworn in this blood ceremony that will change everybody into a Chinese" (*TM*, 145). In this performance, in which everybody becomes a Chinese hero, Wittman will not only seek to steer the country toward unity and fun, away from chaos and fear, but also to create a new and complex picture of the Chinese and Chinese Americans.

As Kingston indicates, Chinese Americans' use of theater to perform their own complex identities, and to integrate a Chinese past into the American present is not Wittman's invention. Rather, he is emulating the vigorous theatrical performances of the first wave of immigrant Chinese who brought Chinese stories and heroes to America with them, who steadied their own sense of self by seeing their heroes alive and well on the American stage.

The heroes who most inspire Wittman and other immigrants are drawn from the well-known story of the Three Kingdoms in the third century A.D., a time when three forces contended for the throne of China. The events of this time provided material for countless tales and plays until the fifteenth century, when storytellers' "prompt books" were woven into a full-length novel, entitled *Romance of Three Kingdoms*. In the seventeenth century the version most read today appeared (Scott, 75–76). In the popular oath scene,[3] which Wittman will perform, the three heroes meet for the first time. The first is Liu Pei, a relative to the emperor and claimant to the throne, who has been reduced to supporting his family by weaving sandals, and who is seen lamenting his inability to fight the rebels alone. The second is Chang Fei, a butcher and farmer with "a blunt head like a panthers," a "thunderous voice," and a "stance like a horse in stride," who offers Liu Pei his support.[4] These two are joined by the most famous figure from the story, Kuan Yu, or, as Kingston renders the name in *Tripmaster Monkey,* Gwan Goong. Originally a historical figure, he has been raised through myth to the status of a god.[5] As he appears in Lo Kuan-chung's version of the story, he has "gleaming skin, glistening lips, eyes like the crimson phoenix, brows like nestling silkworms. His appearance was stately, his bearing awesome" (Lo, 7). The three men agree to fight together to restore proper rule, going into Chang Fei's blooming peach garden to swear an oath of eternal brotherhood, vowing to fight together until the end. Usually, family ties bind the Chinese together; these men show that it is possible to form a new family of mutual protection: "We could not help our separate births, but on the selfsame day we mean to die!" (Lo, 8).[6]

In *China Men* Kingston shows her railroad-building grandfather, himself—like the heroes of *Romance*—disenfranchised in a chaotic time, lonely without village or family. When he sees the heroes on stage, he is instantly heartened as the hope of community and brotherhood is renewed in America: the grandfather's heart "leapt to recognize hero and horse in the wilds of America. . . . [The grandfather] felt refreshed and inspired. . . . Guan Goong, the God of War, also God of War and Literature, had come to America—Guan Goong, Grandfather Guan, our own ancestor" (*CM*, 149). So beloved—so necessary, Kingston implies—was this oath of brotherhood to the Chinese immigrants, and the assurance of mutual support, that it was performed at "every matinee or evening for a hundred years, somewhere in America [where] some acting company was performing *The Oath in the Peach Orchard*" (*TM*, 141).

But this theater, which reassured the immigrants that beloved concepts of brotherhood and courage could still be theirs in the United States, no longer exists in Wittman's time. The Chinese American theater that had once been so visible "disappeared," Wittman says. "I don't know why. The theater has died. The words of [the Peach Garden] oath used to be printed on programs, and it was inscribed on walls for the World War II audience, when we were kids—that recently—to chant along with the actors, community singing." It will be Wittman's job to bring back this Chinese theater which is also "deep-roots American theater. We need it" (*TM*, 141).

The early immigrants not only put on plays, but they also put on parades, in response, Wittman imagines, to being "pogrommed in a drive-out" (*TM*, 211). Unwilling to accept the role of undesirable "other," to act out that part by hiding or fleeing when whites decided they no longer needed Chinese labor, the Chinese of the silver-mining mountain towns performed another version of themselves, showing themselves to be "human beings so beautiful that [residents of the silver towns] won't want to massacre them anymore." Here too Grandfather Gwan, hero of *Romance*, "god of war and theater, rides again," in a show of force that encourages the Chinese and changes the attitude of the whites. In commenting on the parade the *Sacramento Union*, while speaking in the vernacular of racism, still seems to recognize the Chinese determination to define themselves in a land they have come to take as their own: " 'It would appear,' " the newspaper wrote, " 'that John Chinaman means to remain with us for an indefinite period and to enjoy himself the while,' " to which the narrator of *Tripmaster Monkey* replies, "[Y]ou bet your booty and sweet patootie" (*TM*, 216).

Wittman, then, must set out to create a theater piece that will bring together his diverse community and give them all roles in performing the great stories of human valor, loyalty, and even, in the case of Monkey, the search for enlightenment. Wittman wants to incorporate all the complexity of Chinese myth, bringing together on one stage not only the heroes of *Romance* and the trickster, Monkey, but also the "hundred and eight superheroes" of *The Water Margin,* a novel loosely based on a legendary band of outlaws who lived in the twelfth century. The one hundred and eight heroes were known for their ideal of loyal friendship and for their antigovernment stance taking matters of justice into their own hands, defying official authority.[7]

The play that Wittman envisions reflects his belief in inclusion. Not only will all the great heroes appear on stage, but the cast will include everybody Wittman knows because, "Nobody should leave anybody out of anything" (*TM*, 137). Again, Kingston signals that she understands the difficulty readers may have with this unusual project. She lists one of the rules of improvisation: "A new ritual is embarrassing, it's OK" (*TM*, 145).

The very invocation of these heroes creates a kind of miracle. When Wittman and his friends do a speed read-through of the play, they are suffused by the rosy glow of dawn, as if, the narrator says, Gwan Goong were "paying us a visit" (*TM*, 148). As Kingston's narrator sought ancestral help in *The Woman Warrior,* Wittman believes that he has come under the wing of a protective ancestral force by casting himself and his friends in the stories of brotherhood, friendship, audacity, and heroism of Chinese myth: "A feeling went through Wittman that nothing wrong could ever happen again—or *had* ever happened." He looks around at his "chosen family," a group that includes both Asians and Whites, and is sure that, "We're about to change the world for the better" (*TM*, 149).

But changing the world, and oneself, is not accomplished so easily. As Monkey in *Journey to the West* must contend with numerous perils on his path to enlightenment—man-eating monsters, demons, and goblins—so Wittman must face one after another all the obstacles that Kingston suggests the world throws up to prevent individuals from truly knowing themselves and each other in peaceful community.

Is There Drama without War?

A problem that continues to plague Kingston is the apprehension that theatrical drama usually depends on violence and war to move people and inspire them to action. Certainly this is true in the Chinese stories upon which Wittman draws. Although Gwan Goong and the loyal friends of *Romance of Three Kingdoms* are icons of friendship and loyalty, they also exist in the context of constant warfare and violence. Similarly, the 108 rebels of *The Water Margin* who make up a kind of counterculture community, banding together in defiance of authority, live an extremely violent life. And for all his playfulness, Monkey spends a good deal of his time in ferocious battle. One of the obstacles both Kingston and Wittman face, then, is to find a way to use these stories of loyalty and heroism in waging peace, not war.

Kingston underscores the theater's dependence on the excitement of war, as well as its potential to change the course of events, through Wittman's visit to his mother, Ruby (Long Legs) Ah Sing, and her friends. The aunties, World War II–era showgirls, toured the nation in the early 1940s in a review that called attention to the plight of Japanese-occupied China. The showgirls danced and sang, paraded, and gave speeches, raising the money to buy a World War II airplane, which they painted with the flags of China and the United States, and the words, "California Society to Rescue China." This effort, they believe, helped to finally bring the United States into the war and to the aid of China. As Wittman hopes to save the world now, the aunties are convinced they accomplished the same task in the 1940s, that they "rescued China and won World War II" (*TM,* 189).

Although they believe that theater can bring change, they seem not to have found a worthy cause since World War II, the point at which the Chinese theater went dark. One of the tasks facing pacifist Wittman is to uncouple the Chinese American theater from war and to wean theater and theatergoers from the excitement of war. He declares, "The highpoint of a life shouldn't be war. At the war rallies, they performed their last, then the theater died. I have to make a theater for them without a war" (*TM,* 190). He urges his mother and the other former showgirls to use theater to make peace: "Ma, if you can stir up a war with your dancing, you can stop one, right? Why don't you and the aunties make up an Anti-War Bond show, and see what happens?" (*TM,* 270).

But Kingston and Wittman understand that peace may be harder to sell than the thrills and the "surprising gaiety," the explosions and lights of war, "which are more beautiful than anything" (*TM*, 301). And it isn't only men who like war. Women are excited by it as well, and about the "men, sexy in uniform," who are willing to "fight and die for them" (*TM*, 296). Somehow, then, Wittman must uncouple the drama of war and violence from the drama of theater. Kingston's narrator says, "Whatever there is when there isn't war has to be invented. What do people do in peace? Peace has barely been thought" (*TM*, 306).

If Wittman's visit to Ruby Long Legs and her friends portrays the first-generation Chinese American as stuck in the glory days of World War II, unable to contribute to the salvation of the present, his visit to his father, Zeppelin Ah Sing, demonstrates another obstacle to the achievement of a vital sense of community among the Chinese Americans. For the men Wittman's father's age also seem to hang motionless in the amber of past excitements; like the women, the men are still energized by the violence of past conflicts: "Kill the commies," the men yell in tense moments in their card game. "He used to yell, 'Kill the Japs!,' slap down his cards, scoop up his money," Wittman remembers. "If it weren't for the Japanese and the red-hot communists, these old futs would have lost their spirit" (*TM*, 197).

The older Chinese men seem to be stuck in yet another way, becalmed in the immigrant dream of magical gold-mountain wealth. Wittman's father publishes a newsletter called *Find Treasure*, which gives its six subscribers information on abandoned gold mines and speculates about how much wealth might still be found there. And although the fabulous wealth of abandoned mines is probably only a dream, the elder Ah Sing has found enough actual gold to make him a permanent believer: "Gold spoiled him for regular ambition. He lives from gold find to gold find" (*TM*, 199). Even when there are no gold strikes, the overall abundance of America has destroyed ambition, instilling the father with the philosophy that "the world is a generous place . . . full of free stuff," from the food behind the supermarkets to perfectly good mattresses left on the street (*TM*, 204).

The parental generation is so enthralled by the drama of war, Kingston suggests, and so caught up in Gold Mountain dreams, that it is not of much use in helping Wittman to build a community that integrates the imaginations of China and America. For the "ancestral help" that Kingston seems always to seek, Wittman turns to Popo, his ancient grandmother, or at least the woman who may be his grandmother. With this figure Kingston both symbolizes Wittman's search for an elusive Chinese past, about which one can never be entirely certain, and also suggests that it is the desire of his parents' generation to deny or dump that past. The parents symbolically demonstrate this desire by somehow losing Popo; perhaps she wandered away; perhaps they left her in the mountains after a picnic; perhaps she has left on her own, gone to gamble in Las Vegas.

Even in her absence, however, the grandmother is, as Wittman seeks to be, the keeper of a China that must now reside only in the imagination. A visit to her room opens a door into a past that extends well beyond the events of World War II. This is illustrated best by the "memory village" that stands on Popo's dresser. A Chinese village, small enough to sit on the palm of Wittman's hand, the model was devised so that immigrants who had purchased false identity papers could study and describe it for immigration authorities, thus convincing the authorities that they were the legitimate relatives of legal immigrants who had described the same model. The village, like the stories Wittman seeks to stage, both is and is not the real China. It is not, Wittman explains, "a model *of* anything." It is a made-up village, invented to give immigrants a past they can see, and describe in detail, one that is useful in the American context, though it does not represent anything they have personally known. As Wittman seeks to do with his performance, the memory village finds a Chinese past which is of solid, practical use in the Chinese American present. In keeping the memory village, Popo also keeps ties to family members still in China. When she first arrived at the Ah Sings, she brought "news about relatives that we shouldn't have lost touch with." Wittman's parents act as if they understand and remember, but it is a charade: "They didn't want to let on they'd lost their Chinese" (*TM*, 193). In the same way that they've lost or jettisoned "their Chinese," they have also apparently dumped the grandmother, and it is up to Wittman to see that she, and the past she represents, be found.

Killer Ape, Lost Child

Like Monkey on his quest, Wittman must overcome external obstacles and is also sometimes overwhelmed by his own unruly passions. Wittman must continually work to define himself as hero rather than victim, one who builds community rather than seeking revenge. This tension is revealed at the end of the "Ruby Long Legs' and Zeppelin's Song" section of *Tripmaster Monkey,* as Wittman finds himself alone beside a sleeping Tana, the young Caucasian woman whom he has met at the party and married in an impromptu ceremony conducted by a self-ordained Universal Life Church minister the couple happened to meet. Wittman has modeled himself on the trickster Monkey, master of transformations and seeker of enlightenment but is now "panicked" to be left alone in Tana's apartment as she sleeps: "Tana, please don't go. Don't shut me out" (*TM*, 220). For all his audacity, for all his insistence on belonging, Wittman/Monkey suddenly feels that he is an unwanted menace in Tana's white world once her protective companionship is submerged in sleep. In this mood he metamorphoses into a "great killer ape" that is "loose upon America" (*TM*, 221). First, he envisions himself ferociously "crashing" the party that is America, but he instantly slides into the sensation of isolation that those who try to crash must inevitably feel. Thus isolated, Wittman seems to fall prey to the question, always waiting to be asked in a racist society, of whether he is truly the Other, fundamentally different, and not fully human. Looking at himself in Tana's dressing-table mirror, seeing, symbolically, his reflection in the mirror of white society, he glimpses his profile and sees himself in racist terms: "I look like an ape. I have an ape nose" (*TM*, 222). With this he spirals downward into a nightmare of loss and helplessness, war and destruction, as if this, on some psychic level, is an identity that is always waiting to claim him if his grip on his own humanity is ever weakened. Now the sleeping Tana is cast as a dead mother, lying by the side of the road, in a scene that calls up the horrors of World War II, particularly the plight of Chinese refugees fleeing Japanese occupation. Overwhelmed by his sense of isolation, loss, fear, guilt, and helplessness, Wittman becomes a lost child, "clinging to her dead body still warm," sure to die if he stays, leaving his mother "dead alone forever" if he goes (*TM*, 222).

Can You Stand Community?

Like Monkey, who is only temporarily halted by the hazards that block his way, Wittman overcomes this sense of isolation. He manages to regain his audacious self in time to visit the unemployment office the next morning. Here Kingston examines another obstacle that Wittman must overcome, as she studies the tension between the ideal of community on one hand and the belief in the freedom of the individual on the other. The official American position on this question is clear in the hard

light of a California unemployment office, where government hand-
books for job seekers make it clear that to make it in America, one
must go it alone. " 'Come alone to the [job] interview,' " the handbook
instructs. " 'Do not take friends or relatives with you.' " Kingston's
narrator notes, "An American stands alone. Alienated, tribeless, individual. To be a successful American, leave your tribe, your caravan,
your gang, your partner, your village cousins, your refugee family that
you're making the money for, leave them behind" (TM, 246).
Although Wittman does not approve of this official propaganda, which
has the purpose, he believes, of breaking people down into isolated, and
thus more controllable, individual units, Kingston expresses ambiguity
on the question of tribalism versus American individualism. The lack of
tribalism on the part of white Americans can, Kingston suggests, be
read as freedom. Thus, whereas Wittman feels obliged to introduce his
new "wife" to his family, Tana is under no similar compunction. The
narrator observes: "White people don't have families. They're free"
(TM, 176). But Wittman is far from being free of his family. He always
begins to cough as he nears his mother's home and begs, as his mother
begins a litany of advice and criticism, "Just—. Just—. Just—." The
narrator fills in for him: "Just lay off me. Cut me some slack. Let me be.
And let me live" (TM, 183). The narrator underscores the point by noting: "[Poet] Gary Snyder had gone to Japan to meditate for years, and
could now spend five minutes in the same room with his mother. Beat
his record" (TM, 182).

In the unemployment office waiting room, Wittman's status as a
"tribal" Chinese rather than a "free" white American means he can be
commandeered by any elderly Chinese whom he encounters, in this case
one Mrs. Chew. The narrator notes, "When you have a moment of idle-
ness, an old Chinese lady will always appear, and give you something to
do, keep you from going lazy" (TM, 228). The narrator asks: "See what
you have to put up with if you want to have community? Any old Chinese lady comes along, she takes your day, you have to do her beckon-
ing. The hippy-dippies don't know what they're in for. They couldn't
take Communitas" (TM, 231).

But this ambivalence about the desirability of community is one
obstacle that Wittman/Monkey is able to overcome. Despite the annoy-
ance of being responsible for and available to others, he knows that he
has "always wanted a tribe" ever since seeing a night janitor happily at
work in the warmth of his large family, who had accompanied him to
the job (TM, 247). And while the old lady, Mrs. Chew, takes up Wittman's

time and energy, involving him in her complicated dilemmas, assuming that it is his responsibility to help her, she in turn also feels responsible for him, "naming heroes" to lift Wittman and herself from the grim tedium of the unemployment office. Armed with "hero stories," Mrs. Chew is not degraded or demoralized by the depressing government office, the official pronouncements, the deadening regimentation, or her own wearisome outlook as an aged and injured cannery worker. Rather, like the beautiful black woman who has come to the unemployment office dressed like a model, and who has "gladdened" and "inspired" the black men waiting in line, Mrs. Chew imposes her own brand of beauty on the bleak situation, inspiring her cotribalist, with her endless stories of heroism.

Wittman/Monkey's last obstacle is his family benevolent association, which has a space where Wittman's play might be staged but which "hasn't done useful politics anymore since China Relief" (*TM*, 262) and has in his view degenerated like other Chinese organizations into a "law-abiding, super-patriotic do-nothing" (*TM*, 263). Here again, as in dealing with his father, Wittman must overcome the "old fut" factor, where the son, as an American-born Chinese, is dismissed as if he were not quite real, treated as if he were a Caucasian health inspector, salesman, or tourist. But Wittman, who has refused to be defined as an Oriental Other by the United States, also refuses to be defined as American Other by immigrant Chinese. Not only does Wittman need a space for his play, but he also wants to revitalize the benevolent association, giving the association a task other than that of burying old men. He wants to bring it and the old men who run it into the present and into the community Wittman is trying to build. For, as much as he is annoyed by the dismissive attitudes of the "old futs," as well as the possessiveness of the old Chinese women, he also yearns for their nurturing, protective bossiness, lamenting the passing of a time when "any old Chinese stopped you in the intersection and scolded you to be careful crossing streets. Scolded you to be a good boy, like they all took a hand in raising you." Now, Wittman says, "The ethnos is degenerating" (*TM*, 255).

The old man who runs the benevolent association is finally worn down by Wittman's manic, monkeyesque one-man performance of scenes from *The Water Margin*, unable to avoid laughing. Assured that nothing in the play will result in negative advertisement for Chinatown businesses or give an unfavorable impression of the Chinese in general, the association head grudgingly allows Wittman to use the space.

Integrating the American Imagination

Having overcome the barriers standing in the way of his performance of identity and community, Wittman is rewarded by the reappearance of the ancient grandmother, Popo, who represents the unknowable, yet indelible, memory of China, and who, though misplaced, has not been really lost. Despite her age she has heroically survived alone in the wilderness, boosting her morale with quotes from the 108 outlaws of *The Water Margin*. In this she recalls the heroism of Kingston's swordswoman in *The Woman Warrior*, as well as the grandfathers in *China Men*, all of whom must master fear alone in the wilderness. And her heroism has translated into good fortune, as she has found romance and wealth, marrying a rich man and also hitting it big in Las Vegas, providing China-town with another inspiring hero story. She is the past, but she is also the vigorous present, giving thanks for her good fortune in a ceremony that is both anchored in tradition and spontaneously of the moment. Wittman asks her how and to whom she gives thanks. Her explanation aligns her with such other figures in Kingston's work as Ts'ai Yen in *The Woman Warrior* and the brother who went to Vietnam in *China Men*, both insisting on integrating past and present, Chinese and American into a new synthesis: "Pile up some fruit, stick three incense sticks in the pile. You don't have to go to the temple, you can do it anywhere; the kitchen is okay. Oranges, grapefruit, not lemons but. Then hold your hands together like this, and say something . . . whatever you feel like saying. Say it all out" (*TM*, 263). Wittman has been struggling to span a gener-ation gap that seems to separate him from older Chinese, trying to find a way to both incorporate a Chinese past and to live in a Chinese American present; Popo now shows that this is possible. She has done what Wittman hopes to do, richly integrating past and present, facing down fear and loss, living fully, and having fun. She has also shown that with courage and imagination you may survive and prosper richly as yourself, though others may find you useless or burdensome.

Having overcome the obstacles set in his path, Wittman is now ready to rehearse his show, and Kingston is ready to present the sometimes manic tour de force with which she seeks, at last, to perform the her-itage and experience and mind of Chinese America, making it visible to itself and to mainstream America, to integrate China and America and to form a new, inclusive community that celebrates the fullness of expe-rience and the complexity of identity. Community, Kingston posits, is created when people share in each other's imaginative life. And, as

Wittman's shows go on night after night, community building is shown to be a constant process: "Community is not built once-and-for-all; people have to imagine, practice, and re-create it" (*TM, 306*).

For his scenes from the Chinese classics, Wittman enlists everyone he knows to be both performer and audience, from the elderly Chinese showgirls to the lady he met in the unemployment office to the Caucasian Yale Younger poet, who is needed to integrate the cast. Putting on scenes from *Romance of Three Kingdoms* and *Journey to the West*, Wittman shows his intention to integrate these stories into the American experience, bringing the Chinese heroes to America, making them American and thus making America Chinese. With Wittman taking the role of the warrior Gwan Goong, the players enact a speed version of *Romance of Three Kingdoms* in a performance that underscores the sense that in their bravery and brotherhood the heroes are immortal and can cross boundaries of time, space, and culture: "Just because they all die, that isn't the end," Kingston's narrator declares. "Gwan Goong has the ability to travel anywhere. . . . An ocean-going ship will cross the stage behind a scrim of time, and he will be on it. Gwan Goong on Angel Island [where immigrant Chinese arrived in California]. Gwan Goong on Ellis Island" (*TM, 285*).

It is not only Gwan Goong who is brought to America, but also Monkey. Whereas the Gwan Goong figure is always heroic, Kingston's Monkey is possessed of a range of attitudes; sometimes he is insufferably confident, sometimes trapped and helpless. With his complexity and contradictions, Monkey demonstrates the complexity of identity, undermining the notion that the Chinese, Chinese Americans, or for that matter, anybody can be reduced to a set of cultural stereotypes. In one of his American incarnations he is King Kong atop the Empire State Building, Fay Wray in his arms. In another he is the "toy monkey" that James Dean finds "broken in the gutter," the first shot of the 1950s classic motion picture *Rebel without a Cause*. If Monkey—the Other—can be a ferocious invader, he can also be a mirror of broken-hearted, misunderstood young America.

As has been his intention throughout, Wittman responds to the soullessness and isolation he perceives as plaguing everyone in postwar corporate America by staging scenes from the Chinese classics with their message of heroic, defiant brotherhood. But his travels through his own psyche, as well as Chinese America, have prompted him to include other performances as well. In the "Bones and Jones" section, he puts on a set of Siamese twins, a parody of an old-fashioned freak show to address the way in which those of dual heritage are seen as oddities in American life. Playing the Siamese twins, the Yale Younger poet and Wittman's Japanese friend, Lance Kamiyama, roll onto stage, tied together. In a vaudeville patter routine, the twins begin as Chang and Eng, but change their names to the more American Chang Bunker and Eng Bunker, in hopes of being "more like the normal American person" (*TM*, 290). The routine explores various problems of identity: Should the twins take on a "Japanese identity" because "Americans adore cherry blossoms and silk fans and tea ceremony and geisha girls"? (292). And the performance echoes an idea found in "The Brother from Vietnam" section of *China Men*, that the identification of an enemy is a much more complex problem for those of a mixed heritage than for those who view themselves as "pure" American. Drafted, the twins utter a line often attributed to the Lone Ranger's sidekick Tonto when the two are surrounded by hostile Indians, as well as to black Americans drafted to fight the Vietnamese: "What do you mean 'we' white man?" (*TM*, 293). Although the twins' comedy routine alludes to a number of such issues, the "circus crowd" is not really interested, fascinated only by the "freakyness" of the exotic creatures. Chang yells to the audience: "We know damned well what you came for to see—the angle we're joined at. . . . You want to look at the hyphen. You want to look at it bare" (*TM*, 293).

The second half of the "Bones and Jones" section is devoted to the excitement of war, which Wittman has discovered in his travels to have been a key component in both Chinese and Chinese American drama and community building. Here Kingston seems to regard the experience of the Chinese and the Chinese Americans during centuries of war, and the way in which they have come to love its excitement and drama, with a combination of affection and mockery. As always, she works to integrate the myths of China and America. Scenes from the 108 outlaws of *The Water Margin* merge with scenes from the American west; a runaway slave in a poke bonnet has a Chinese face. A lynching turns into the Opium War. And discrimination against the Chinese is seen as another form of warfare, as Kingston shows the Chinese captured and imprisoned for everything from carrying baskets on poles (in violation of an early California ordinance) to being "restaurateurs and launderers who didn't pass health inspections" and for working at less than the minimum wage (*TM*, 301).

The section concludes with a "climactic free-for-all—everybody fights everybody everywhere at once" (*TM*, 301), as Wittman stages a "fake war" in hopes of "displacing real war" (*TM*, 306). So appealing is the melee that the audience joins in, chasing one another outside the theater and onto the street. Again Chinese and American myth is integrated as "gunslingers and archers" join the battle. As a climax Wittman sets off a series of explosions, which in turn set off a series of associations: the awful thrill of World War II bombs, the fear of which so permeated Kingston's childhood; the radical 1960s cry of "Burn, baby, burn"; the war in Vietnam; and even Chinese opera, suggested by the fire engines that come wailing and clanging to the scene. For the audience, and one suspects on some level for Kingston herself, the "awful gaiety" of war is hard to kick. Even Wittman feels like blowing things up sometimes, setting off the explosives after having revisited a racist Rudyard Kipling story about his experiences in Chinatown. But Kingston, who particularly despises Kipling's "east is east and west is west" slogan—which was played upon in numerous reviews of her first book—acknowledges that even the "magnificence" of Wittman's explosions has failed to "bust through Kipling" (*TM*, 308). Finally, war is put in its place. It has been a traditional expression of human passions, but it can not serve as a tool for the bettering of human life: "What's crazy is the idea that revolutionaries must shoot and bomb and kill, that revolution is the same as war. We keep losing our way on the short cut—killing for freedom and liberty and community and a better economy" (*TM*, 305).

With this performance, Wittman takes over the process by which the stories of the powerful invent the identity of the powerless. He assumes the task of making the stories by which Americans—Chinese and non-Chinese—may know themselves and one another. If America is defined by its frontier myths of heroism and patriotism, Wittman will insert Chinese story into that myth. If the "freakishness" of duality is a part of the American defining story, then Wittman will intervene in that story, undercutting it with his mockery. If we are all enthralled by the romance and bright lights of war, Wittman will show war at its ludicrous extreme and in all of its ultimate uselessness—everybody fighting everybody and blowing up everything.

The show is concluded with Wittman's performance of himself in the final monologue, drawing on a variety of models. He seems in part Lenny Bruce, the stand-up comedian who dragged his audience into a confrontation with social issues, part beat poet, like Allen Ginsberg, who confessed his pain and alienation in "Howl." At the same time he draws from the Chinese talk-story tradition, telling the old stories. In this he is reminiscent of the young Maxine who in *The Woman Warrior* tells her list of desires, guilts, and grievances, which keep "pouring out" of her "in a voice like the Chinese opera" (*WW,* 203).

Finally, Wittman posits that the way to build community and know who you are is not through war or through cultural hostilities, which teach people to define themselves in terms of an Other. Rather one must tell and listen, engaging in the long, slow process of learning who you are and who others are. To do that, Wittman says, one must drop the notion that others are "exotic" and "inscrutable" and at the same time insist on being "scrutable" oneself. In his performances, the Chinese become scrutable, deluging the audience not only with their myths but with their American experiences. It is up to Wittman—and Kingston— to teach, to provide the stories in their human complexity, to perform the Chinese American self. It is up to America to watch and to listen, to let go of the "perversion of willful innocence" (*TM,* 310).

For all her use of magic, Kingston insists at the end of *Tripmaster Monkey* that the key to identity and community is not acquired through a haze of romantic magic. Tana and Wittman, whose marriage symbol- izes the difficult but not impossible union that can occur over bound- aries, should love each other across the space that separates them not because of the magic of romance but because their souls are big enough to love across cultural barriers: "We're going to prove that any two ran- dom people can get together and learn to care for each other. I'm against magic; I go into despair over things happening that skip causa- tion. The superior man loves anyone he sets his mind to. Otherwise, we're fucked" (*TM,* 337).

Kingston began her intervention in the process by which narratives of the powerful define the powerless by transforming Chinese women, outsiders in the male kinship system, into heroes and saviors. In *China Men* Kingston transforms men who have been seen as soulless coolies into figures of sensitivity and passion. In *Tripmaster Monkey* she continues to insist on the need to find and express an inner life and to refuse to be defined by others. With Wittman, Kingston brings her study of Chinese America into the counterculture 1960s, building identity and commu- nity through complexity, through playfulness, and through the determi- nation to speak for oneself, to be, finally, "scrutable."

Appendix:
A Conversation with
Maxine Hong Kingston

Maxine Hong Kingston spoke with Diane Simmons on a spring morning in Oakland in 1997, in the new home Maxine and Earll Kingston built on the site of a house lost to a 1991 wildfire. Earll Kingston was still working with landscapers whose difficult task it would be to replace the dense foliage lost to the fire, examples of which were blooming in fragrant profusion only a few blocks down the hill. On the desk in Kingston's study, in a double Plexiglas frame, were two small black and white photographs that had been in the Kingstons' Hawaii home and thus survived the fire. One was of Tom Hong, a young man in a Western suit, looking out from a perch on what appears to be the rocks of New York's Brighton Beach. The other was of Kingston's mother, a striking young woman in Chinese dress posing gravely against the formal background of a photographer's studio in China. "Aren't they beautiful," Kingston said.

Kingston is at work on what she calls *The Fifth Book of Peace* but says she is not trying to replicate exactly the manuscript that was lost in the fire: "To me it's the pleasure of writing to be constantly discovering, going into the new. For me to recall word by word what I had written before sounds like torture and agony for me. I know I can do it. I'm sure I can do it if I wanted to. One of my former students volunteered to hypnotize me so I could recall but that seemed so wrong to me."

Kingston says her present book is similar in theme to the lost work, although she is approaching the same ideas differently: "The one big difference is that *The Book of Peace* [which was destroyed in the fire] was a work of fiction. I was imagining fictional characters. But after the fire I wanted to use writing for my personal self. I wanted to write directly what I was thinking and feeling. I didn't want to imagine fictional other people. I wanted to write myself. I wanted to write the way I wrote when I was a child, which is to say my deepest feelings and thoughts [that would] come out in a personal way and not for public consumption. It's not even for other people to read but for myself, to express myself."

The fire, she says, as well as the loss of her father at around the same time caused her to "want to say what I felt about all that, about all my losses. And I don't see that as writing for publication. I see that as writing for myself, to put into words my losses. And so I started there and wrote and wrote and wrote. But as I was writing it became some of the things I was thinking in the book that burned, those [thoughts] would come into the writing. . . . So all this stuff that I wrote down is going to be part of *The Fifth Book of Peace*."

Despite her present desire to write more personally, Kingston sees a sense of expanding mission in her work: "There's the existential creation of the self through art. Then I began to see really clearly the self is always in context with society and community. The sense of mission in *China Men* is that I was responsible for history. *China Men* was written in order to give us a history and to educate everyone as to our Chinese American history. And I saw my mission that I needed to educate a very ignorant America. Creating the self also means to create oneself as a good citizen, a citizen of America and a citizen of the world. There's a social and political responsibility. I think I express it in *China Men* and in *Tripmaster Monkey*.

"And that same sense of mission now is global. I think that the only way I can integrate East and West is thinking about global politics or a global peace-making mission, and so what I'm working on now has to do with: How do you make peace in the world? How do you stop war? How do you write a book of peace? And of course this brings up all kinds of literary problems. I think a lot about Aristotle writing about action, and that dramatic action comes from conflict. So does conflict have to be violent? Does conflict have to be war? I see myself writing counterpoint to *The Odyssey*, which is about a human consciousness that finds its heroism in war. So how do I write about woman warriors, peace warriors?"

Are you a Western individualist or a Confucian, for whom the individual exists in relation to the community?
Of course we have to be both. We need to be the individual self and also need to be the communal woman, the family woman. Life wouldn't be worth living if you didn't have other people.

Do you feel that you owe a debt to the community? Do you have to save the world, as you get in position to do so?
Yeah.

You have to?
Yeah. You have to.

I guess my sense of social responsibility comes from all my life, as far back as I can remember, my parents telling me those stories of the man with the writing on his back and of the woman warrior going into battle for her father. So I was raised with those stories. I think those stories passed on social responsibility to the children and to the young writer.

I think I've made readjustments and realignments so we can see things correctly. Like Confucianism has . . . a bad rap against it when we look at it in a certain feminist way, and also people who are Confucians will use the basic ideas [of Confucian philosophy] and put women down, and say, "Oh little sister doesn't belong here. She has to be under the thumb of somebody else." What I've done is let us really look at the main point of Confucianism, which is that everybody has an honorable right place in society and it doesn't mean that little sister has to be crushed. It means she has a place. And she has power in that place and from her place she can influence the whole structure.

So you're fixing Confucianism.
Yes, I'm fixing it. And then I'm fixing the story of Yue Fei and Fa Mu Lan. I'm saying, wait a minute. She comes home, now what happens. I have always admired Cincinnatus. I always like it that he could come home and that he could not remain a soldier, a killer, a brute. He found a way to come home so that he could be in normal peaceful society again. That story has been really important when I think about the homecoming of the Vietnam vet. Are we going to be Rambo 1, 2, 3, 4, 5, 6, 7, 8, 9? How many Rambos? All those stories are about his trying to come home. He goes to Chinatown. He goes back to Vietnam. But he can't come home; he never can make it.

And so look at these stories of Fa Mu Lan. . . . The wonderful part of Fa Mu Lan is that she does come home. She's able to be with her husband; she's able to put the flowers in her hair again. So what I'm working on now is to make that homecoming honorable, that it's not a failure for a woman to come home from work and cook dinner and raise the kids. It's not a failure to quit her job and stay home with the kids.

But how do you manage it? How do you do it? That's part of the work right now, the book of peace. How to come home from war? How to come home from Vietnam? How to come home as a woman from work?

They did a remake of *The Odyssey* on television. I watched it [because] I wanted to look at how they [portrayed the end, when Odysseus] gets home. He's supposed to be home now. Penelope has recognized him; he and his son have recognized each other; there's a wonderful recognition from his old nurse. And the next thing he does he just goes berserk and he slaughters all those people. They didn't even show it on TV, but in *The Odyssey* the book, the poem, he also has the women killed, all those servants that have allowed all those men to come in. So there's the most tremendous horrible slaughter at the end and I think, "Oh my gosh, so he doesn't really come home in the sense that he's still this butcher." And then at one point Athena comes in and she says, "Okay, that's enough now, enough killing, you're home." And so its solved like that, by Athena coming in and saying it's enough.

Do women save the world?
The vets I have been working with, again and again, they say, "Well, it's the women that are going to save the world. You're saving the world. You saved me. It's women that do this."

Why do women save the world?
I don't think about why. I think about how.

Women are *the world in* The Woman Warrior.
Yes, there aren't any men there.

In China Men *the mother comes to New York and she yanks these guys back. The holidays come back. She pulls Ed back out of this kind of frivolous fantasy world. And then you, the author, are pulling the father back.*
I'm giving him his whole history.

Then in Tripmaster Monkey *the female narrator keeps Wittman on track.*
It's true. That's just the way it is. Maybe it's just that I look around and that does seem to be what's happening. I've never stopped to think why. I've only thought how, how do I save the world?

All those women are like Penelope. Penelope's men come back. It just feels like that, when I look around, that seems the situation, all these ancestors, my mother's like that.

What comes to my mind is that there is actually a saving and nurturing force in the universe, and it is embodied in Kuan Yin, for example. These are names for that saving force and Kuan Yin is sometimes seen as a woman, sometimes as a man. She has many masculine incarnations in India, and she can be embodied in human imagination in these mythic figures. I think that it is easy for women to incorporate that force, and this is because women actually create life. We have babies; we actually hold a human being inside of ourselves, both in birth and in sex, and so I think that women's bodies are very naturally able to hold this force of salvation.

And then as I look at actual women around me, and as I feel my own deepest feelings, I can feel an incarnation of Kuan Yin, just like I identify with Penelope standing there saying to Odysseus, "Cut it out. You're home now." And Penelope saying those words to him, she's very much like a writer saying those words to people. Of course she's also able to say, "Get in there and fight."

Notes and References

Chapter One

1. Maxine Hong Kingston, *Hawai'i One Summer* (San Francisco: Meadow Press, 1987), 24; hereafter cited in the text as *HS*.

2. Suzanne Juhasz, "Toward a Theory of Form in Feminist Autobiography: Kate Millet's *Flying* and *Sita;* Maxine Hong Kingston's *The Woman Warrior*," in *Women's Autobiography*, ed. Estelle C. Jelineck (Bloomington: Indiana University Press, 1980), 221.

3. Edward Iwata, "Word Warriors," *Los Angeles Times*, 24 June 1990, sec. E, pp. 1, 9; hereafter cited in the text.

4. Judy Hoy, "To Be Able to See the Tao," in *Interviews with Women in the Creative Arts* (n.p.: Global City Press, 1995), 125; hereafter cited in the text.

5. Alvin P. Sanoff, "Chinese Mythology, '60s California," *U.S. News and World Report*, 22 May 1989, BC-4.

6. Kay Ann Johnson, *Women, the Family, and Peasant Revolution in China* (Chicago: University of Chicago Press, 1983), 24; hereafter cited in the text.

7. Bill Moyers, *A Conversation with Maxine Hong Kingston* (Alexandria, Va.: Public Broadcasting Service, Public Affairs Television, 1990), videocassette; hereafter cited in the text.

8. Diane Simmons, interview with Maxine Hong Kingston, Oakland, Calif., 31 May 1997; hereafter cited in the text.

9. Shelley Fisher Fishkin, "Interview with Maxine Hong Kingston," *American Literary History* 2 (Winter 1991): 784; hereafter cited in the text.

10. William Carlos Williams, *In the American Grain* (1925; reprint, New York: New Directions, 1956).

11. Donna Perry, *Backtalk: Women Writers Speak Out, Interviews by Donna Perry* (New Brunswick, N.J.: Rutgers University Press, 1993), 174; hereafter cited in the text.

12. I follow Kingston's romanization of the poet's name as Ts'ai Yen. In the pinyin system of romanization, generally considered standard, the name is rendered Cai Yan. Here and throughout the book I follow Kingston's usage. I give names in pinyin as an aid to readers. For this and advice in all matters of romanization I am indebted to Jeffrey Kinkley, Professor of Asian Studies at St. Johns University, Jamaica, Queens. Professor Kinkley is not, of course, responsible for any errors I may have made in giving Chinese names.

13. Rendered Cai Yan in the pinyin system.

14. Jeffrey Kinkley, letter to author, 31 August 1997.

15. Janet Nomura Morey and Wendy Dunn, *Famous Asian Americans* (New York: Dutton, 1992), 70; hereafter cited in the text.

16. Susan Brownmiller, "Susan Brownmiller Talks with Maxine Hong Kingston," *Mademoiselle,* March 1977, p. 210, hereafter cited in the text.

17. D. C. Denison, "Maxine Hong Kingston," *Boston Globe Magazine,* 18 June 1989, p. 3.

18. Kay Bonetti, "Maxine Hong Kingston Interview" (Columbia, Mo.: American Audio Prose Library, 1986), audiocassette; hereafter cited in the text.

19. Tu Fu is rendered Du Fu in the pinyin system; Li Po is rendered Li Bo.

20. Marilyn Chin, "A *MELUS* Interview: Maxine Hong Kingston," *MELUS* 16 (Winter 1989–1990): 70; hereafter cited in the text.

21. Stephen Talbot, "Talking Story: Maxine Hong Kingston Rewrites the American Dream," *San Francisco Chronicle,* 24 June 1990, sec. 6, p. 1; hereafter cited in the text.

22. Maxine Hong Kingston, *The Woman Warrior: Memoirs of a Girlhood among Ghosts* (New York: Vintage, 1989), 46; hereafter cited in the text as *WW.*

23. Maxine Hong Kingston, *Through the Black Curtain* (Berkeley, Calif.: Friends of the Bancroft Library, 1987), 5; hereafter cited in the text as *BC.*

24. Joan Saffa, *Maxine Hong Kingston Talking Story* (San Francisco, Calif.: National Asian American Telecommunications Association, 1990), videocassette; hereafter cited in the text.

25. Maxine Hong Kingston, "Rupert Garcia: Dancing between Realms," *Mother Jones,* October 1988, p. 32.

26. Neila C. Seshachari, "An Interview with Maxine Hong Kingston," *Weber Studies* 12 (Winter 1995): 20: hereafter cited in the text.

27. Margarett Loke, "The Tao Is Up," *New York Times Magazine,* 30 April 1989, p. 55; hereafter cited in the text.

28. Tom Vitale, "Maxine Hong Kingston Reads from *Tripmaster Monkey: His Fake Book* and Talks About Psychedelic Experience of Theatre and Life in the 1960s," *A Moveable Feast no. 207* (Columbia, Mo.: American Audio Prose Library), audiocassette; hereafter cited in the text.

29. John Leonard, "In Defiance of Two Worlds," *New York Times,* 17 September 1976, sec. 3, p. 21.

30. Gloria Chun, "The High Note of the Barbarian Reed Pipe: Maxine Hong Kingston," *Journal of Ethnic Studies* 19, no. 3 (1991): 85.

31. Maxine Hong Kingston, "Cultural Mis-Readings by American Reviewers," in *Asian and Western Writers in Dialogue: New Cultural Identities,* ed. Guy Amirthanayagam (London: Macmillan, 1982), 55; hereafter cited in the text.

32. Cited in Kingston's "Cultural Mis-Readings by American Reviewers," the phrase is that of Michael T. Malloy writing in *The National Observer.*

33. Maxine Hong Kingston, *Tripmaster Monkey: His Fake Book* (New York: Vintage, 1990), 308; hereafter cited in the text as *TM.*

170 NOTES AND REFERENCES

34. Frederic Wakeman Jr., *"China Men* by Maxine Hong Kingston," *New York Review of Books,* 14 August 1980, p. 42; hereafter cited in the text.
35. *Contemporary Authors,* Vol. 38 (Detroit: Gale Research, 1993), 209.
36. "Maxine Hong Kingston: From an Interview between Kingston and Arturo Islas October 1, 1980," in *Women Writers of the West Coast: Speaking of Their Lives and Careers,* ed. Marilyn Yalom (Santa Barbara, Calif.: Capra Press, 1980), 14.
37. Kingston gives the name for this historical figure who has been elevated to the status of an immortal as Guan Goong in *China Men* and as Gwan Goong in *Tripmaster Monkey.* The pinyin rendering is Guan Gong. In the introduction to Frank Chin's play *The Chickencoop Chinaman* (Dorothy Ritsuko McDonald, introduction to *"The Chickencoop Chinaman" and "The Year of the Dragon": Two Plays by Frank Chin* [Seattle: University of Washington Press, 1981]; hereafter cited in the text), the name is given as Kwan Kung.
38. Maxine Hong Kingston, *China Men* (New York: Ballantine Books, 1981), 149; hereafter cited in the text as *CM.*
39. From an introduction to the re-issued edition of *Hawai'i One Summer,* Honolulu: University of Hawaii Press, 1999. Kingston sent the introduction to the author in manuscript form.
40. Timothy Pfaff, *New York Times Book Review,* 15 June 1980, p. 25; hereafter cited in the text.
41. Quentin Anderson, "The Emergence of Modernism," in *Columbia Literary History of the United States,* ed. Emory Elliott (New York: Columbia University Press, 1998), 709.
42. David Leiwei Li, *"China Men:* Maxine Hong Kingston and the American Canon," *American Literary History* 2 (Fall 1990): 496, hereafter cited in the text.
43. Paula Rabinowitz, "Eccentric Memories: A Conversation with Maxine Hong Kingston," *Michigan Quarterly Review* 26 (Winter 1987): 179; hereafter cited in the text.
44. Harrison Salisbury, "On the Literary Road: American Writers in China," *New York Times Book Review,* 20 January 1985, p. 25; hereafter cited in the text.
45. Maxine Hong Kingston, "Discussions: Sau-ling Wong and Karen Meißenburg Papers," in *Autobiographie & Avant-garde: Alain Robbe-Grillet, Serge Doubrovsky, Rachid Boudjedra, Maxine Hong Kingston, Raymond Federman, Ronald Sukenick,* ed. G. Alfred Hornung and G. Ernstpeter Ruhe (Tübingen, Germany: Narr, 1977), 318.
46. C. T. Hsia, *The Classic Chinese Novel: A Critical Introduction* (New York: Columbia University Press, 1968), 133; hereafter referred to in the text.
47. LeAnne Schreiber, *New York Times Book Review,* 23 April 1989, p. 1.
48. John Leonard, "Of Thee Ah Sing," *Nation,* 5 June 1989, p. 768; hereafter referred to in the text.

49. Ann Tyler, "Manic Monologue," *New Republic,* 17 April 1989, pp. 46, 45; hereafter referred to in the text.
50. Rendered Liu Bei in pinyin.
51. Kuan Yin, or Guan Yin, Chinese goddess of mercy, was a male before he/she came to China.
52. The title of one of Frank Chin's essays is "Come All Ye Asian American Writers of the Real and the Fake" (in *The Big Aiiieeeee!: An Anthology of Chinese American and Japanese American Literature,* ed. Jeffrey Paul Chan, Frank Chin, Lawson Fusao Inada, and Shawn Wong [New York: Meridian Books, 1991].); hereafter cited in the text
53. Amy Ling, *Between Worlds: Women Writers of Chinese Ancestry* (New York: Pergamon, 1990), 149.
54. Rendered Cao Cao in pinyin.
55. Wm. Satake Blauvelt, "Talking with 'The Woman Warrior,' " *Pacific Reader: International Examiner Literary Supplement* 1 (17 July 1989): 8.
56. Frank Chin repeatedly describes Kingston—along with other Asian American writers—as Christian. In "Come All Ye Asian American Writers," he charges that Kingston and "the other Christian American publishing sensations" David Henry Hwang and Amy Tan are themselves Christian, that "the only form of literature written by Chinese Americans that major publishers will publish (other than a cookbook) is autobiography, an "exclusively Christian form," and that "they all write to the specifications of the Christian stereotype of Asia being as opposite morally from the West as it is geographically" (8). In Chin's "This Is Not an Autobiography," he writes: "It's the quality of submission, not assertion that counts, in the confession and autobiography. The autobiography combines the thrills and guilt of masturbation and the porno movie" (*GENRE* 18 [Summer 1985]: 13). According to Kingston, however, neither she nor her family has ever accepted or practiced Christianity (Simmons).

King-Kok Cheung has responded to Chin's charge that autobiography is necessarily a Christian, confessional form: "Feminist critics . . . believe that women have always appropriated autobiography for *asserting,* however tentatively, their subjectivity" (King-Kok Cheung, "The Woman Warrior versus the Chinaman Pacific: Must a Chinese American Critic Choose between Feminism and Heroism?" in *Conflicts in Feminism,* ed. Marianne Hirsch and Evelyn Fox Keller [New York: Routledge, 1990], 238; hereafter cited in the text). Sharon Shih-Jiuan Hou, in an article on Ts'ai Yen, "the first great woman poet" of China who lived around A.D. 190, writes that Ts'ai Yen's poems "share autobiographical import with a nationwide political and social significance [as they] chronicle personal experience against a background of turmoil" (Sharon Shih-Jiuan Hou, "Women's Literature," in *Indiana Companion to Traditional Chinese Literature,* ed. William Nienhauser, [Bloomington: Indiana University Press, 1987], 175). Finally, it is not only women who have written autobiographically within the Chinese tradition. In analyzing *A Red Mansion,* one of the best-known Chinese novels, which is also translated as *Dream of the Red Chamber, A Red Mansion Dream*, and *Story of the Stone*, James J. Y. Liu writes that the author, Ts'ao Chan (also rendered Ts'ao Hsueh-ch'in), who professes to accept Buddhist doctrine, still "is unable to detach himself totally from the human world," pointing out that "much of the material in the novel is based on the author's own experience or that of his family" (James J. Y. Liu, *Essentials of Chinese Literary Art* [North Scituate, Mass.: Duxbury Press, 1979], 77; hereafter cited in the text).

57. Maxine Hong Kingston, "The Novel's Next Step," *Mother Jones*, December 1989, p. 37; hereafter cited in the text.

58. Eric James Schroeder, " 'As Truthful as Possible': An Interview with Maxine Hong Kingston," *Writing on the Edge* 7 (1989): 93; hereafter cited in the text.

Chapter Two

1. The woman warrior's name is Fa Mu Lan in Cantonese, Hua Mulan in Mandarin. She is also known simply by her given name, Mulan. I use "Fa Mu Lan" when referring to Kingston's character. I use "Mulan" when I refer to the subject of "The Ballad of Mulan" or the traditional figure.

2. Wu-Chi Liu and Irving Lo, *Sunflower Splendor: Three Thousand Years of Chinese Poetry* (Bloomington: Indiana University Press, 1975), 77; hereafter cited in the text.

3. Edward W. Said, *Orientalism* (New York: Vintage, 1979), 47, 40.

4. Françoise Lionnet, *Autobiographical Voices: Race, Gender, Self-Portraiture* (Ithaca, N.Y.: Cornell University Press, 1989), 5.

5. Robert G. Lee, "*The Woman Warrior* as an Intervention in Asian American Historiography," in *Approaches to Teaching Kingston's "The Woman Warrior,"* ed. Shirley Geok-Lin Lim (New York: Modern Language Association, 1991), 56; hereafter cited in the text.

6. In *One Hundred and Seventy Chinese Poems*, trans. Arthur Waley (New York: Alfred A. Knopf, 1919).

7. The author and title rendered in the pinyin system are Tieyun Yun, *The Travels of Lao Can*.

8. Liu Tieh Yun, *The Travels of Lao Ts'an* (New York: Columbia University Press, 1990), 158.

9. Lu Xun, "New Year's Sacrifice," in *Lu Xun: Diary of a Madman and Other Stories* (Honolulu: University of Hawaii Press, 1990), 1538.

10. Ye Weilin, "Five Girls and One Rope," *Fiction* 8 (1987): 96–114.

11. Li Ju-chen, *Flowers in the Mirror*, trans. Lin Tai-yi (Berkeley: University of California Press, 1965); hereafter cited in the text. The author's name is also given as Li Ruzhen.

12. Tsao Hsueh-chin, *Dream of the Red Chamber* (New York: Doubleday, 1958).

13. Wu Ch'eng-En, *Monkey: A Journey to the West*, ed. David Kherdian (Boston, Mass.: Shambhala, 1992). Kherdian's edition is described as a "retelling of the Chinese folk novel by Wu Ch'eng-En."

14. Margery Wolf and Roxane Witke, *Women in Chinese Society* (Stanford, Calif.: Stanford University Press, 1975), 32–41; hereafter cited in the text.

15. Emily Ahern, "Chinese Ritual and Politics," in *Women in Chinese Society*, ed. Margery Wolf and Roxane Witke (Stanford, Calif.: Stanford University Press, 1975), 200; hereafter cited in the text.

16. Louise Edwards, "Women Warriors and Amazons of the Mid Qing Texts *Jinghua yuan* and *Honglou meng*," *Modern Asian Studies* 29 (1995): 226; hereafter cited in the text.

17. According to Liu and Lo, *Sunflower Splendor*, 77, the historical figure upon whom the poem is based "was of northern, i.e., non-Chinese, stock and lived during the Six Dynasties period (A.D. 220–588)."

18. His name is sometimes rendered Gnak Fei.

19. Frank Chin, who has accused Kingston of incorporating the Yue Fei story because she is grasping for ways to show Chinese "misogynistic cruelty toward women" ("Come All Ye Asian American Writers," 6), seems to entirely misunderstand Kingston's use of the carved back episode.

Chapter Three

1. See Jack M. Potter, "Cantonese Shamanism," in *Religion and Ritual in Chinese Society*, ed. Arthur P. Wolfe (Stanford, Calif.: Stanford University Press, 1974); hereafter referred to in the text.

2. Although the difficulties facing immigrant Chinese men are implicit throughout Kingston's work, she details legal restrictions placed on the immigrants in the United States in "The Laws" section of *China Men* (*CM*, 150–59). These restrictions denied the Chinese men many of the rights and responsibilities accorded to both Chinese and American men at the time.

Chapter Four

1. See Dorothea Hayward Scott, *Chinese Popular Literature and the Child* (Chicago: American Library Association, 1980), 30; hereafter cited in the text.

2. Kathryn VanSpanckeren, "The Asian Literary Background of *The Woman Warrior*," in *Approaches to Teaching Kingston's "The Woman Warrior*," ed. Shirley Geok-Lin Lim (New York: Modern Language Association, 1991), 49.

3. *A Cycle of Chinese Festivities* (Singapore: Malaysia Publishing House, 1967), 148; hereafter cited as *Cycle*.

4. Amy Tan, *The Joy Luck Club* (New York: Ivy Books, 1989); hereafter cited in the text.

Chapter Five

1. King-Kok Cheung, *Articulate Silences: Hisaye Yamamoto, Maxine Hong Kingston, Joy Kogawa* (Ithaca, N.Y.: Cornell University Press, 1993.
2. Kenneth Rexroth and Ling Chung, *The Orchid Boat: Women Poets of China* (New York: McGraw Hill, 1972), 134; hereafter cited in the text.
3. "The Lamentation" can be found in Liu and Lo, *Sunflower Splendor.* "From 18 Verses Sung to a Tatar Reed Whistle" is in Rexroth and Chung, *The Orchid Boat.*

Chapter Six

1. Cyril Birch, ed., *Anthology of Chinese Literature* (New York: Grove, 1967), 57; hereafter cited in the text.
2. Maxine Hong Kingston, "On Understanding Men," *Hawaii Review* 77 (1977): 43; hereafter referred to in the text as "OUM."
3. Shu-Mei Shih, "Exile and Intertextuality in Maxine Hong Kingston's *China Men,*" in *The Literature of Emigration and Exile,* ed. James Whitlark and Wendell Aycock (Lubbock: Texas Tech University Press, 1992), 66.
4. Rendered Chu in pinyin.
5. Yang Hsienyi and Gladys Yang, ed. and trans., *Li Sao: The Lament* (Singapore: Asiapac, 1994), 2.
6. Rendered Du Fu in pinyin.
7. Qing-yun Wu, "A Chinese Reader's Response to Maxine Hong Kingston's *China Men,*" *MELUS* 17 (Fall 1991): 97
8. Ralph Ellison, *Invisible Man* (New York: Vintage, 1990), 3; hereafter cited in the text.
9. Rendered Gao Qi in pinyin.
10. In *China Men* Kingston spells the name Guan Goong. In *Tripmaster Monkey* the spelling is changed to Gwan Goong.

Chapter Seven

1. The way in which jazz is an expression and agent of altered consciousness is portrayed in Ellison's *Invisible Man,* as Ellison's narrator describes the complex subliminal message of pain and anger he hears in Louis Armstrong's apparently benign rendition of "What Did I Do to Be So Black and Blue" (8–12).
2. A. Noelle Williams, "Parody and Pacifist Transformations in Maxine Hong Kingston's *Tripmaster Monkey: His Fake Book,*" *MELUS* 20 (Spring 1995): 90.
3. In Lo Kuan-chung's version of the story, the oath takes place in a peach orchard. In Kingston's account it is a pear garden.
4. Lo Kuan-chung, *Three Kingdoms: China's Epic Drama,* trans. Moss Roberts (New York: Random House, 1976), 7; hereafter cited in the text.

5.   Kingston gives the historical figure who became the god of war and literature as Guan Goong in *China Men* and as Gwan Goong in *Tripmaster Monkey*. In standard pinyin the name is given Guan Gong.

6.   In the pinyin style of romanization the characters' names undergo the following changes: Liu Pei, Liu Bei; Chang Fei, Zhang Fei. The author's name, Lo Kuan-chung, would be given as Luo Guanzhong.

7.   Kingston apparently has chosen to include the heroes of *The Water Margin* for their ideals of brotherhood and opposition to governmental authority, and to overlook what C. T. Hsia and others have pointed out as the deep-seated misogyny of the book in which sexually puritanical heroes "harbor a subconscious hatred of women as their worst enemy" and who indulge in "misogyny and sadism" (Hsia, 106).

Selected Bibliography

PRIMARY WORKS

China Men. New York: Alfred A. Knopf, 1980.
Hawai'i One Summer. San Francisco: Meadow Press, 1987. Reprint, Honolulu: Univeristy of Hawaii Press, 1999.
Through the Black Curtains. Berkeley, Calif.: Friends of the Bancroft Library, 1987.
Tripmaster Monkey: His Fake Book. New York: Alfred A. Knopf, 1989.
The Woman Warrior: Memoirs of a Girlhood Among Ghosts. New York: Alfred A. Knopf, 1976.

SECONDARY SOURCES

Chapters in Books

Cheung, King-Kok. "The Woman Warrior versus the Chinaman Pacific: Must a Chinese American Critic Choose between Feminism and Heroism?" In *Conflicts in Feminism,* ed. Marianne Hirsch and Evelyn Fox Keller, 234–51. New York: Routledge, 1990. Examines the attacks on Kingston by a group of male Asian American writers.

―――. "Provocative Silence: *The Woman Warrior* and *China Men.*" In *Articulate Silences: Hisaye Yamamoto, Maxine Hong Kingston, Joy Kogawa,* by King-Kok Cheung, 74–125. Ithaca, N.Y.: Cornell University Press, 1993. Discusses the many forms of silence imposed on a Chinese American female that enable the "creative writer to dispense with time-honored authority and invent a braver world."

Lee, Robert G. "*The Woman Warrior* as an Intervention in Asian American Historiography." In *Approaches to Teaching Kingston's "The Woman Warrior,"* ed. Shirley Geok-Lin Lim, 52–63. New York: Modern Language Association, 1991. Claims that Kingston "stands Orientalism on its head" by rejecting imposed, fixed identities and telling hidden stories that continually complicate meaning and identity.

Perry, Donna. "Maxine Hong Kingston." In *Backtalk: Women Writers Speak Out: Interviews by Donna Perry,* ed. Donna Perry, 172–93. New Brunswick, N.J.: Rutgers University Press, 1983. Kingston discusses *Tripmaster Mon-*

key: His Fake Book and considers why "feminists are mad at me" for creating a male protagonist in the macho Wittman Ah Sing.

VanSpanckeren, Kathryn. "The Asian Literary Background of *The Woman Warrior.*" In *Approaches to Teaching Kingston's "The Woman Warrior,"* ed. Shirley Geok-Lin Lim, 44–51. New York: Modern Language Association, 1991. A valuable examination of Kingston's work as it reflects Chinese literature.

Journal Articles

Chin, Marilyn. "A *MELUS* Interview: Maxine Hong Kingston." *MELUS* 16 (Winter 1989–1990): 57–74. Kingston discusses *Tripmaster Monkey: His Fake Book,* which she describes in part as a struggle between Wittman Ah Sing's "macho spirit," and the "great female" who narrates the story.

Fishkin, Shelley Fisher. "Interview with Maxine Hong Kingston." *American Literary History* 2 (Winter 1991): 782–91. Kingston discusses *Tripmaster Monkey: His Fake Book,* acknowledging her debt to Walt Whitman and also to Virginia Woolf's *Orlando,* which "broke through constraints of time, of gender, of culture."

Li, David Leiwei. "*China Men:* Maxine Hong Kingston and the American Canon." *American Literary History* 2 (Fall 1990): 482–502. Shows Kingston combating "invisibility of the ethnic" in America by telling stories of Chinese Americans that both "assert cultural independence as well as interdependence in the American grain."

Lin, Patricia. "Clashing Constructs of Reality: Reading Maxine Hong Kingston's *Tripmaster Monkey: His Fake Book* as Indigenous Ethnography." In *Reading the Literature of Asian America,* ed. Shirley Geok-Lin Lim and Amy Ling, 333–47. Philadelphia: Temple University Press, 1992. Discusses the "retrieval of the self-as-subject" as the main theme of *Tripmaster Monkey: His Fake Book.*

Rabinowitz, Paula. "Eccentric Memories: A Conversation with Maxine Hong Kingston." *Michigan Quarterly Review* 26 (Winter 1987): 177–87. Kingston discusses the connection between *The Woman Warrior* and *China Men* and also describes her first impressions of China.

Schueller, Malini. "Questioning Race and Gender Definitions: Dialogic Subversions in *The Woman Warrior.*" *Criticism* 31 (Fall 1989): 421–37. Discusses *The Woman Warrior* as a "sustained subversion of cultural, racial and gender definitions."

Seshachari, Neila C. "An Interview with Maxine Hong Kingston." *Weber Studies* 12 (Winter 1995): 7–26. Kingston discusses her work with Vietnam veterans, as well as the novel that was lost in a wildfire that destroyed her home in 1991.

Sledge, Linda Ching. "Oral Tradition in Kingston's *China Men.*" In *Redefining American Literary History,* ed. A. La Vonne Brown Ruoff and Jerry W.

Ward Jr., 142–54. New York: Modern Language Association, 1990. Describes Kingston's *China Men* as a "throwback" to Chinese oral tradition and one that "changes the direction of American letters" by introducing this tradition to a large audience of readers.

Williams, A. Noelle. "Parody and Pacifist: Transformations in Maxine Hong Kingston's *Tripmaster Monkey: His Fake Book.*" *MELUS 20* (Spring 1995): 83–100. Shows that Kingston's use of irony, subversion, and doubleness is designed to "protect her text from the quick, essentializing mis-readings that her work has suffered in the past from both the Asian American and feminist communities as well as critics from the mainstream."

Index

The Author

Diane Simmons is an assistant professor of English at The City University of New York–Borough of Manhattan Community College in New York City. Her book on the West Indian author Jamaica Kincaid was published in 1994. Her second novel, *Dreams like Thunder,* won the 1993 Oregon Book Award for Fiction.

The Editor

Frank Day is a professor of English and head of the English Department at Clemson University. He is the author of *Sir William Empson: An Annotated Bibliography* (1984) and *Arthur Koestler: A Guide to Research* (1985). He was a Fulbright lecturer in American literature in Romania (1980–1981) and in Bangladesh (1986–1987).